THE THIRTY YEARS' WAR 1618-1648
BY

Samu...

FOREWORD

Samuel Rawson Gardiner was an English historian and writer. Gardiner wrote an extensive book on the Thrity Years' War, one of the longest and most destructive wars in European history, which involved most European countries. This edition includes a table of contents.

The Thirty Years' War

PREFACE.

If the present work should appear to be written for more advanced students than those for whom most if not all the other books of the series are designed, the nature of the subject must be pleaded in excuse. The mere fact that it relates exclusively to Continental history makes it unlikely that junior pupils would approach it in any shape, and it is probably impossible to make the very complicated relations between the German states and other European nations interesting to those who are for the first time, or almost the first time, attempting to acquire historical knowledge. Every history, to be a history, must have a unity of its own, and here we have no unity of national life such as that which is reflected in the institutions of England and France, not even the unity of a great race of sovereigns handing down the traditions of government from one generation to another. The unity of the subject which I have chosen must be sought in the growth of the principle of religious toleration as it is adopted or repelled by the institutions under which Germany and France, the two principal nations with which we are concerned, are living. Thus the history of the period may be compared to a gigantic dissolving view. As we enter upon it our minds are filled with German men and things. But Germany fails to find the solution of the problem before it. Gradually France comes with increasing distinctness before us. It succeeds where Germany had failed, and occupies us more and more till it fills the whole field of action.

But though, as I have said, the present work is not intended for young children, neither is it intended for those who require the results of original research. The data for a final judgment on the story are scattered in so many repositories that the Germans themselves have now discovered that a complete investigation into one or other of the sections into which the war naturally falls, is sufficient work for any man. There must surely, however, be many, as well in the upper classes of schools as in more advanced life, who would be glad to know at second hand what is the result of recent inquiry in Germany into the causes of the failure of the last attempt, before our own day, to constitute a united German nation. The writer who undertakes such a task encounters, with his eyes open, all the hazards to which a second-hand narrative is liable. His impressions are less sharp, and are exposed to greater risk of error than those of one who goes direct to the fountain head. He must be content to be the retailer rather than the manufacturer of history, knowing that each kind of work has its use.

Not that the present book is a mere collection of other men's words. If I have often adopted without much change the narrative or opinions of German writers, I have never said any thing which I have not made my own, by passing it through my own mind. To reproduce with mere paste and scissors passages from the writings of men so opposed to one another as Ranke, Gindely, Ritter, Opel, Hurter, Droysen, Gfrörer, Klopp, Förster, Villermont, Uetterodt, Koch, and others, would be to bewilder, not to instruct. And in forming my own opinions I have had the advantage not merely of being in the habit of writing from original documents, but of having studied at least some of the letters and State papers of the time. I have thus, for example, been able, from my knowledge of the despatches of Sir Robert Anstruther, to neglect Droysen's elaborate argument that Christian IV. took part in the war through jealousy of Gustavus

Adolphus; and to speak, in opposition to Onno Klopp, of the persistence of the Dukes of Mecklenburg in the support which they gave to the King of Denmark.

More valuable than the little additional knowledge thus obtained is the insight into the feelings and thoughts of the Catholic princes gained by a very slight acquaintance with their own correspondence. To start by trying to understand what a man appears to himself, and only when that has been done, to try him by the standard of the judgment of others, is in my opinion the first canon of historical portraiture; and it is one which till very recent times has been more neglected by writers on the Thirty Years' War than by students of any other portion of history.

My teachers in Germany from whom I have borrowed so freely, and according to the rules of the series, without acknowledgment in foot-notes, will, I hope, accept this little book, not as an attempt to do that which they are so much better qualified to execute, but as an expression of the sympathy which an Englishman cannot but feel for the misfortunes as well as the achievements of his kindred on the Continent, and as an effort to tell something of the by-gone fortunes of their race to those amongst his own countrymen to whom, from youth or from circumstances of education, German literature is a sealed book.

I have only to add that the dates are according to the New Style. Ten days must be deducted to bring them in accordance with those used at the time in England.

CHAPTER I. CAUSES OF THE THIRTY YEARS' WAR.

SECTION I.—Political Institutions of Germany.

§ 1. Want of national institutions in Germany.

It was the misfortune of Germany in the sixteenth and seventeenth centuries that, with most of the conditions requisite for the formation of national unity, she had no really national institutions. There was an emperor, who looked something like an English king, and a Diet, or General Assembly, which looked something like an English Parliament, but the resemblance was far greater in appearance than in reality.

§ 2. The Emperor.

The Emperor was chosen by three ecclesiastical electors, the Archbishops of Mentz, Treves and Cologne, and four lay electors, the Elector Palatine, the Electors of Saxony and Brandenburg, and the King of Bohemia. In theory he was the successor of the Roman Emperors Julius and Constantine, the ruler of the world, or of so much of it at least as he could bring under his sway. More particularly, he was the successor of Charles the Great and Otto(Pg 2) the Great, the lay head of Western Christendom. The Emperor Sigismund, on his death-bed, had directed that his body should lie in state for some days, that men might see 'that the lord of all the world was dead.' 'We have chosen your grace,' said the electors to Frederick III., 'as head, protector, and governor of all Christendom.' Yet it would be hard to find a single fragment of reality corresponding to the magnificence of the claim.

As far, however, as the period now under review is concerned, though the name of Emperor was retained, it is unnecessary to trouble ourselves with the rights, real or imaginary, connected with the imperial dignity. Charles the Great, before the imperial crown was conferred on him, ruled as king, by national assent or by conquest, over a great part of Western Europe. When his dominions were divided amongst his successors, the rule of those successors in Germany or elsewhere had no necessary connexion with the imperial crown. Henry the Fowler, one of the greatest of the Kings of the Germans, was never an emperor at all, and though, after the reign of his son Otto the Great, the German kings claimed from the Pope the imperial crown as their right, they never failed also to receive a special German crown at Aachen (*Aix-la-Chapelle*) or at Frankfort as the symbol of their headship over German lands and German men.

§ 4. Its connexion with the Empire.

When, therefore, the writers of the 16th or 17th centuries speak of the rights of the Emperor in Germany, they really mean to speak of the rights of the Emperor in his capacity of German king, just as, when they speak of the Empire, they mean what we call Germany, together with certain surrounding districts, such as Switzerland, the Netherlands, Lorraine, and Eastern Burgundy or Franche Comté, which(Pg 3) are not now, if Alsace and the newly-conquered part of Lorraine be excepted, included under that name. In the same way the mere fragments of feudal supremacy, and the payment of feudal dues which the emperors claimed in Italy, belonged to them, not as emperors, but simply as Italian kings, and as wearers of the iron crown of Lombardy, which, as the legends told, was formed of nails taken from the Saviour's cross.

§ 5. Some confusion unavoidable.

Not that it would be wise, even if it were possible, to do otherwise than to follow the practice of contemporaries. The strange form, Emperor of Germany, by which, at a later period, men unfamiliar with Germany history strove to reconcile the old claims with something like the actual fact, had not been yet invented. And, after all, the confusions of history, the use of words and titles when their meaning is changed, are so many tokens to remind us of the unity of successive generations, and of the impossibility of any one of them building anew without regarding the foundations of their fathers. All that is needed is to remember that the emperor of later times is a personage whose rights and functions can be profitably compared with those of Henry VIII. of England or Lewis XIV. of France, not with Julius or Constantine whose successor he professed himself to be.

§ 6. The great vassals.

'Take away the rights of the Emperor,' said a law book of the fifteenth century, in language which would have startled an old Roman legislator, 'and who can say, "This house is mine, this village belongs to me?"' But the princes and bishops, the counts and cities, who were glad enough to plead on their own behalf that their lands were held directly from the head of the Empire, took care to allow him scarcely any real authority. This kingly dignity(Pg 4) which passed under the name of the Empire was indeed very weak. It had never outgrown the needs of the Middle Ages, and was still essentially a feudal kingship. From circumstances which it would take too much space to notice here, it had failed in placing itself at the head of a national organization, and in becoming the guardian of the rights of the tillers of the soil and the burghers of the towns, who found no place in the ranks of the feudal chivalry.

§ 7. Their independence.

The immediate vassals of the Empire, in fact, were almost independent sovereigns, like the Dukes of Normandy in the France of the tenth century, or the Dukes of Burgundy in the France of the fifteenth century. They quarrelled and made war with one another like the Kings of England and France. Their own vassals, their own peasants, their own towns could only reach the Emperor through them, if anybody thought it worth while to reach him at all.

§ 8. Prospect of order.

The prospect of reviving the German kingship which was veiled under the august title of Emperor seemed far distant at the beginning of the fifteenth century. But whilst the Empire, in its old sense, with its claims to universal dominion, was a dream, this German kingship needed but wisdom in the occupant of the throne to seize the national feeling, which was certain sooner or later to call out for a national ruler, in order to clothe itself in all the authority which was needed for the maintenance of the unity and the safety of the German people. That, when the time came, the man to grasp the opportunity was not there, was the chief amongst the causes of that unhappy tragedy of disunion which culminated in the Thirty Years' War.

§ 9. Attempts to introduce order.

In the middle of the fifteenth century an effort was made to introduce a system of regular assemblies, un(Pg 5)der the name of a Diet, in order to stem the tide of anarchy. But it never entered into the mind of the wisest statesman living to summon any general representation of the people. In the old feudal assemblies no one had taken part who was not an immediate vassal of the Empire, and the Diet professed to be only a more regular organization of the old feudal assemblies.

§ 10. The Diet, or general assemblies of the Empire.

From the Diet, therefore, all subjects of the territorial princes were rigorously excluded. Whatever their wishes or opinions might be, they had neither part nor lot in the counsels of the nation. There was nothing in the Diet answering to those representatives of English counties, men not great enough to assume the state of independent princes, nor small enough to be content simply to register without question the decrees of those in authority who with us did more than any other class to cement town and country, king and people together. Nor did even the less powerful of the immediate vassals take part in the meetings. Like the lesser barons of the early Plantagenet reigns, they slipped out of a position to which they seemed to have a right by the fact that they held their few square miles of land as directly from the Emperor as the Dukes of Bavaria or the Electors of Saxony held the goodly principalities over which they ruled.

§ 11. The princes care little for the Diet.

Such a body was more like a congress of the representatives of European sovereigns than an English Parliament. Each member came in his own right. He might or might not speak the sentiments of his subjects, and, even if he did, he naturally preferred deciding pretty much as he pleased at home to allowing the question to be debated(Pg 6) by an assembly of his equals. An Elector of Saxony, a Landgrave of Hesse, or an Archduke of Austria knew that taxes were levied, armies trained, temporal and spiritual wants provided for at his own court at Dresden, at Cassel, or at Vienna, and he had no wish that it should be otherwise. Nor was it easy, even when a prince had made himself so obnoxious as to call down upon himself the condemnation of his fellows, to subject him to punishment. He might, indeed, be put to the ban of the Empire, a kind of secular excommunication. But if he were powerful himself, and had powerful friends, it might be difficult to put it in execution. It would be necessary to levy war against him, and that war might not be successful.

§ 12. Some sort of order established.

Still, at the end of the fifteenth and the beginning of the sixteenth centuries some progress was made. An Imperial Court (*Reichskammergericht*) came into existence, mainly nominated by the princes of the Empire, and authorized to pronounce judgment upon cases arising between the rulers of the various territories. In order to secure the better execution of the sentences of this court, Germany was divided into circles, in each of which the princes and cities who were entitled to a voice in the Diet of the Empire were authorized to meet together and to levy troops for the maintenance of order.

§ 13. The three Houses of the Diet.

These princes, lay and ecclesiastical, together with the cities holding immediately from the Empire, were called the Estates of the Empire. When they met in the general Diet they voted in three houses. The first house was composed of the seven Electors, though it was only at an Imperial election that the number was complete. At all ordinary meetings for legislation, or for the dispatch of busi(Pg 7)ness, the king of Bohemia was excluded, and six Electors only appeared. The next house was the House of Princes, comprising all those persons, lay or ecclesiastical, who had the right of sitting in the Diet. Lastly, came the Free Imperial Cities, the only popular element in the Diet. But they were treated as decidedly inferior to the other two houses. When the Electors and the Princes had agreed upon a proposition, then and not till then it was submitted to the House of Cities.

§ 14. The cities too weak.

The special risk attending such a constitution was that it provided almost exclusively for the wants of the princes and electors. In the Diet, in the circles, and in the Imperial Court, the princes and electors exercised a preponderating, if not quite an exclusive influence. In ordinary times there might be no danger. But if extraordinary times arose, if any great movement swept over the surface of the nation, it might very well be that the nation would be on one side and the princes and the electors on the other. And if this were the case there would be great difficulty in bringing the nation into harmony with its institutions. In England the sovereign could alter a hostile majority in the House of Lords by a fresh creation of peers, and the constituencies could alter a hostile majority of the House of Commons by a fresh election. In Germany there was no House of Commons, and an emperor who should try to create fresh princes out of the immediate vassals who were too weak to be summoned to the Diet would only render himself ridiculous by an attempt to place in check the real possessors of power by the help of those who had the mere appearance of it.

Section II.—Protestantism in Germany.

§ 1. The German people in favor of Protestantism; the Diet opposed to it.

When, in the sixteenth century, Protestantism sud(Pg 8)denly raised its head, the institutions of the Empire were tried to the uttermost. For the mass of the nation declared itself in favour of change, and the Diet was so composed as to be hostile to change, as soon as it appeared that it was likely to take the direction of Lutheranism. In the Electoral House, indeed, the votes of the three ecclesiastical electors were met by the votes of the three lay electors. But in the House of Princes there were thirty-eight ecclesiastical dignitaries and but eighteen laymen. It was a body, in short, like the English House of Lords before the Reformation, and there was no Henry VIII. to bring it into harmony with the direction which lay society was taking, by some act equivalent to the dissolution of the monasteries, and the consequent exclusion of the mitred abbots from their seats in Parliament. To pass measures favourable to Protestantism through such a house was simply impossible. Yet it can hardly be doubted that a really national Parliament would have adopted Lutheranism, more or less modified, as the religion of the nation. Before Protestantism was fifty years old, in spite of all difficulties, ninety per cent. of the population of Germany were Protestant.

§ 2. Most of the lay princes adopt it.

In default of national action in favor of Protestantism, it was adopted and supported by most of the lay princes and electors. A new principle of disintegration was thus introduced into Germany, as these princes were forced to act in opposition to the views adopted by the Diet.

§ 3. The Emperor Charles V.

If the Diet was unlikely to play the part of an English Parliament, neither was the Emperor likely to play the part of Henry VIII. For the interests of Germany, Charles V., who(Pg 9) had been elected in 1519, was weak where he ought to have been strong, and strong where he ought to have been weak. As Emperor, he was nothing. As feudal sovereign and national ruler, he was very little. But he was also a prince of the Empire, and as such he ruled over the Austrian duchies and Tyrol. Further than this, he was one of the most powerful sovereigns of Europe. He was king of Spain, and of the Indies with all their mines. In Italy, he disposed of Naples and the Milanese. Sicily and Sardinia were his, and, under various titles, he ruled over the fragments of the old Burgundian inheritance, Franche Comté, and the seventeen provinces of the Netherlands. Such a man would influence the progress of affairs in Germany with a weight out of all proportion to his position in the German constitution. And unhappily, with the power of a foreign sovereign, he brought the mind of a foreigner. His mother's Spanish blood beat in his veins, and he had the instinctive aversion of a Spaniard to anything which savoured of opposition to the doctrines of the Church. 'That man,' he said, when he caught sight of Luther for the first time, 'shall never make me a heretic.'

1552.
§ 4. The Convention of Passau.

Of this antagonism between the minority of the princes backed by the majority of the nation, and the majority of the princes backed by an Emperor who was also a foreign sovereign, civil war was the natural result. In the end, the triumph of the Protestants was so far secured that they forced their opponents in 1552 to yield to the Convention of Passau, by which it was arranged that a Diet should be held as soon as possible for a general pacification.

1555

§ 5. The peace of Augsburg.

That Diet, which was assembled at Augsburg in 1555, met under remarkably favourable circumstances. Charles V., baffled(Pg 10) and disappointed, had retired from the scene, and had left behind him, as his representative, his more conciliatory brother Ferdinand, who was already King of Hungary and Bohemia, and was his destined successor in the German possessions of the House of Austria. Both he and the leading men on either side were anxious for peace, and were jealous of the influence which Philip, the son of Charles V., and his successor in Spain, Italy, and the Netherlands, might gain from a continuance of the war.

§ 6. Its terms.

There was little difficulty in arranging that the Protestant princes, who, before the date of the Convention of Passau, had seized ecclesiastical property within their own territories, either for their own purposes or for the support of Protestant worship, should no longer be subject to the law or authority of the Catholic clergy. The real difficulty arose in providing for the future. With Protestantism as a growing religion, the princes might be inclined to proceed further with the secularizing of the Church property still left untouched within their own territories; and besides this, it was possible that even bishops or abbots themselves, being princes of the Empire, might be inclined to abandon their religion, and to adopt Protestantism.

§ 7. Might the princes seize more lands?

The first of these difficulties was left by the treaty in some obscurity; but, from the stress laid on the abandonment by the Catholics of the lands secularized before the Convention of Passau, it would seem that they might fairly urge that they had never abandoned their claims to lands which at that date had not been secularized.

§ 8. Might the ecclesiastics turn Protestants?

The second difficulty led to long discussions. The Protestants wished that any bishop or abbot who pleased might be allowed to turn Protestant, and might then(Pg 11) establish Protestantism as the religion of his subjects. The Catholics insisted that any bishop or abbot who changed his religion should be compelled to vacate his post, and this view of the case prevailed, under the name of the Ecclesiastical Reservation. It was further agreed that the peace should apply to the Lutheran Church alone, no other confession having been as yet adopted by any of the princes.

§ 9. Dangers of the future.

Such a peace, acceptable as it was at the time, was pregnant with future evil. Owing its origin to a Diet in which everything was arranged by the princes and electors, it settled all questions as if nobody but princes and electors had any interest in the matter. And, besides this, there was a most unstatesmanlike want of provision for future change. The year 1552 was to give the line by which the religious institutions of Germany were to be measured for all time. There was nothing elastic about such legislation. It did not, on the one hand, adopt the religion of the vast majority as the established religion of the Empire. It did not, on the other hand, adopt the principle of religious liberty. In thinking of themselves and their rights, the princes had forgotten the German people.

§ 10. Fresh encroachments upon Church lands.

The barriers set up against Protestantism were so plainly artificial that they soon gave way. The princes claimed the right of continuing to secularize Church lands within their territories as inseparable from their general right of providing for the religion of their subjects. At all events they had might on their side. About a hundred monasteries are said to have fallen victims in the Palatinate alone, and an almost equal number, the gleanings of a richer harvest which had been reaped before the(Pg 12) Convention of Passau, were taken possession of in Northern Germany.

§ 11. The Ecclesiastical Reservation.

The Ecclesiastical Reservation applied to a different class of property, namely, to the bishoprics and abbeys held immediately of the Empire. Here, too, the Protestants found an excuse for evading the Treaty of Augsburg. The object of the reservation, they argued, was not to keep the bishoprics in Catholic hands, but to prevent quarrels arising between the bishops and their chapters. If, therefore, a bishop elected as a Catholic chose to turn Protestant, he must resign his see in order to avoid giving offence to the Catholic chapter. But where a chapter, itself already Protestant, elected a Protestant bishop, he might take the see without hesitation, and hold it as long as he lived.

§ 12. The northern bishoprics Protestant.

In this way eight of the great northern bishoprics soon came under Protestant rule. Not that the Protestant occupant was in any real sense of the word a bishop. He was simply an elected prince, calling himself a bishop, or often more modestly an administrator, and looking after the temporal affairs of his dominions.

§ 13. Good and bad side of the arrangement.

In some respects the arrangement was a good one. The populations of these territories were mainly Protestant, and they had no cause to complain. Besides, if only a sufficient number of these bishoprics could be gained to Protestantism, the factitious majority in the Diet might be reversed, and an assembly obtained more truly representing the nation than that which was in existence. But it must be acknowledged that the whole thing had an ugly look; and it is no wonder that Catholics pronounced these administrators to be no bishops at all, and to have no right(Pg 13) to hold the bishops' lands, or to take their seat as bishops in the Diet of the Empire.

SECTION III.—Reaction against Protestantism.

§ 1. Theological disputes among Protestants.

In course of time Protestantism, in its turn, exposed itself to attack. Each petty court soon had its own school of theologians, whose minds were dwarfed to the limits of the circle which they influenced with their logic and their eloquence. The healthful feeling which springs from action on a large stage was wanting to them. Bitterly wrangling with one another, they were eager to call in the secular arm against their opponents. Seizing the opportunity, the newly-constituted order of Jesuits stepped forward to bid silence in the name of the renovated Papal Church, alone, as they urged, able to give peace instead of strife, certainty instead of disputation. The Protestants were taken at a disadvantage. The enthusiasm of a national life, which repelled the Jesuits in the England of the sixteenth century, and the enthusiasm of scientific knowledge which repels them in the Germany of the nineteenth century, were alike wanting to a Germany in which national life was a dream of the past, and science a dream of the future. Luther had long ago passed away from the world. Melanchthon's last days were spent in hopeless protest against the evil around him. 'For two reasons,' he said, as he lay upon his death-bed, 'I desire to leave this life: First, that I may enjoy the sight, which I long for, of the Son of God and of the Church in Heaven. Next, that I may be set free from the monstrous and implacable hatreds of the theologians.'

§ 2. The Catholics make progress.

In the face of a divided people, or self-seeking princes, and of conflicting theories, the Jesuits made(Pg 14) their way. Step by step the Catholic reaction gained ground, not without compulsion, but also not without that moral force which makes compulsion possible. The bishops and abbots gave their subjects the choice between conversion and exile. An attempt made by the Archbishop of Cologne to marry and turn Protestant was too plainly in contradiction to the Ecclesiastical Reservation to prosper, and when the Protestant majority of the Chapter of Strasburg elected a Protestant bishop they were soon overpowered. A Protestant Archbishop of Magdeburg offering to take his place amongst the princes of the Empire at the Diet was refused admission, and though nothing was done to dispossess him and the other northern administrators of their sees, yet a slur had been cast upon their title which they were anxious to efface. A few years later a legal decision was obtained in the cases of four monasteries secularized after the Convention of Passau, and that decision was adverse to the claim of the Protestants.

§ 3. The disputes which led finally to war.

Out of these two disputes—the dispute about the Protestant administrators and the dispute about the secularized lands—the Thirty Years' War arose. The Catholic party stood upon the strict letter of the law, according, at least, to their own interpretation, and asked that everything might be replaced in the condition in which it was in 1552, the date of the Convention of Passau. The Protestant view, that consideration should be taken for changes, many of which at the end of the sixteenth century were at least a generation old, may or may not have been in accordance with the law, but it was certainly in accordance with the desires of the greater part of the population affected by them.

(Pg 15)

§ 4. No popular representation.

There is every reason to believe that if Germany had possessed anything like a popular representation its voice would have spoken in favour of some kind of compromise. There is no trace of any mutual hostility between the populations of the Catholic and Protestant districts apart from their rulers.

SECTION IV.—Three Parties and Three Leaders.

§ 1. The leaders of parties.

Two men stood forward to personify the elements of strife—Maximilian, the Catholic Duke of Bavaria, and the Calvinist Prince Christian of Anhalt, whilst the warmest advocate of peace was John George, the Lutheran Elector of Saxony.

§ 2. Maximilian of Bavaria.

Maximilian of Bavaria was the only lay prince of any importance on the side of the Catholics. He had long been known as a wise administrator of his own dominions. No other ruler was provided with so well-filled a treasury, or so disciplined an army. No other ruler was so capable of forming designs which were likely to win the approbation of others, or so patient in waiting till the proper time arrived for their execution. 'What the Duke of Bavaria does,' said one of his most discerning opponents, 'has hands and feet.' His plans, when once they were launched into the world, seemed to march forwards of themselves to success.

§ 3. His love of legality.

Such a man was not likely to take up the wild theories which were here and there springing up, of the duty of uprooting Protestantism at all times and all places, or to declare, as some were declaring, that the Peace of Augsburg was invalid because it had never been confirmed by the Pope. To him the Peace of Augsburg was the legal settlement by which all(Pg 16) questions were to be tried. What he read there was hostile to the Protestant administrators and the secularizing princes. Yet he did not propose to carry his views into instant action. He would await his opportunity. But he would do his best to be strong, in order that he might not be found wanting when the opportunity arrived, and, in spite of his enthusiasm for legal rights, it was by no means unlikely that, if a difficult point arose, he might be inclined to strain the law in his own favour.

§ 4. Danger of the Protestants.

Such an opponent, so moderate and yet so resolute, was a far more dangerous enemy to the Protestants than the most blatant declaimer against their doctrines. Naturally, the Protestants regarded his views as entirely inadmissible. They implied nothing less than the forcible conversion of the thousands of Protestants who were inhabitants of the administrators' dominions, and the occupation by the Catholic clergy of points of vantage which would serve them in their operations upon the surrounding districts. It is true that the change, if effected would simply replace matters in the position which had been found endurable in 1552. But that which could be borne when the Catholics were weak and despondent might be an intolerable menace when they were confident and aggressive.

§ 5. Danger of the Protestants.

Resistance, therefore, became a duty, a duty to which the princes were all the more likely to pay attention because it coincided with their private interest. In the bishoprics and chapters they found provision for their younger sons, from which they would be cut off if Protestants were hereafter to be excluded.

§ 6. Protestants of the north and south.

The only question was in what spirit the resistance should be offered. The tie which bound the Empire to(Pg 17)gether was so loose, and resistance to law, or what was thought to be law, was so likely to lead to resistance to law in general, that it was the more incumbent on the Protestants to choose their ground well. And in Germany, at least, there was not likely to be any hasty provocation to give Maximilian an excuse for reclaiming the bishoprics. Far removed from the danger, these northern Lutherans found it difficult to conceive that there was any real danger at all. The states of the south, lying like a wedge driven into the heart of European Catholicism, were forced by their geographical position to be ever on the alert. They knew that they were the advanced guard of Protestantism. On the one flank was the Catholic duchy of Bavaria, and the bishoprics of Würzburg and Bamberg. On the other flank were the ecclesiastical electorates on the Rhine and the Moselle, the bishoprics of Worms, Spires, and Strasburg, the Austrian lands in Swabia and Alsace, and the long line of the Spanish frontier in Franche Comté and the Netherlands garrisoned by the troops of the first military monarchy in Europe. What wonder if men so endangered were in haste to cut the knot which threatened to strangle them, and to meet the enemy by flying in his face rather than by awaiting the onslaught which they believed to be inevitable.

§ 7. Spread of Calvinism.

Under the influence of this feeling the princes of these southern regions for the most part adopted a religion very different from the courtly Lutheranism of the north. If Würtemberg continued Lutheran under the influence of the University of Tübingen, the rulers of the Palatinate, of Hesse Cassel, of Baden-Durlach, of Zwei-Brücken, sought for strength in the iron discipline of Calvinism, a form of(Pg 18) religion which always came into favour when there was an immediate prospect of a death-struggle with Rome.

§ 8. Courtly character of Calvinism in Germany.

Unhappily, German Calvinism differed from that of Scotland and the Netherlands. Owing to its adoption by the princes rather than by the people, it failed in gaining that hardy growth which made it invincible on its native soil. It had less of the discipline of an army about it, less resolute defiance, less strength altogether. And whilst it was weaker it was more provocative. Excluded from the benefits of the Peace of Augsburg, which knew of no Protestant body except the Lutheran, the Calvinists were apt to talk about the institutions of the Empire in a manner so disparaging as to give offence to Lutherans and Catholics alike.

§ 9. Frederick IV., Elector Palatine.

Of this Calvinist feeling Christian of Anhalt became the impersonation. The leadership of the Calvinist states in the beginning of the seventeenth century would naturally have devolved on Frederick IV., Elector Palatine. But Frederick was an incapable drunkard, and his councillors, with Christian at their head, were left to act in his name.

§ 10. Christian of Anhalt.

Christian of Anhalt possessed a brain of inexhaustible fertility. As soon as one plan which he had framed appeared impracticable, he was ready with another. He was a born diplomatist, and all the chief politicians of Europe were intimately known to him by report, whilst with many of them he carried on a close personal intercourse. His leading idea was that the maintenance of peace was hopeless, and that either Protestantism must get rid of the House of Austria, or the House of Austria would get(Pg 19) rid of Protestantism. Whether this were true or false, it is certain that he committed the terrible fault of underestimating his enemy. Whilst Maximilian was drilling soldiers and saving money, Christian was trusting to mere diplomatic finesse. He had no idea of the tenacity with which men will cling to institutions, however rotten, till they feel sure that some other institutions will be substituted for them, or of the strength which Maximilian derived from the appearance of conservatism in which his revolutionary designs were shrouded even from his own observation. In order to give to Protestantism that development which in Christian's eyes was necessary to its safety, it would be needful to overthrow the authority of the Emperor and of the Diet. And if the Emperor and the Diet were overthrown, what had Christian to offer to save Germany from anarchy? If his plan included, as there is little doubt that it did, the seizure of the lands of the neighbouring bishops, and a fresh secularization of ecclesiastical property, even Protestant towns might begin to ask whether their turn would not come next. A return to the old days of private war and the law of the strongest would be welcome to very few.

1607

§ 11. The occupation of Donauwörth.

In 1607 an event occurred which raised the alarm of the southern Protestants to fever heat. In the free city of Donauwörth the abbot of a monastery saw fit to send out a procession to flaunt its banners in the face of an almost entirely Protestant population. Before the starting-point was regained mud and stones were thrown, and some of those who had taken part in the proceedings were roughly handled. The Imperial Court (*Reichskammergericht*), whose duty it was to settle such quarrels, was out of working order in consequence of the(Pg 20) religious disputes; but there was an Imperial Council (*Reichshofrath*), consisting of nominees of the Emperor, and professing to act out of the plenitude of imperial authority. By this council Donauwörth was put to the ban of the Empire without due form of trial, and Maximilian was appointed to execute the decree. He at once marched a small army into the place, and, taking possession of the town, declared his intention of retaining his hold till his expenses had been paid, handing over the parish church in the meanwhile to the Catholic clergy. It had only been given over to Protestant worship after the date of the Convention of Passau, and Maximilian could persuade himself that he was only carrying out the law.

1608

§ 12. The Diet of 1608.

It was a flagrant case of religious aggression under the name of the law. The knowledge that a partial tribunal was ready to give effect to the complaints of Catholics at once threw the great Protestant cities of the South—Nüremberg, Ulm, and Strasburg into the arms of the neighbouring princes of whom they had hitherto been jealous. Yet there was much in the policy of those princes which would hardly have reassured them. At the Diet of 1608 the representatives of the Elector Palatine were foremost in demanding that the minority should not be bound by the majority in questions of taxation or religion; that is to say, that they should not contribute to the common defence unless they pleased, and that they should not be subject to any regulation about ecclesiastical property unless they pleased. Did this mean only that they were to keep what they had got, or that they might take more as soon as it was convenient? The one was the Protestant, the other the Catholic interpretation of their theory.

(Pg 21)

§ 13. Formation of the Union.

On May 14, 1608, the Protestant Union, to which Lutherans and Calvinists were alike admitted, came into existence under the guidance of Christian of Anhalt. It was mainly composed of the princes and towns of the south. Its ostensible purpose was for self-defence, and in this sense it was accepted by most of those who took part in it. Its leaders had very different views.

§14. Formation of the League.

A Catholic League was at once formed under Maximilian. It was composed of a large number of bishops and abbots, who believed that the princes of the Union wished to annex their territories. Maximilian's ability gave it a unity of action which the Union never possessed. It, too, was constituted for self-defence, but whether that word was to include the resumption of the lands lost since the Convention of Passau was a question probably left for circumstances to decide.

§ 15. Revolutionary tendencies of the Union.

Whatever the majority of the princes of the Union may have meant, there can be no doubt that Christian of Anhalt meant aggression. He believed that the safety of Protestantism could not be secured without the overthrow of the German branch of the House of Austria, and he was sanguine enough to fancy that an act which would call up all Catholic Europe in arms against him was a very easy undertaking.

1609
§ 16. The succession of Cleves.
Scarcely had the Union been formed when events occurred which almost dragged Germany into war. In the spring of 1609 the Duke of Cleves died. The Elector of Brandenburg and the son of the Duke of Neuburg laid claim to the succession. On the plea that the Emperor had the right to settle the point, a Catholic army advanced(Pg 22) to take possession of the country. The two pretenders, both of them Lutherans, made common cause against the invaders. 1610. Henry IV. of France found in the dispute a pretext for commencing his long-meditated attack upon Spain and her allies. But his life was cut short by an assassin, and his widow only thought of sending a small French force to join the English and the Dutch in maintaining the claims of the two princes, who were ready to unite for a time against a third party.

1613
§ 17. The box on the ear.

It was not easy to bring the princes to an arrangement for the future. One day the young Prince of Neuburg proposed what seemed to him an excellent way out of the difficulty. 'He was ready,' he said, 'to marry the Elector's daughter, if only he might have the territory.' Enraged at the impudence of the proposal, the Elector raised his hand and boxed his young rival's ears. The blow had unexpected consequences. The injured prince renounced his Protestantism, and invoked, as a good Catholic, the aid of Spain and the League. The Elector passed from Lutheranism to Calvinism, and took a more active part than before in the affairs of the Union. That immediate war in Germany did not result from the quarrel is probably the strongest possible evidence of the reluctance of the German people to break the peace.

1612
§ 18. John George, Elector of Saxony.

The third party, the German Lutherans, looked with equal abhorrence upon aggression on either side. Their leader, John George, Elector of Saxony, stood aloof alike from Christian of Anhalt, and from Maximilian of Bavaria. He was attached by the traditions of his house as well as by his own character to the Empire and the House of Austria. But he was anxious to obtain security for(Pg 23) his brother Protestants. He saw there must be a change; but he wisely desired to make the change as slight as possible. In 1612, therefore, he proposed that the highest jurisdiction should still be retained by the Imperial Council, but that the Council, though still nominated by the Emperor, should contain an equal number of Catholics and Protestants. Sentences such as that which had deprived Donauwörth of its civil rights would be in future impossible.

§ 19. His weakness of character.

Unhappily, John George had not the gift of ruling men. He was a hard drinker and a bold huntsman, but to convert his wishes into actual facts was beyond his power. When he saw his plan threatened with opposition on either side he left it to take care of itself. In 1613 a Diet met, and broke up in confusion, leaving matters in such a state that any spark might give rise to a general conflagration.

(Pg 24)

CHAPTER II. THE BOHEMIAN REVOLUTION.

SECTION I.—The House of Austria and its Subjects.

§ 1. The Austrian dominions.

At the beginning of the seventeenth century the dominions of the German branch of the House of Austria were parcelled out amongst the various descendants of Ferdinand I., the brother of Charles V. The head of the family, the Emperor Rudolph II., was Archduke of Austria—a name which in those days was used simply to indicate the archduchy itself, and not the group of territories which are at present ruled over by the Austrian sovereign—and he was also King of Bohemia and of Hungary. His brother Maximilian governed Tyrol, and his cousin Ferdinand ruled in Styria, Carinthia, and Carniola.

§ 2. Aristocracy and Protestantism.

The main difficulty of government arose from the fact that whilst every member of the family clung firmly to the old creed, the greater part of the population, excepting in Tyrol, had adopted the new; that is to say, that on the great question of the day the subjects and the rulers had no thoughts in common. And this difficulty was aggravated by the further fact that Protestantism prospered mainly from the support given to it by a powerful aristocracy, so that political disagreement was added to the difference in religion. Ferdinand had, indeed, contrived to put down with a strong hand the exercise of Protestantism in his own dominions so easily as almost to suggest the inference that it had not taken very deep root in those Alpine regions. But Rudolph was quite incapable of(Pg 25) following his example. If not absolutely insane, he was subject to sudden outbursts of temper, proceeding from mental disease.

1606
§ 3. Rudolph and Matthias.

In 1606, a peace having been concluded with the Turks, Rudolph fancied that his hands were at last free to deal with his subjects as Ferdinand had dealt with his. The result was a general uprising, and if Rudolph's brother Matthias had not placed himself at the head of the movement, in order to save the interests of the family, some stranger would probably have been selected as a rival to the princes of the House of Austria.

In the end, two years later, Austria and Hungary were assigned to Matthias, whilst Bohemia, Moravia and Silesia were left to Rudolph for his lifetime.

1609
§ 4. The Royal Charter of Bohemia.

The result of Rudolph's ill-advised energy was to strengthen the hands of the Protestant nobility. In Hungary the Turks were too near to make it easy for Matthias to refuse concessions to a people who might, at any time, throw themselves into the arms of the enemy, and in Austria he was driven, after some resistance, to agree to a compromise. In Bohemia, in 1609, the Estates extorted from Rudolph the Royal Charter (*Majestätts brief*) which guaranteed freedom of conscience to every inhabitant of Bohemia, as long as he kept to certain recognised creeds. But freedom of conscience did not by any means imply freedom of worship. A man might think as he pleased, but the building of churches and the performance of divine service were matters for the authorities to decide upon. The only question was, who the authorities were.

§ 5. Position of the landowner.

By the Royal Charter this authority was given over to members of the Estates, that is to say, to about 1,400 of(Pg 26) the feudal aristocracy and 42 towns. In an agreement attached to the charter, a special exception was made for the royal domains. A Protestant landowner could and would prohibit the erection of a Catholic church on his own lands, but the king was not to have that privilege. On his domains worship was to be free.

§ 6. Rudolph tries to get rid of it.

From this bondage, as he counted it, Rudolph struggled to liberate himself. There was fresh violence, ending in 1611 in Rudolph's dethronement in favour of Matthias, who thus became king of Bohemia. The next year he died, and Matthias succeeded him as Emperor also.

§ 7. Christian of Anhalt hopes for general confusion.

During all these troubles, Christian of Anhalt had done all that he could to frustrate a peaceful settlement. 'When Hungary, Moravia, Austria, and Silesia are on our side,' he explained, before the Royal Charter had been granted, to a diplomatist in his employment, 'the House of Hapsburg will have no further strength to resist us, except in Bohemia, Bavaria, and a few bishoprics. Speaking humanly, we shall be strong enough not only to resist these, but to reform all the clergy, and bring them into submission to our religion. The game will begin in this fashion. As soon as Bavaria arms to use compulsion against Austria,' (that is to say, against the Austrian Protestants, who were at that time resisting Matthias) 'we shall arm to attack Bavaria, and retake Donauwörth. In the same way, we shall get hold of two or three bishops to supply us with money. Certainly, it seems that by proceeding dexterously we shall give the law to all, and set up for rulers whom we will.'

§ 8. Matthias King of Bohemia.

For the time Christian was disappointed. The dominions of Matthias settled down into quietness. But(Pg 27) Matthias was preparing another opportunity for his antagonist. Whether it would have been possible in those days for a Catholic king to have kept a Protestant nation in working order we cannot say. At all events, Matthias did not give the experiment a fair trial. He did not, indeed, attack the Royal Charter directly on the lands of the aristocracy. But he did his best to undermine it on his own. The Protestants of Braunau, on the lands of the Abbot of Braunau and the Protestants of Klostergrab, on the lands of the Archbishop of Prague, built churches for themselves, the use of which was prohibited by the abbot and the archbishop. A dispute immediately arose as to the rights of ecclesiastical landowners, and it was argued on the Protestant side, that their lands were technically Crown lands, and that they had therefore no right to close the churches. Matthias took the opposite view.

§ 9. He evades the charter.

On his own estates Matthias found means to evade the charter. He appointed Catholic priests to Protestant churches, and allowed measures to be taken to compel Protestants to attend the Catholic service. Yet for a long time the Protestant nobility kept quiet. Matthias was old and infirm, and when he died they would, as they supposed, have an opportunity of choosing their next king, and it was generally believed that the election would fall upon a Protestant. The only question was whether the Elector Palatine or the Elector of Saxony would be chosen.

1617
§ 10. Ferdinand proposed as king of Bohemia.

Suddenly, in 1617, the Bohemian Diet was summoned. When the Estates of the kingdom met they were told that it was a mistake to suppose that the crown of Bohemia was elective. Evidence was pro(Pg 28)duced that for some time before the election of Matthias the Estates had acknowledged the throne to be hereditary, and the precedent of Matthias was to be set aside as occurring in revolutionary times. Intimidation was used to assist the argument, and men in the confidence of the court whispered in the ears of those who refused to be convinced that it was to be hoped that they had at least two heads on their shoulders.

§ 11. The Bohemians acknowledge him as their king.

If ever there was a moment for resistance, if resistance was to be made at all, it was this. The arguments of the court were undoubtedly strong, but a skilful lawyer could easily have found technicalities on the other side, and the real evasion of the Royal Charter might have been urged as a reason why the court had no right to press technical arguments too closely. The danger was all the greater as it was known that by the renunciation of all intermediate heirs the hereditary right fell upon Ferdinand of Styria, the man who had already stamped Protestantism out in his own dominions. Yet, in spite of this, the Diet did as it was bidden, and renounced the right of election by acknowledging Ferdinand as their hereditary king.

§ 12. His character.

The new king was more of a devotee and less of a statesman than Maximilian of Bavaria, his cousin on his mother's side. But their judgments of events were formed on the same lines. Neither of them were mere ordinary bigots, keeping no faith with heretics. But they were both likely to be guided in their interpretation of the law by that which they conceived to be profitable to their church. Ferdinand was personally brave; but except when his course was very clear before him, he was apt to let difficulties settle themselves rather than come to a decision.

(Pg 29)

§ 13. He takes the oath to the Royal Charter.

He had at once to consider whether he would swear to the Royal Charter. He consulted the Jesuits, and was told that, though it had been a sin to grant it, it was no sin to accept it now that it was the law of the land. As he walked in state to his coronation, he turned to a nobleman who was by his side. 'I am glad,' he said, 'that I have attained the Bohemian crown without any pangs of conscience.' He took the oath without further difficulty.

The Bohemians were not long in feeling the effects of the change. Hitherto the hold of the House of Austria upon the country had been limited to the life of one old man. It had now, by the admission of the Diet itself, fixed itself for ever upon Bohemia. The proceedings against the Protestants on the royal domains assumed a sharper character. The Braunau worshippers were rigorously excluded from their church. The walls of the new church of Klostergrab were actually levelled with the ground.

Section II.—The Revolution at Prague.

1618. § 1. The Bohemians petition Matthias.

The Bohemians had thus to resist in 1618, under every disadvantage, the attack which they had done nothing to meet in 1617. Certain persons named Defensors had, by law, the right of summoning an assembly of representatives of the Protestant Estates. Such an assembly met on March 5, and having prepared a petition to Matthias, who was absent from the kingdom, adjourned to May 21.

§ 2. Reply of Matthias.

Long before the time of meeting came, an answer was sent from Matthias justifying all that had been done, and declaring the assembly illegal. It was believed at(Pg 30) the time, though incorrectly, that the answer was prepared by Slawata and Martinitz, two members of the regency who had been notorious for the vigour of their opposition to Protestantism.

§ 3. Violent counsels.

In the Protestant assembly there was a knot of men, headed by Count Henry of Thurn, which was bent on the dethronement of Ferdinand. They resolved to take advantage of the popular feeling to effect the murder of the two regents, and so to place an impassable gulf between the nation and the king.

§ 4. Martinitz and Slawata thrown out of window.

Accordingly, on the morning of May 23, the 'beginning and cause,' as a contemporary calls it, 'of all the coming evil,' the first day, though men as yet knew it not, of thirty years of war, Thurn sallied forth at the head of a band of noblemen and their followers, all of them with arms in their hands. Trooping into the room where the regents were seated, they charged the obnoxious two with being the authors of the king's reply. After a bitter altercation both Martinitz and Slawata were dragged to a window which overlooked the fosse below from a dizzy height of some seventy feet. Martinitz, struggling against his enemies, pleaded hard for a confessor. 'Commend thy soul to God,' was the stern answer. 'Shall we allow the Jesuit scoundrels to come here?' In an instant he was hurled out, crying, 'Jesus, Mary!' 'Let us see,' said some one mockingly, 'Whether his Mary will help him.' A moment later he added: 'By God, his Mary has helped him.' Slawata followed, and then the secretary Fabricius. By a wonderful preservation, in which pious Catholics discerned the protecting hand of God, all three crawled away from the spot without serious hurt.

(Pg 31)

§ 5. A bad beginning.

There are moments when the character of a nation or party stands revealed as by a lightning flash, and this was one of them. It is not in such a way as this that successful revolutions are begun.

§ 6. The revolutionary government.

The first steps to constitute a new government were easy. Thirty Directors were appointed, and the Jesuits were expelled from Bohemia. The Diet met and ordered soldiers to be levied to form an army. But to support this army money would be needed, and the existing taxes were insufficient. A loan was accordingly thought of, and the nobles resolved to request the towns to make up the sum, they themselves contributing nothing. The project falling dead upon the resistance of the towns, new taxes were voted; but no steps were taken to collect them, and the army was left to depend in a great measure upon chance.

§ 7. The Elector of Saxony wishes for peace.

Would the princes of Germany come to the help of the Directors? John George of Saxony told them that he deeply sympathized with them, but that rebellion was a serious matter. To one who asked him what he meant to do, he replied, 'Help to put out the fire.'

§ 8. The Elector Palatine holds out hopes of assistance.

There was more help for them at Heidelberg than at Dresden. Frederick IV. had died in 1610, and his son, the young Frederick V., looked up to Christian of Anhalt as the first statesman of his age. By his marriage with Elizabeth, the daughter of James I. of England, he had contracted an alliance which gave him the appearance rather than the reality of strength. He offered every encouragement to the Bohemians, but for the time held back from giving them actual assistance.

(Pg 32)

Section III.—The War in Bohemia.

§ 1. Outbreak of war.

The Directors were thus thrown on their own resources. Ferdinand had secured his election as king of Hungary, and, returning to Vienna, had taken up the reins of government in the name of Matthias. He had got together an army of 14,000 men, under the command of Bucquoi, an officer from the great school of military art in the Netherlands, and on August 13, the Bohemian frontier was invaded. War could hardly be avoided by either side. Budweis and Pilsen, two Catholic towns in Bohemia, naturally clung to their sovereign, and as soon as the Directors ordered an attack upon Budweis, the troops of Matthias prepared to advance to its succour.

§ 2. The Bohemians vote men, but object to paying taxes.

The Directors took alarm, and proposed to the Diet that new taxes should be raised and not merely voted, and that, in addition to the army of regular soldiers, there should be a general levy of a large portion of the population. To the levy the Diet consented without difficulty. But before the day fixed for discussing the proposed taxes arrived, the majority of the members deliberately returned to their homes, and no new taxes were to be had.

§ 3. They are not likely to prosper.

This day, August 30, may fairly be taken as the date of the political suicide of the Bohemian aristocracy. In almost every country in Europe order was maintained by concentrating the chief powers of the State in the hands of a single governor, whether he were called king, duke, or elector. To this rule there were exceptions in Venice, Switzerland, and the Netherlands, and by-and-by there would be an exception on a grander scale in England. But the peoples who formed these exceptions had proved(Pg 33)themselves worthy of the distinction, and there would be no room in the world for men who had got rid of their king without being able to establish order upon another basis.

§ 4. Help from Savoy.

Still there were too many governments in Europe hostile to the House of Austria to allow the Bohemians to fall at once. Charles Emmanuel, Duke of Savoy, had just brought a war with Spain to a close, but he had not become any better disposed towards his late adversary. He accordingly entered into an agreement with the leaders of the Union, by which 2,000 men who had been raised for his service were to be placed at the disposal of the Bohemian Directors.

§ 5. Mansfeld.

The commander of these troops was Count Ernest of Mansfeld, an illegitimate son of a famous general in the service of Spain. He had changed his religion and deserted his king. He now put himself forward as a champion of Protestantism. He was brave, active, and versatile, and was possessed of those gifts which win the confidence of professional soldiers. But he was already notorious for the readiness with which he allowed his soldiers to support themselves on the most unbridled pillage. An adventurer himself, he was just the man to lead an army of adventurers.

§ 6. A forced loan.

Soon after his arrival in Bohemia, Mansfeld was employed in the siege of Pilsen, whilst Thurn was occupied with holding Bucquoi in check. The failure in obtaining additional taxes had led the Directors to adopt the simple expedient of levying a forced loan from the few rich.

§ 7. Success of the Bohemians.

For a time this desperate expedient was successful. The help offered to Ferdinand by Spain was not great, and it was long in coming. The prudent Maximilian re(Pg 34)fused to ruin himself by engaging in an apparently hopeless cause. At last the Silesians, who had hesitated long, threw in their lot with their neighbours, and sent their troops to their help early in November. Bucquoi was in full retreat to Budweis. On the 21st Pilsen surrendered to Mansfeld. Further warfare was stopped as winter came on—a terrible winter for the unhappy dwellers in Southern Bohemia. Starving armies are not particular in their methods of supplying their wants. Plunder, devastation and reckless atrocities of every kind fell to the lot of the doomed peasants, Bucquoi's Hungarians being conspicuous for barbarity.

§ 8. Scheme of Christian of Anhalt.

Meanwhile, Christian of Anhalt was luring on the young Elector Palatine to more active intervention. The Bohemian leaders had already begun to talk of placing the crown on Frederick's head. Frederick, anxious and undecided, consented on the one hand, at the Emperor's invitation, to join the Duke of Bavaria and the Electors of Mentz and Saxony in mediating an arrangement, whilst, on the other hand, he gave his assent to an embassy to Turin, the object of which was to dazzle the Duke of Savoy with the prospect of obtaining the imperial crown after the death of Matthias, and to urge him to join in an attack upon the German dominions of the House of Austria.

§ 9. Coolness of the Union.

The path on which Frederick was entering was the more evidently unsafe, as the Union, which met at Heilbronn in September, had shown great coolness in the Bohemian cause. Christian of Anhalt had not ventured even to hint at the projects which he entertained. If he was afterwards deserted by the Union he could not say that its members as a body had engaged to support him.

(Pg 35)

1619
§ 10. The Duke of Savoy gives hopes.

The Duke of Savoy, on the other hand, at least talked as if the Austrian territories were at his feet. In August 1618 he had given his consent to the proposed elevation of Frederick to the Bohemian throne. In February 1619 he explained that he wished to have Bohemia for himself. Frederick might be compensated with the Austrian lands in Alsace and Swabia. He might, perhaps, have the Archduchy of Austria too, or become King of Hungary. If he wished to fall upon the bishops' lands, let him do it quickly, before the Pope had time to interfere. This sort of talk, wild as it was, delighted the little circle of Frederick's confidants. The Margrave of Anspach, who, as general of the army of the Union, was admitted into the secret, was beyond measure pleased: 'We have now,' he said, 'the means of upsetting the world.'

§ 11. Conservative feeling alienated.

For the present, these negotiations were veiled in secresy. They engendered a confident levity, which was certain to shock that conservative, peace-loving feeling which the Bohemians had already done much to alienate.

SECTION IV.—Ferdinand on his Defence.

§ 1. The Bohemians look for aid from foreign powers.

If the assistance of the Union was thus likely to do more harm than good to the Bohemians, their hopes of aid from other powers were still more delusive. The Dutch, indeed, sent something, and would willingly have sent more, but they had too many difficulties at home to be very profuse in their offers. James of England told his son-in-law plainly that he would have nothing to do with any encroachment upon the rights of others, and he had undertaken at the instigation of Spain a formal mediation between the Bohemians and their king—a mediation(Pg 36) which had been offered him merely in order to keep his hands tied whilst others were arming.

§ 2. Attack upon Vienna.

On March 20, before the next campaign opened, Matthias died. Ferdinand's renewed promises to respect the Royal Charter—made doubtless under the reservation of putting his own interpretation upon the disputed points—were rejected with scorn by the Directors. The sword was to decide the quarrel. With the money received from the Dutch, and with aid in money and munitions of war from Heidelberg, Thurn and Mansfeld were enabled to take the field. The latter remained to watch Bucquoi, whilst the former undertook to win the other territories, which had hitherto submitted to Matthias, and had stood aloof from the movement in Bohemia. Without much difficulty he succeeded in revolutionizing Moravia, and he arrived on June 5 under the walls of Vienna. Within was Ferdinand himself, with a petty garrison of 300 men, and as many volunteers as he could attach to his cause. Thurn hoped that his partisans inside the cities would open the gates to admit him. But he lost time in negotiations with the Austrian nobility. The estates of the two territories of Upper and Lower Austria were to a great extent Protestant, and they had refused to do homage to Ferdinand on the death of Matthias. The Lower Austrians now sent a deputation to Vienna to demand permission to form a confederation with the Bohemians, on terms which would practically have converted the whole country, from the Styrian frontier to the borders of Silesia, into a federal aristocratic republic.

§ 3. Ferdinand resists the demands of the Lower Austrian Estates.

In Ferdinand they had to do with a man who was not to be overawed by personal danger. He knew well that by yielding he would be giving a legal basis to a system which he regarded as opposed to all law, human(Pg 37) and divine. Throwing himself before the crucifix, he found strength for the conflict into which he entered on behalf of his family, his church, and, as he firmly believed, of his country and his God—strength none the less real because the figure on the cross did not, as men not long afterwards came fondly to believe, bow its head towards the suppliant, or utter the consoling words: 'Ferdinand, I will not forsake thee.'

§ 4. Rescue arrives.

To a deputation from the Austrian Estates he was firm and unbending. They might threaten as they pleased, but the confederation with Bohemia he would not sign. Rougher and rougher grew the menaces addressed to him. Some one, it is said, talked of dethroning him and of educating his children in the Protestant religion. Suddenly the blare of a trumpet was heard in the court below. A regiment of horses had slipped in through a gate unguarded by Thurn, and had hurried to Ferdinand's defence. The deputation, lately so imperious, slunk away, glad enough to escape punishment.

§ 5. The siege raised.

Little would so slight a reinforcement have availed if Thurn had been capable of assaulting the city. But, unprovided with stores of food or siege munitions, he had counted on treason within. Disappointed of his prey, he returned to Bohemia, to find that Bucquoi had broken out of Budweis, and had inflicted a serious defeat on Mansfeld.

§ 6. The Imperial election.

Ferdinand did not linger at Vienna to dispute his rights with his Austrian subjects. The election of a new Emperor was to take place at Frankfort, and it was of importance to him to be on the spot. To the German Protestants the transfer of the Imperial crown to his head could not be(Pg 38) a matter of indifference. If he succeeded, as there seemed every probability of his succeeding, in re-establishing his authority over Bohemia, he would weigh with a far heavier weight than Matthias upon the disputes by which Germany was distracted. The Elector Palatine and his councillors had a thousand schemes for getting rid of him, without fixing upon any. John George of Saxony, in 1619 as in 1612, had a definite plan to propose. Ferdinand, he said, was not in possession of Bohemia, and could not, therefore, vote as King of Bohemia at the election. The election must, therefore, be postponed till the Bohemian question had been settled by mediation. If only the three Protestant electors could have been brought to agree to this course, an immediate choice of Ferdinand would have been impossible.

§ 7. Ferdinand chosen Emperor.

Whatever might be the merits of the proposal itself, it had the inestimable advantage of embarking the Lutherans of the North and the Calvinists of the South in a common cause. But Frederick distrusted John George, and preferred another plan of his own. John George lost his temper, and voted unconditionally for Ferdinand. Frederick, if he did not mean to be left alone in impotent isolation, had nothing for it but to follow his example. He had no other candidate seriously to propose; and on August 28, 1619, Ferdinand was chosen by a unanimous vote. He was now known as the Emperor Ferdinand II.

§ 8. Frederick elected King of Bohemia.

Two days before, another election had taken place at Prague. The Bohemians, after deposing Ferdinand from the throne, which in 1617 they had acknowledged to be his, chose Frederick to fill the vacant seat.

§ 9. He accepts the throne.

Would Frederick accept the perilous offer? Opinions(Pg 39) round him were divided on the advisability of the step. The princes of the Union, and even his own councillors, took opposite sides. In his own family, his mother raised a voice of warning. His wife, Elizabeth of England, the beautiful and high-spirited, urged him to the enterprise. The poor young man himself was well-nigh distracted. At last he found a consolation in the comfortable belief that his election was the act of God. Amidst the tears of the good people of Heidelberg he set out from the proud castle, magnificent even now in its ruins as it looks down upon the rushing stream of the Neckar. 'He is carrying the Palatinate into Bohemia,' said his sorrowing mother. On November 4 he was crowned at Prague, and the last act of the Bohemian Revolution was accomplished.

CHAPTER III. IMPERIALIST VICTORIES IN BOHEMIA AND THE

PALATINATE.

Section I.—The Attack upon Frederick.

§ 1. Maximilian prepares for war.

The news of Frederick's acceptance of the Bohemian crown sent a thrill of confidence through the ranks of his opponents. 'That prince,' said the Pope, 'has cast himself into a fine labyrinth.' 'He will only be a winter-king,' whispered the Jesuits to one another, certain that the summer's campaign would see his pretensions at an end. Up to that time the Bohemian cause stood upon its own merits. But if one prince of the Empire was to be allowed, on any pretext, to seize upon the territories of another, what bulwark was there against a return of the(Pg 40) old fist-right, or general anarchy? Frederick had attacked the foundations on which the institutions of his time rested, without calling up anything to take their place.

§ 2. Makes use of Frederick's mistakes.

Maximilian saw more clearly than any one the mistake that had been committed. In an interview with the new Emperor he engaged to forsake his inaction. Hitherto he had kept quiet, because he knew well that the apparent aggressor would have the general opinion of the world against him. Now that the blunder had been committed, he was ready to take advantage of it. At the same time, he did not forget his own interests, and he stipulated that, when all was over, Frederick's electoral dignity—not necessarily his territory—should be transferred to himself, and that he should retain Upper Austria in pledge till his military expenses had been repaid.

§ 3. Bethlen Gabor attacks Austria.

The effect of the change from the passive endurance of Ferdinand to the active vigour of Maximilian was immediately perceptible. His first object was to gain over or neutralize the German Protestants, and events in the East were seconding him to a marvel. About one-fifth only of Hungary was in Ferdinand's possession. The rest was about equally divided between the Turks and Bethlen Gabor, the Protestant Prince of Transylvania, a semi-barbarous but energetic chieftain, who hoped, with Turkish support, to make himself master of all Hungary, if not of Austria as well. In the first days of November, his hordes, in friendly alliance with the Bohemians, were burning and plundering round the walls of Vienna. But such armies as his can only support themselves by continuous success; and Bethlen Gabor found the capture of Vienna(Pg 41) as hopeless in the winter as Thurn had found it in the summer. Retiring eastwards, he left behind him a bitter indignation against those who had abetted his proceedings, and who had not been ashamed, as their adversaries declared, to plant the Crescent upon the ruins of Christianity and civilization.

§ 4. The Union refuses to support Frederick.

Such declamation, overstrained as it was, was not without its effect. German Protestantism had no enthusiasm to spare for Frederick's enterprise in Bohemia. At a meeting of the Union at Nüremberg, Frederick's cause found no support. Maximilian could well afford to leave the Union to its own hesitation, and to think only of conciliating the Elector of Saxony and the North German princes.

1620

§ 5. The agreement of Mühlhausen.

That John George should have taken serious alarm at his rival's increase of power is not surprising. Not only did it assail whatever shadow still remained of the protecting institutions of the Empire, but it did so in a way likely to be especially disagreeable at Dresden. The revolution at Prague did not simply raise an otherwise powerless person into Ferdinand's place. It gave the crown of Bohemia to a man whose territories were already so extensive that if he managed to consolidate his new dominion with them he would unite in his hands a power which would be unequalled in the Empire, and which would bring with it the unheard-of accumulation of two votes upon one person at imperial elections. John George would descend from being one of the first of the German princes to a mere second-rate position.

§ 6. The ecclesiastical lands held by Protestants guaranteed under conditions.

John George was not to be won for nothing. At an assembly held at Mühlhausen in March 1620, the League promised that they would never attempt to(Pg 42) recover by force the lands of the Protestant administrators, or the secularized lands in the northern territories, as long as the holders continued to act as loyal subjects; and this promise was confirmed by the Emperor.

§ 7. Spinola prepares to attack the Palatinate.

That this engagement was not enough, later events were to show. For the present it seemed satisfactory to John George, and Maximilian was able to turn his attention to the actual preparations for war. In May orders had been issued from Madrid to Spinola, the Spanish general in the Netherlands, to make ready to march to the Emperor's defence; and on June 3 the frightened Union signed the treaty of Ulm, by which they promised to observe neutrality towards the League, thus securing to Maximilian freedom from attack in the rear during his march into Bohemia. The Union, however, if it should be attacked, was to be allowed to defend its own territories, including the Palatinate.

§ 8. The invasions.

At the head of Maximilian's army was the Walloon Tilly, a man capable of inspiring confidence alike by the probity of his character and by the possession of eminent military capacity. On June 23 he crossed the Austrian frontier. On August 20 the Estates of Upper Austria unconditionally bowed to Ferdinand as their lord and master. Lower Austria had already submitted to its fate. About the same time John George had entered Lusatia, and was besieging Bautzen in Ferdinand's name. Spinola, too, had marched along the Rhine, and had reached Mentz by the end of August.

§ 9. Spinola subdues the Western Palatinate.

The army of the Union was drawn up to oppose the Spaniards. But there was no harmony amongst the(Pg 43) leaders; no spirit in the troops. Falling upon one town after another, Spinola now brought into his power nearly the whole of that portion of the Palatinate which lay on the left bank of the Rhine. The army of the Union retreated helplessly to Worms, waiting for what might happen next.

§ 10. Invasion of Bohemia.

Maximilian was now ready to attack Bohemia. He soon effected a junction with Bucquoi. Frederick's position was deplorable.

§ 11. Growing unpopularity of Frederick.

At first he had been received at Prague with the liveliest joy. When a son was born to him, who was in after days to become the Prince Rupert of our English civil wars, every sign of rejoicing accompanied the child to the font. But it was not long before Frederick's Lutheran subjects were offended by his Calvinistic proceedings. In the royal chapel pictures of the saints were ruthlessly torn down from the walls, and the great crucifix, an object of reverence to the Lutheran as well as the Catholic, was tossed aside like a common log of wood. The treasures of art which Rudolph II. had collected during his life of seclusion were catalogued that they might be offered for sale; and it is said that many of them were carried off by the officials entrusted with the duty. And besides real grievances, there were others that were purely imaginary. A story has been told which, whether true or false, is a good illustration of the impracticable nature of the Bohemian aristocracy. Frederick is said to have convened some of them to council early in the morning and to have received an answer that it was against their privileges to get up so soon.

§ 12. Frederick brings no strength to the Bohemians.

The Bohemians were not long in discovering that no real strength had been brought to them by Frederick.(Pg 44) He had been set upon the throne, not for his personal qualities, but because he was supposed to have good friends, and to be able to prop up the falling cause of Bohemia by aid from all parts of Protestant Europe. But his friends gave him little or no help, and he was himself looking tranquilly on whilst the storm was gathering before his eyes. In his ranks there was neither organization nor devotion. Christian of Anhalt had been placed in command of the army, but, though personally brave he did not inspire confidence. The other generals were quarrelling about precedence. New levies were ordered, but the men either remained at home or took the earliest opportunity to slink away. Those who remained, scantily provided with the necessities of life, were on the verge of mutiny.

§ 13. March of Tilly and Bucquoi.

On September 28 Frederick joined the army. He still cherished hope. Bethlen Gabor, who had deserted his cause a few months before, had repented his defection, and was now coming to his aid. Sickness was raging in the enemy's camp. Yet, in spite of sickness, Tilly pressed on, taking town after town, and choosing his positions too skilfully to be compelled to fight unless it suited him. On the morning of November 8 the Imperialists were close upon Prague. The enemy was posted on the White Hill, a rising ground of no great height outside the walls. The Imperial army had been weakened by its sufferings; and Bucquoi still counselled delay. But Tilly knew better, and urged an immediate advance. As the commanders were disputing, a Dominican friar, who accompanied the armies, stepped forward. 'Sons of the church,' he said, 'why do you hang back? We ought to march straight forward, for the Lord hath delivered the enemy into our hands. We shall overcome them as(Pg 45) sure as we are alive.' Then showing them a figure of the Virgin which had been defaced by Protestant hands, 'See here,' he said, 'what they have done. The prayers of the Holy Virgin shall be yours. Trust in God, and go boldly to the battle. He fights on your side, and will give you the victory.' Before the fiery utterances of the friar Bucquoi withdrew his opposition.

§ 14. The battle of the White Hill.

It was a Sunday morning, and the gospel of the day contained the words, 'Render unto Cæsar the things that be Cæsar's,' and the warriors of the Cæsar at Vienna felt themselves inspired to fulfil the Saviour's words. The task which they had before them was more difficult in appearance than in reality. Frederick was inside the city entertaining two English ambassadors at dinner whilst the blow was being struck. Some Hungarians on whom he chiefly relied set the example of flight, and the day was irretrievably lost. Frederick fled for his life through North Germany, till he found a refuge at the Hague.

§ 15. Submission of Bohemia.

The reign of the Bohemian aristocracy was at an end. Tilly, indeed, had mercifully given time to the leaders to make their escape. But, blind in adversity as they had been in prosperity, they made no use of the opportunity. The chiefs perished on the scaffold. Their lands were confiscated, and a new German and Catholic nobility arose, which owed its possessions to its sovereign, and which, even if the Royal Charter had remained in existence, would have entered into the privileges which allowed their predecessors to convert the churches in their domains to what use they pleased. But the Royal Charter was declared to have been forfeited by rebellion, and the Protestant churches in the towns and on the royal estates had nothing to depend on but the will of the con(Pg 46)queror. The ministers of one great body,—the Bohemian Brethren— were expelled at once. The Lutherans were spared for a time.

§ 16. Frederick put to the ban.

Was it yet possible to keep the Bohemian war from growing into a German one? Ferdinand and Maximilian were hardly likely to stop of themselves in their career of victory. To them Frederick was a mere aggressor, on whom they were bound to inflict condign punishment. Would he not, if he were allowed to recover strength, play the same game over again? Besides, the expenses of the war had been heavy. Ferdinand had been obliged to leave Upper Austria in pledge with Maximilian till his share of those expenses had been repaid to him. It would be much pleasanter for both parties if Maximilian could have a slice of the Palatinate instead. With this and the promised transference of the electorate to Maximilian, there would be some chance of securing order and a due respect for the Catholic ecclesiastical lands. On January 22, therefore, Frederick was solemnly put to the ban, and his lands and dignities declared to be forfeited.

§ 17. Danger of the Protestants.

Whether Ferdinand was justified in doing this was long a moot point. He had certainly promised at his election that he would not put anyone to the ban without giving him the benefit of a fair trial. But he argued that this only applied to one whose guilt was doubtful, and that Frederick's guilt had been open and palpable. However this may have been, something of far greater importance than a legal or personal question was at issue. For Frederick there was little sympathy in Germany; but there was a strong feeling that it would not do to allow a Protestant country to fall into Catholic hands, both for its own sake and for the sake of its Protestant neighbours.

(Pg 47)

Section II.—The War in the Upper Palatinate.

§ 1. Frederick does not give up hope.

If Frederick could only have made it clear that he had really renounced all his pretensions to meddle with other people's lands he might possibly have ended his days peaceably at Heidelberg. But he could not give up his hopes of regaining his lost kingdom. One day he talked of peace; another day he talked of war. When he was most peaceably inclined he would give up his claim if he could have an amnesty for the past. But he would not first give up his claim and then ask for an amnesty.

§ 2. Part taken by James of England.

Even to this he had been driven half unwillingly by his father-in-law. The King of England charged himself with the office of a mediator, and fancied that it was unnecessary to arm in the meantime.

§ 3. Dissolution of the Union.

The states of the Union were in great perplexity. The Landgrave of Hesse Cassel was compelled by his own subjects to come to terms with Spinola. The cities of Strasburg, Ulm, and Nüremberg were the next to give way. On April 12 a treaty was signed at Mentz, by which the Union dissolved itself, and engaged to withdraw its troops from the Palatinate. On the other hand, Spinola promised to suspend hostilities till May 14.

§ 4. Chances in Frederick's favour.

The danger to which the Palatinate was exposed, and the hints let drop that the conquest of the Palatinate might be followed by the transference of the electorate, caused alarm in quarters by no means favourable to Frederick. John George began to raise objections, and even the Catholic ecclesiastics were frightened at the prospects of the enlargement of the war, and at the risk of seeing many powers,(Pg 48) hitherto neutral, taking the part of the proscribed Elector.

§ 5. He still holds places in Bohemia.

The claim kept up by Frederick to Bohemia was something more than a claim to an empty title. He had appointed Mansfeld to act there as his general; and, though Mansfeld had lost one post after another, at the end of April he still held Tabor and Wittingau in Frederick's name.

§ 6. Mansfeld's army.

The appointment of Mansfeld was unfortunately in itself fatal to the chances of peace. Ever since the capture of Pilsen, his troops, destitute of support, had been the terror of the country they were called upon to defend. In those days, indeed, the most disciplined army was often guilty of excesses from which in our days the most depraved outcasts would shrink. The soldiers, engaged merely for as long a time as they happened to be wanted, passed from side to side as the prospect of pay or booty allured them. No tie of nationality bound the mercenary to the standard under which accident had placed him. He had sold himself to his hirer for the time being, and he sought his recompense in the gratification of every evil passion of which human nature in its deepest degradation is capable.

§ 7. Soldiers of the Thirty Years' War.

Yet, even in this terrible war, there was a difference between one army and another. In an enemy's country all plundered alike. Tilly's Bavarians had been guilty of horrible excesses in Bohemia. But a commander like Tilly, who could pay his soldiers, and could inspire them with confidence in his generalship, had it in his power to preserve some sort of discipline; and if, as Tilly once told a complaining official, his men were not nuns, they were at all events able to refrain on occasion from outrageous vil(Pg 49)lany. A commander, like Mansfeld, who could not pay his soldiers, must, of necessity, plunder wherever he was. His movements would not be governed by military or political reasons. As soon as his men had eaten up one part of the country they must go to another, if they were not to die of starvation. They obeyed, like the elements, a law of their own, quite independent of the wishes or needs of the sovereign whose interests they were supposed to serve.

§ 8. Mansfeld takes the offensive.

Before the end of May the breaking up of the army of the Union sent fresh swarms of recruits to Mansfeld's camp. He was soon at the head of a force of 16,000 men in the Upper Palatinate. The inhabitants suffered terribly, but he was strong enough to maintain his position for a time. Nor was he content with standing on the defensive. He seized a post within the frontiers of Bohemia, and threatened to harry the lands of the Bishop of Bamberg and Würzburg if he did not withdraw his troops from the army of the League. He then fell upon Leuchtenberg, and carried off the Landgrave a prisoner to his camp.

§ 9. A truce impossible for him.

The first attack of the Bavarians failed entirely. Bethlen Gabor, too, was again moving in Hungary, had slain Bucquoi, and was driving the Emperor's army before him. Under these circumstances, even Ferdinand seems to have hesitated, and to have doubted whether he had not better accept the English offer of mediation. Yet such was the character of Mansfeld's army that it made mediation impossible. It must attack somebody in order to exist.

§ 10. Vere in the Lower Palatinate.

Yet it was in the Lower, not in the Upper, Palatinate that the first blow was struck. Sir Horace Vere, who had gone out the year before, with a regiment of English volunteers, was now in(Pg 50) command for Frederick. But Frederick had neither money nor provisions to give him, and the supplies of the Palatinate were almost exhausted. The existing truce had been prolonged by the Spaniards. But the lands of the Bishop of Spires lay temptingly near. Salving his conscience by issuing the strictest orders against pillage, he quartered some of his men upon them.

§ 11. War recommenced in the Lower Palatinate.

The whole Catholic party was roused to indignation. Cordova, left in command of the Spanish troops after Spinola's return to Brussels, declared the truce to have been broken, and commenced operations against Vere.

§ 12. Mansfeld driven from the Upper Palatinate.

By this time Mansfeld's power of defending the Upper Palatinate was at an end. The magistrates of the towns were sick of his presence, and preferred coming to terms with Maximilian to submitting any longer to the extortions of their master's army. Mansfeld, seeing how matters stood, offered to sell himself and his troops to the Emperor. But he had no real intention of carrying out the bargain. On October 10 he signed an engagement to disband his forces. Before the next sun arose he had slipped away, and was in full march for Heidelberg.

Tilly followed hard upon his heels. But Mansfeld did not stop to fight him. Throwing himself upon Alsace, he seized upon Hagenau, and converted it into a place of strength.

SECTION III.—Frederick's Allies.

§ 1. Proposal to take Mansfeld into English pay.

The winter was coming on, and there would be time for negotiations before another blow was struck. But to give negotiations a chance it was necessary that Mansfeld's army should be fed, in order that he might be able to keep quiet while the diplomatists were disputing. James, therefore, wise(Pg 51)ly proposed to provide a sum of money for this purpose. But a quarrel with the House of Commons hurried on a dissolution, and he was unable to raise money sufficient for the purpose without a grant from Parliament.

§ 2. England and Spain.

James, poor and helpless, was thus compelled to fall back upon the friendship of Spain, a friendship which he hoped to knit more closely by a marriage between his son, the Prince of Wales, and a Spanish Infanta. The Spanish Government was anxious, if possible, to avoid an extension of the war in Germany. Though all the riches of the Indies were at its disposal, that government was miserably poor. In a land where industry, the source of wealth, was held in dishonour, all the gold in the world was thrown away. Scarcely able to pay the armies she maintained in time of peace, Spain had now again to find money for the war in the Netherlands. In 1621 the twelve years' truce with the Dutch had come to an end, and Spinola's armies in Brabant and Flanders could not live, like Mansfeld's at the expense of the country, for fear of throwing the whole of the obedient provinces, as they were called, into the enemies' hands. If possible, therefore, that yawning gulf of the German war, which threatened to swallow up so many millions of ducats, must be closed. And yet how was it to be done? The great difficulty in the way of peace did not lie in Frederick's pretensions. They could easily be swept aside. The great difficulty lay in this—that the Catholics, having already the institutions of the Empire in their hands, were now also in possession of a successful army. How, under such circumstances, was Protestantism, with which so many temporal interests were bound up, to feel itself secure? And without giving security to Protestantism, how could a permanent peace be obtained?

(Pg 52)

§ 3. Spanish plans.

To this problem the Spanish ministers did not care to address themselves. They thought that it would be enough to satisfy personal interests. They offered James a larger portion with the Infanta than any other sovereign in Europe would have given. They opposed tooth and nail the project for transferring the Electorate to Maximilian, as likely to lead to endless war. But into the heart of the great question they dared not go, tied and bound as they were by their devotion to the Church. Could not Frederick and James, they asked, be bought off by the assurance of the Palatinate to Frederick's heirs, on the simple condition of his delivering up his eldest son to be educated at Vienna? Though they said nothing whatever about any change in the boy's religion, they undoubtedly hoped that he would there learn to become a good Catholic.

§ 4. Frederick not likely to accede to them.

Such a policy was hopeless from the beginning. Frederick had many faults. He was shallow and obstinate. But he really did believe in his religion as firmly as any Spaniard in Madrid believed in his; and it was certain that he would never expose his children to the allurements of the Jesuits of Vienna.

§ 5. A conference to be held at Brussels.

It was settled that a conference should be held at Brussels, the capital of the Spanish Netherlands, first to arrange terms for a suspension of arms, and then to prepare the way for a general peace. The Spanish plan of pacification was not yet announced. But Frederick can hardly be blamed for suspecting that no good would come from diplomacy, or for discerning that a few regiments on his side would weigh more heavily in his favour than a million of words.

§ 6. Where was Frederick to expect help?

The only question for him to decide was the quarter(Pg 53) in which he should seek for strength. His weakness had hitherto arisen from his confidence in physical strength alone. To get together as many thousand men as possible and to launch them at the enemy had been his only policy, and he had done nothing to conciliate the order-loving portion of the population. The cities stood aloof from his cause. The North German princes would have nothing to say to him. If he could only have renounced his past, if he could have acknowledged that all he had hitherto done had been the fruitful root of disaster, if he could, with noble self-renunciation, have entreated others to take up the cause of German Protestantism, which in his hands had suffered so deeply, then it is not impossible that opinion, whilst opinion was still a power in Germany, would have passed over to his side, and that the coming mischief might yet have been averted.

§ 7. His preparations for war.

But Frederick did not do this. If he had been capable of doing it he must have been other than he was. In 1622, as in 1619, the pupil of Christian of Anhalt looked to the mere development of numerical strength, without regard to the moral basis of force.

§ 8. Frederick's allies.

It must be acknowledged that if numbers could give power, Frederick's prospects were never better than in the spring of 1622. Mansfeld's army was not, this time, to stand alone. In the south the Margrave of Baden-Durlach was arming in Frederick's cause. In the north, Christian of Brunswick was preparing to march to the aid of the Palatinate. Such names as these call up at once before us the two main difficulties which would have remained in the way of peace even if the question of the Palatinate could have been laid aside.

(Pg 54)

§ 9. The Margrave of Baden.

The Margrave of Baden-Durlach had long been notorious for the skill with which he had found excuses for appropriating ecclesiastical property, and for defeating legal attempts to embarrass him in his proceedings.

1616
§ 10. Christian of Brunswick.

Christian of Brunswick was a younger brother of the Duke of Brunswick-Wolfenbüttel. By the influence of his family he secured in 1616 his election to the bishopric or administratorship of Halberstadt. The ceremonies observed at the institution of the youth, who had nothing of the bishop but the name, may well have seemed a degrading profanation in the eyes of a Catholic of that day. As he entered the Cathedral the *Te Deum* was sung to the pealing organ. He was led to the high altar amidst the blaze of lighted candles. Then, whilst the choir sang 'Oh Lord! save thy people,' the four eldest canons placed him upon the altar. Subsequently he descended and, kneeling with the canons before the altar, three times intoned the words 'Oh Lord, save thy servant.' Then he was placed again upon the altar whilst a hymn of praise was sung. Lastly, he took his place opposite the pulpit whilst the courtly preacher explained that Christian's election had been in accordance with the express will of God. 'This,' he cried triumphantly, 'is the bishop whom God himself has elected. This is the man whom God has set as the ruler of the land.'

§ 11. Christian's fondness for fighting.

Christian's subsequent proceedings by no means corresponded with the expectations of his enthusiastic admirers. Like one who has been handed down to evil renown in early English history, he did nought bishoplike. He was not even a good ruler of his domain. He left his people to be misgoverned by officials, whilst he(Pg 55) wandered about the world in quest of action. As brainless for all higher purposes as Murat, the young Bishop was a born cavalry officer. He took to fighting for very love of it, just as young men in more peaceful times take to athletic sports.

§ 12. He takes up the cause of Elizabeth.

And, if he was to fight at all, there could be no question on which side he would be found. There was a certain heroism about him which made him love to look upon himself as the champion of high causes and the promoter of noble aims. To such an one it would seem to be altogether debasing to hold his bishopric on the mere tenure of the agreement of Mühlhausen, to be debarred from taking the place due to him in the Diet of the Empire, and to be told that if he was very loyal and very obedient to the Emperor, no force would be employed to wrest from him that part of the property of the Church which he held through a system of iniquitous robbery. Then, too, came a visit to the Hague, where the bright eyes of his fair cousin the titular Queen of Bohemia chained him for ever to her cause, a cause which might soon become his own. For who could tell, when once the Palatinate was lost, whether the agreement of Mühlhausen would be any longer regarded?

§ 13. His ravages in the diocese of Paderborn.

In the summer of 1621 Christian levied a force with which he marched into the Catholic bishopric of Paderborn. The country was in the course of forcible conversion by its bishop, and there was still in it a strong Lutheran element, which would perhaps have answered the appeal of a leader who was less purely an adventurer. But except in word, Catholic and Protestant were alike to Christian, so long as money could be got to support his army. Castles, towns, farmhouses were ransacked(Pg 56) for the treasure of the rich, and the scanty hoard of the poor. We need not be too hard on him if he tore down the silver shrine of a saint in the cathedral of Paderborn, and melted it into coin bearing the legend:—'The friend of God and the enemy of the priests.' But it is impossible to forget he was the enemy of the peasants as well. Burning-masters appear among the regular officers of his army; and many a village, unable to satisfy his demands, went up in flames, with its peaceful industry ruined for ever. At last, satiated with plunder, he turned southward to the support of Mansfeld.

§ 14. Mansfeld will not make peace.

Such were the commanders into whose hands the fortunes of German Protestantism had fallen. Mansfeld told Vere plainly that whether there were a truce or not, he at least would not lay down his arms unless he were indemnified for his expenses by a slice out of the Austrian possession of Alsace.

§ 15. Tilly in the midst of his enemies.

If the three armies of the Margrave of Baden, of Christian of Brunswick, and of Mansfeld, could be brought to co-operate, Tilly, even if supported by Cordova's Spaniards, would be in a decided numerical inferiority. But he had the advantage of a central situation, of commanding veteran troops by whom he was trusted, and above all of being able to march or remain quiet at his pleasure, as not being dependent on mere pillage for his commissariat. He was inspired, too, by a childlike faith in the cause for which he was fighting as the cause of order and religion against anarchy and vice.

Section IV.—The Fight for the Lower Palatinate.

§ 1. Frederick joins Mansfeld in the Palatinate.

By the middle of April the hostile armies were in movement, converging upon the Palatinate, where the(Pg 57) fortresses of Heidelberg, Mannheim, and Frankenthal were safe in Vere's keeping. Frederick himself had joined Mansfeld's army in Alsace, and his first operations were attended with success. Effecting a junction with the Margrave of Baden he inflicted a severe check upon Tilly at Wiesloch. The old Walloon retreated to Wimpfen, calling Cordova to his aid, and he did not call in vain. Mansfeld, on the other hand, and the Margrave could not agree. Each had his own plan for the campaign, and neither would give way to the other. Besides, there were no means of feeding so large an army if it kept together. Mansfeld marched away, leaving the Margrave to his fate.

§ 2. Battle of Wimpfen.

The battle of Wimpfen was the result. On May 6 Tilly and Cordova caught the Margrave alone, and defeated him completely. As soon as the action was over, Cordova left the field to resist the progress of Mansfeld; and Mansfeld, whose men were almost starving, was unable to overcome serious resistance. There was nothing for it but a speedy retreat to Alsace.

§ 3. The Congress at Brussels.

In the meantime the diplomatists had met at Brussels. After some difficulties of form had been got over, Sir Richard Weston, the representative of England, sent to ask Frederick to agree to a truce. When the message reached him the battle of Wimpfen had not been fought, and his hopes were still high. A truce, he wrote to his father-in-law, would be his utter ruin. The country was exhausted. Unless his army lived by plunder it could not exist. A few days later he was a beaten man. On May 13 he gave way, and promised to agree to the truce. On the 28th all was again changed. He had learned that the(Pg 58) Margrave of Baden hoped to bring back his army into the field. He knew that Christian of Brunswick was approaching from beyond the Main; and he informed Weston that he could do nothing to assist the negotiations at Brussels.

§ 4. Seizure of the Landgrave of Darmstadt.

On June 1 Frederick and Mansfeld marched out of Mannheim to meet Christian. On their way they passed by Darmstadt. The Landgrave was especially obnoxious to them, as a Lutheran prince who had warmly adopted the Emperor's side. Love of peace, combined with pretensions to lands in dispute with the Landgrave of Hesse Cassel, in which he hoped to be supported by Ferdinand, had made him a bitter enemy of Mansfeld and his proceedings; and though it was not known at the time that he was actually in receipt of a Spanish pension, Frederick was not likely to attribute to other than interested motives a line of action which seemed so incomprehensible.

§ 5. Mansfeld unable to pass the Main.

As soon as the troops reached Darmstadt, they commenced their usual work, ravaging the country, and driving off the cattle. To the Landgrave, who recommended submission to the Emperor as the best way of recovering peace, Frederick used high language. It was not in quest of peace that he had come so far. The Landgrave had a fortified post which commanded a passage over the Main, and its possession would enable the army to join Christian without difficulty. But the Landgrave was firm; and finding that a denial would not be taken, tried to avoid his importunate guests by flight. He was overtaken and brought back a prisoner. But even in this plight he would give no orders for the surrender of the post, and its commander resolutely refused to give it up(Pg 59) without instructions. Before another passage could be found, Tilly had received reinforcements, and Frederick, carrying the Landgrave with him, was driven to retreat to Mannheim, not without loss.

§ 6. Condition of Mansfeld's army.

Once more Frederick was ready to consent to the cessation of arms proposed at Brussels. But Cordova and Tilly were now of a different opinion. Christian, they knew, would soon be on the Main, and they were resolved to crush him whilst he was still unaided. Lord Chichester, who had come out to care for English interests in the Palatinate, and who judged all that he saw with the eye of an experienced soldier, perceived clearly the causes of Frederick's failure. 'I observe,' he wrote, 'so much of the armies of the Margrave of Baden and of Count Mansfeld, which I have seen, and of their ill discipline and order, that I must conceive that kingdom and principality for which they shall fight to be in great danger and hazard. The Duke of Brunswick's, it is said, is not much better governed: and how can it be better or otherwise where men are raised out of the scum of the people by princes who have no dominion over them, nor power, for want of pay, to punish them, nor means to reward them, living only upon rapine and spoil as they do?'

§ 7. Battle of Höchst.

On June 20, the day before these words were written, Tilly and Cordova had met with Christian at Höchst, and though they did not prevent him from crossing the Main, they inflicted on him such enormous losses that he joined Mansfeld with the mere fragments of his army.

§ 8. Mansfeld abandons the Palatinate.

Great was the consternation at Mannheim when the truth was known. The Margrave of Baden at once(Pg 60) abandoned his associates. Mansfeld and Christian, taking Frederick with them, retreated into Alsace, where Frederick formally dismissed them from his service, and thus washed his hands of all responsibility for their future proceedings.

§ 9. Frederick goes back to the Hague.

Retiring for a time to Sedan, he watched events as they passed from that quiet retreat. 'Would to God,' he wrote to his wife, 'that we possessed a little corner of the earth where we could rest together in peace.' The destinies of Germany and Europe had to be decided by clearer heads and stronger wills than his. After a short delay he found his way back to the Hague, to prove, as many a wiser man had proved before him, how bitter a lot it is to go up and down on the stairs which lead to the antechambers of the great: to plead for help which never is given, and to plan victories which never come.

CHAPTER IV. MANSFELD AND CHRISTIAN IN NORTH GERMANY.

SECTION I.—Mansfeld's March into the Netherlands.

§ 1. Reduction of the Palatinate.

When once Tilly had got the better of the armies in the field, the reduction of the fortresses in the Palatinate was merely a work of time. Heidelberg surrendered on September 16. On November 8 Vere found Mannheim no longer tenable. Frankenthal alone held out for a few months longer, and was then given up to the Spaniards.

§ 2. Aims of the Catholics.

James still hoped that peace was possible, though the conference at Brussels had broken up in September. In(Pg 61) the meanwhile, Ferdinand and Maximilian were pushing on to the end which they had long foreseen; and an assembly of princes was invited to meet at Ratisbon in November to assent to the transference of the electorate to the Duke of Bavaria.

1623
§ 3. The Electorate transferred to Maximilian.

Constitutional opposition on the part of the Protestants was impossible. In addition to the majority against them amongst the princes, there was now, by the mere fact of Frederick's exclusion, a majority against them amongst the Electors, a majority which was all the more firmly established when, on February 13, the transfer was solemnly declared. Maximilian was to be Elector for his lifetime. If any of Frederick's relations claimed that the electorate ought rather to pass over to them, they would be heard, and if their case appeared to be a good one, they would receive what was due to them after Maximilian's death. If, in the meanwhile, Frederick chose to ask humbly for forgiveness, and to abandon his claim to the electoral dignity, the

Emperor would take his request for the restitution of his lands into favourable consideration. Against all this the Spanish ambassador protested; but the protest was evidently not meant to be followed by action.

§ 4. The North German Protestants.

The question of peace or war now depended mainly on the North German Protestants. Nobody doubted that, if they could hit upon a united plan of action, and if they vigorously set to work to carry it out, they would bring an irresistible weight to bear upon the points at issue. Unfortunately, however, such uniformity of action was of all things most improbable. John George, indeed, had more than once been urged in different directions during the past years by(Pg 62) events as they successively arose. The invasion of the Palatinate had shaken him in his friendship for the Emperor. Then had come the kidnapping of the Landgrave of Darmstadt to give him a shock on the other side. Later in the year the news that an excuse had been found for driving the Lutheran clergy out of Bohemia had deeply exasperated him, and his exasperation had been increased by the transference of the electorate, by which the Protestants were left in a hopeless minority in the Electoral House. But the idea of making war upon the Emperor, and unsettling what yet remained as a security for peace, was altogether so displeasing to John George that it is doubtful whether anything short of absolute necessity would have driven him to war. What he would have liked would have been a solemn meeting, at which he might have had the opportunity of advancing his views. But if those views had been seriously opposed he would hardly have drawn the sword to uphold them.

§ 5. Mansfeld and Christian of Brunswick.

If the only danger to be apprehended by the North Germans had been the march of Tilly's army, it is not unlikely that the war would here have come to an end. Ferdinand and Maximilian would doubtless have respected the agreement of Mühlhausen, and there would hardly have been found sufficient determination in the northern princes to induce them to arm for the recovery of the Palatinate. But a new danger had arisen. Mansfeld and Christian had not laid down their arms when Frederick dismissed them in July, and so far from being ready to make sacrifices for peace, they were ready to make any sacrifices for the sake of the continuance of the war.

1622
§ 6. They establish themselves in Lorraine.

It was not long before the adventurers were forced to leave Alsace. They had eaten up everything that was(Pg 63) to be eaten there, and the enemy was known to be on their track. Throwing themselves into Lorraine, they settled down for a time like a swarm of locusts upon that smiling land. But where were they to turn next? The French government hurried up reinforcements to guard their frontier. That road, at all events, was barred to them, and Christian, whose troops were in a state of mutiny, tried in vain to lead them towards the Lower Rhine. Whilst the leaders hardly knew what to do, they received an invitation to place themselves for three months at the disposal of the Dutch Republic.

§ 7. Battle of Fleurus.

Matters had not been going well with the Dutch since the re-opening of the war in 1621. Their garrison at Juliers had surrendered to Spinola in the winter, and the great Spanish commander was now laying siege to Bergen-op-Zoom, with every prospect of reducing it. To come to its relief Mansfeld would have to march across the Spanish Netherlands. On August 28 he found Cordova on his way to Fleurus, as he had stood in his way in the Palatinate the year before. Worse than all, two of his own regiments broke out into mutiny, refusing to fight unless they were paid. At such a time Mansfeld was at his best. He was a man of cool courage and infinite resource, and he rode up to the mutineers, entreating them if they would not fight at least to look as if they meant to fight. Then, with the rest of his force, he charged the enemy. Christian seconded him bravely at the head of his cavalry, fighting on in spite of a shot in his left arm. Three horses were killed under him. The loss was enormous on both sides, but Mansfeld gained his object, and was able to pursue his way in safety.

§ 8. Christian loses his arm.

Christian's arm was amputated. He ordered that the(Pg 64) operation should be performed to the sound of trumpets. 'The arm that is left,' he said, 'shall give my enemies enough to do.' He coined money out of the silver he had taken from the Spaniards, with the inscription '*Altera restat.*'

§ 9. Mansfeld in Münster and East Friesland.

Bergen-op-Zoom was saved. Spinola raised the siege. But Mansfeld's disorderly habits did not comport well with the regular discipline of the Dutch army. Those whom he had served were glad to be rid of him. In November he was dismissed, and marched to seek his fortune in the diocese of Münster. But the enemy was too strong for him there, and he turned his steps to East Friesland, a land rich and fertile, easily fortified against attack, yet perfectly helpless. There he settled down to remain till the stock of money and provisions which he was able to wring from the inhabitants had been exhausted.

SECTION II.—Christian of Brunswick in Lower Saxony.

§ 1. Difficulties of the Lower Saxon circle.

Here then was a new rock of offence, a new call for the Emperor to interfere, if he was in any way to be regarded as the preserver of the peace of the Empire. But a march of Tilly against an enemy in East Friesland was not a simply military operation. Not a few amongst the northern princes doubted whether a victorious Catholic army would respect the agreement of Mühlhausen. Christian of Brunswick, of course, lost no time in favouring the doubt. For, whatever else might be questionable there was no question that the diocese of Halberstadt was no longer secured by the provisions of that agreement. Neither the League nor the Emperor had given any promise to those administrators who did not continue loyal to the Emperor, and no one could for a moment contend that Christian had ever shown a spark of loyalty.

(Pg 65)

§ 2. Christian and Tilly urge them to opposite courses.

On the one side was Christian, assuring those poor princes that neutrality was impossible, and that it was their plain duty to fight for the bishoprics and Protestantism. On the other side was Tilly, equally assuring them that neutrality was impossible, but asserting that it was their plain duty to fight for their Emperor against Mansfeld and brigandage. The princes felt that it was all very hard. How desirable it would be if only the war would take some other direction, or if Tilly and Christian would mutually exterminate one another, and rid them of the difficulty of solving such terrible questions!

§ 3. Halberstadt in danger.

But the question could not be disposed of. Halberstadt was a member of the Lower Saxon circle, one of those districts of which the princes and cities were legally bound together for mutual defence. The Lower Saxon circle, therefore, was placed between two fires. The Catholic troops were gathering round them on the south. Mansfeld was issuing forth from his fastness in East Friesland and threatening to occupy the line of the Weser on the north.

§ 4. Warlike preparations.

In February the circle determined to levy troops and prepare for war. But the preparations were rather directed against Mansfeld than against Tilly. If the Emperor could only have given satisfaction about the bishoprics, he would have had no vassals more loyal than the Lower Saxon princes. But in Ferdinand's eyes to acknowledge more than had been acknowledged at Mühlhausen would be to make himself partaker in other men's sins. It would have been to acknowledge that robbery might give a lawful title to possession.

§ 5. Christian invited to take service under his brother.

Almost unavoidably the circle became further involved in opposition to the Emperor. Christian's brother, Frederick Ulric, the reigning Duke of Bruns(Pg 66)wick-Wolfenbüttel, was a weak and incompetent prince much under his mother's guidance. Anxious to save her favourite son, the dashing Christian, from destruction, the Duchess persuaded the Duke to offer his brother a refuge in his dominions. If he would bring his troops there, he and they would be taken into the service of the Duke, a respectable law-abiding prince, and time would be afforded him to make his peace with the Emperor.

§ 6. The Battle of Stadtlohn.

Christian at once accepted the offer, and entered into negotiations with Ferdinand. But he had never any thought of really abandoning his adventurous career. Young princes, eager for distinction, levied troops and gathered round his standard. Every week the number of his followers increased. At last the neighbouring states could bear it no longer. The authorities of the circle told him plainly to be gone. Reproaching them for their sluggishness in thus abandoning the cause of the Gospel, he started for the Dutch Netherlands, with Tilly following closely upon him. On August 6 he was overtaken at Stadtlohn, within a few hours' march of the frontier, behind which he would have been in safety. His hastily levied recruits were no match for Tilly's veterans. Of 20,000 men only 6,000 found their way across the border.

Section III.—Danger of the Lower Saxon Circle.

§ 1. Danger of the Northern bishoprics.

Christian's defeat, however disastrous, settled nothing. Mansfeld was still in East Friesland. The princes of Lower Saxony were still anxious about the bishoprics. Even if the agreement of Mühlhausen were scrupulously observed, was it so very certain that the bishoprics might not be wrenched from them in another way than by(Pg 67) force of arms? The administrators held the sees simply because they had been elected by the chapters, and if only a Catholic majority could be obtained in a chapter the election at the next vacancy would be certain to fall upon a Catholic. Often it happened that the Protestant majority had taken care to perpetuate its power by methods of very doubtful legality, and it would be open to the Emperor to question those methods. It might even come to pass that strict law might turn the majority into a minority. Already, on April 18, the chapter of Osnabrück had chosen a Catholic to succeed a Protestant bishop, perhaps not altogether uninfluenced by the near neighbourhood of a Catholic army. Christian of Brunswick, certain that he would not be allowed to retain his see, had formally given in his resignation, and it was not impossible that with some manipulation the chapter of Halberstadt might be induced to follow the example of Osnabrück. The question of the bishoprics had, no doubt, its low and petty side. It may be spoken of simply as a question interesting to a handful of aristocratic sinecurists, who had had the luck to reap the good things of the old bishops without doing their work. But this would be a very incomplete account of the matter. Scattered as these bishoprics were over the surface of North Germany, their restitution meant nothing less than the occupation by the Emperor and his armies of points of vantage over the whole of the north. No one who casts his eyes over the map can doubt for an instant that, with these bishoprics open to the troops of the League, or it might be even to the troops of the King of Spain, the independence of the princes would have been a thing of the past; and it must never be forgotten that, as matters stood, the cause of the independence of the princes was inextricably bound up with the independ(Pg 68)ence of Protestantism. If Ferdinand and Maximilian had their way, German Protestantism would exist merely upon sufferance; and whatever they and the Jesuits might say, German Protestantism was, in spite of all its shortcomings, too noble a creed to exist on sufferance.

§ 2. The Lower Saxon circle does nothing.

Would the members of the circle of Lower Saxony be strong enough to maintain their neutrality? They sent ambassadors to the Emperor, asking him to settle the question of the bishoprics in their favour, and to John George to ask for his support. The Emperor replied that he would not go beyond the agreement of Mühlhausen. John George gave them good advice, but nothing more. And, worse than all, they were disunited amongst themselves. Princes and towns, after agreeing to support troops for the common defence, had done their best to evade their duties. As few men as possible had been sent, and the money needed for their support was still slower in coming in. As usual, unpaid men were more dangerous to the country which they were called upon to protect than to the enemy. The circle came to the conclusion that it would be better to send the troops home than to keep them under arms. By the beginning of the new year, Lower Saxony was undefended, a tempting prey to him who could first stretch out his hand to take it.

§ 3. Low state of public feeling.

It was the old story. With the Empire, the Diet and the Church in the hands of mere partisans, there was nothing to remind men of their duty as citizens of a great nation. Even the idea of being members of a circle was too high to be seriously entertained. The cities strove to thrust the burden of defence upon the princes, and the princes(Pg 69) thrust it back upon the cities. The flood was rising rapidly which was to swallow them all.

Section IV.—England and France.

§ 1. Foreign powers ready to interfere.

In the spring of 1624 there was rest for a moment. Mansfeld, having stripped East Friesland bare, drew back into the Netherlands. The only army still on foot was the army of the League, and if Germany had been an island in the middle of the Atlantic, exercising no influence upon other powers and uninfluenced by them, the continuance in arms of those troops might fairly be cited in evidence that the Emperor and the League wished to push their advantages still further, in spite of their assertions that they wanted nothing more than assurance of peace.

§ 2. Ferdinand's weakness.

But Germany was not an island. Around it lay a multitude of powers with conflicting interests, but all finding in her distractions a fair field for pursuing their own objects. Ferdinand, in fact, had made himself just strong enough to raise the jealousy of his neighbours, but not strong enough to impose an impassible barrier to their attacks. He had got on his side the legal and military elements of success. He had put down all resistance. He had frightened those who dreaded anarchy. But he had not touched the national heart. He had taught men to make it a mere matter of calculation whether a foreign invasion was likely to do them more damage than the success of their own Emperor. Whilst he affected to speak in the name of Germany, more than half of Germany was neutral if not adverse in the struggle.

1623
§ 3. Breach between England and Spain.

England, at last, was giving signs of warlike preparation. Prince Charles had paid a visit to Madrid in hopes of bringing home a Spanish bride, and of(Pg 70) regaining the Palatinate for his brother-in-law. He had come back without a wife, and with the prospect of getting back the Palatinate as distant as ever. He had learned what the Spanish plan was, that wonderful scheme for educating Frederick's children at Vienna, with all ostensible guarantees for keeping them in their father's faith, which were, however, almost certain to come to nothing when reduced to practice. And so he came back angry with the Spaniards, and resolved to urge his father to take up arms. In the spring of 1624 all negotiations between England and Spain were brought to an end, and Parliament was discussing with the king the best means of recovering the Palatinate.

§ 4. English plans.

In the English House of Commons there was but little real knowledge of German affairs. The progress of the Emperor and the League was of too recent a date to be thoroughly comprehended. Men, remembering the days of Philip II., were inclined to overestimate the power of Spain, and to underestimate the power of the Emperor. They therefore fancied that it would be enough to attack Spain by sea, and to send a few thousand soldiers to the aid of the Dutch Republic.

§ 5. Question between the king and the House of Commons.

James, if he was not prompt in action, at all events knew better than this. He believed that the Imperial power was now too firmly rooted in Germany to fall before anything short of a great European confederacy. From this the Commons shrunk. A war upon the continent would be extremely expensive, and, after all, their wrath had been directed against Spain, which had meddled with their internal affairs, rather than against the Emperor, who had never taken the slightest interest in English politics.(Pg 71) The utmost they would do was to accept the king's statement that he would enter into negotiations with other powers and would lay the results before them in the winter.

§ 6. The French Government and the Huguenots.

James first applied to France. He saw truly that the moment the struggle in Germany developed into a European war the key to success would lie in the hands of the French government. In that great country, then as now, ideas of the most opposite character were striving for the mastery. Old thoughts which had been abandoned in England in the sixteenth century were at issue with new thoughts which would hardly be adopted in England before the eighteenth. In France as well as in England and Germany, the question of the day was how religious toleration could be granted without breaking up the national unity. In England that unity was so strong that no party in the state could yet be brought to acknowledge that toleration should be granted at all. But for that very reason the question was on the fair way to a better settlement than it could have in France or Germany. When the nation was once brought face to face with the difficulty, men would ask, not whether one religion should be established in Northumberland and another in Cornwall, but what amount of religious liberty was good for men as men all over England. In Germany it could not be so. There the only question was where the geographical frontier was to be drawn between two religions. Neither those who wished to increase the power of the princes, nor those who wished to increase the power of the Emperor, were able to rise above the idea of a local and geographical division. And to some extent France was in the same condition. The Edict of Nantes had recognised some hundreds of the country(Pg 72) houses of the aristocracy, and certain cities and towns, as places where the reformed religious doctrines might be preached without interference. But in France the ideal of national unity, though far weaker than it was in England, was far stronger than it was in Germany. In order to give security to the Protestant, or Huguenot towns as they were called in France, they had been allowed the right of garrisoning themselves, and of excluding the royal troops. They had thus maintained themselves as petty republics in the heart of France, practically independent of the royal authority.

SECTION V.—Rise of Richelieu.

§ 1. Lewis XIII.

Such a state of things could not last. The idea involved in the exaltation of the monarchy was the unity of the nation. The idea involved in the maintenance of these guarantees was its disintegration. Ever since the young king, Lewis XIII., had been old enough to take an active part in affairs he had been striving to establish his authority from one end of the kingdom to the other.

§ 2. His ideas.

The supremacy and greatness of the monarchy was the thought in which he lived and moved. His intellect was not of a high order, and he was not likely to originate statesmanlike projects, or to carry them out successfully to execution. But he was capable of appreciating merit, and he would give his undivided confidence to any man who could do the thing which he desired to have done, without himself exactly knowing how to do it.

§ 3. Early years of his reign.

During the first years of his reign everything seemed falling to pieces. As soon as his father's strong hand was removed some of the nobility fell back into half-independence of the Crown, whilst others submitted to it in considera(Pg 73)tion of receiving large pensions and high positions in the state. To this Lewis was for the time obliged to submit. But the privileges of the Huguenot towns roused his indignation. It was not long before he levied war upon them, determined to reduce them to submission to the royal authority.

§ 4. The intolerant party at Court.

All this foreboded a future for France not unlike the future which appeared to be opening upon Germany. There were too many signs that the establishment of the king's authority over the towns would be followed by the forcible establishment of his religion. There was a large party at Court crying out with bigoted intolerance against any attempt to treat the Huguenots with consideration, and that cry found an echo in the mind of the king. For he was himself a devout Catholic, and nothing would have pleased him better than to see the victories of his arms attended by the victories of the Church to which he was attached.

§ 5. Lewis jealous of Spain.

If Lewis was not a Ferdinand, it was not because he was a nobler or a better man, but because he had his eye open to dangers from more quarters than one. When the troubles in Germany first broke out, French influence was exerted on the side of the Emperor. French ambassadors had taken part in the negotiations which preceded the treaty of Ulm, and had thrown all their weight in the scale to secure the safety of Maximilian's march into Bohemia. But in 1622 the conquest of the Palatinate brought other thoughts into the mind of the King of France. His monarchical authority was likely to suffer far more from the victorious union between the two branches of the House of Austria than from a few Huguenot towns. For many a long year Spain had planted her standards not(Pg 74) only beyond the Pyrenees, but in Naples, Milan, Franche Comté, and the Netherlands. Frankenthal and the Western Palatinate were now garrisoned by her troops, and behind those troops was the old shadowy empire once more taking form and substance, and presenting itself before the world as a power hereafter to be counted with. In 1622, accordingly, Lewis made peace with the Huguenots at home. In 1623 he sent some slight aid to Mansfeld. In 1624 he called Richelieu to his counsels.

§ 6. Richelieu's accession to power.

It would be a mistake to suppose that the cool and far-sighted Cardinal who was thus suddenly placed at the head of the French ministry had it all his own way from the first. He had to take into account the ebb and flow of feeling in the Court and the country, and the ebb and flow of feeling in Lewis himself. There was still with Lewis the old anxiety to crush the Huguenots and to make himself absolute master at home, alongside with the new anxiety to shake off the superiority of the House of Austria abroad. It was Richelieu's task to show him how to satisfy both his longings; how to strike down rebellion whilst welcoming religious liberty, and how, by uniting Catholic and Protestant in willing obedience to his throne, he might make himself feared abroad in proportion as he was respected at home.

§ 7. Marriage of Henrietta Maria.

Richelieu's first idea was not altogether a successful one. He encouraged Lewis to pursue the negotiation which had been already commenced for a marriage between his sister and the Prince of Wales. At the wish either of Lewis himself or of Richelieu the marriage was hampered with conditions for the religious liberty of the English Catholics, to which the prince, when he afterwards(Pg 75) came to the throne as Charles I., was unwilling or unable to give effect. These conditions were therefore the beginning of an ill feeling between the two crowns, which helped ultimately to bring about a state of war.

§ 8. Foreign policy of Lewis and Richelieu.

Nor were other causes of dispute wanting. James and his son expected France to join them in an avowed league for the recovery of the Palatinate. But to this Lewis and Richelieu refused to consent. Lewis was proud of the name of Catholic, and he was unwilling to engage in open war with the declared champions of the Catholic cause. But he was also King of France, and he was ready to satisfy his conscience by refusing to join the league, though he had no scruple in sending money to the support of armies who were fighting for Protestantism. He agreed to pay large subsidies to the Dutch, and to join the King of England in promoting an expedition which was to march under Mansfeld through France to Alsace, with the object of attacking the Palatinate. At the same time he was ready to carry on war in Italy. The Spaniards had taken military possession of the Valtelline, a valley through which lay the only secure military road from their possessions in Italy to the Austrian lands in Germany. Before the end of the year a French army entered the valley and drove out the Spaniards with ease.

§ 9. Mansfeld's expedition.

Mansfeld's expedition, on the other hand, never reached Alsace at all. Before the troops of which it was composed were ready to sail from England, Richelieu had found an excuse for diverting its course. Spinola had laid siege to Breda, and the Dutch were as anxiously seeking for means to succour it as they had sought for means to succour Bergen-op-Zoom when it was besieged in 1622. The French averred that Mansfeld would be far better employed(Pg 76) at Breda than in Alsace. At all events, they now declined positively to allow him to pass through France.

1625
§ 10. Failure of the expedition.

James grumbled and remonstrated in vain. At last, after long delays, Mansfeld was allowed to sail for the Dutch coast, with strict orders to march to the Palatinate without going near Breda. He had with him 12,000 English foot, and was to be accompanied by 2,000 French horse under Christian of Brunswick. No good came of the expedition. James had consented to conditions appended to his son's marriage contract which he did not venture to submit to discussion in the House of Commons, and Parliament was not, therefore, allowed to meet. Without help from Parliament the Exchequer was almost empty, and James was unable to send money with Mansfeld to pay his men. Upon their landing, the poor fellows, pressed a few weeks before, and utterly without military experience, found themselves destitute of everything in a hard frost. Before long they were dying like flies in winter. The help which they were at last permitted to give could not save Breda from surrender, and the handful which remained were far too few to cross the frontier into Germany.

§ 11. The rising of the French Huguenots.

Richelieu had hoped to signalize the year 1625 by a larger effort than that of 1624. He had mastered the Valtelline in alliance with Venice and Savoy, and French troops were to help the Duke of Savoy to take Genoa, a city which was in close friendship with Spain. There was further talk of driving the Spaniards out of the Duchy of Milan, and even intervention in Germany was desired by Richelieu, though no decision had been come to on the subject. In the midst of these thoughts(Pg 77) he was suddenly reminded that he was not completely master at home. The peace made with the Huguenots in 1622 had not been fairly kept: royal officials had encroached upon their lands, and had failed to observe the terms of the treaty. On a sudden, Soubise, a powerful Huguenot nobleman with a fleet of his own, swooped down upon some of the king's ships lying at Blavet, in Brittany, and carried them off as his prize. Sailing to Rochelle, he persuaded that great commercial city to come to an understanding with him, and to declare for open resistance to the king's authority.

§ 12. Interruption to Richelieu's plans for intervening in Germany.

If Richelieu intended seriously to take part in the German war, this was cause enough for hesitation. Cleverly availing himself of the expectations formed of the French alliance in England and Holland, he contrived to borrow ships from both those countries, and before the autumn was over Soubise was driven to take refuge in England. But Rochelle and the Huguenots on land were still unconquered, and Ferdinand was safe for the moment from any considerable participation of France in the German war. Whether Richelieu would at any time be able to take up again the thread of his plans depended in the first place upon his success in suppressing rebellion, but quite as much upon the use which he might make of victory if the event proved favourable to him. A tolerant France might make war with some chances in its favour. A France composed of conquerors and conquered, in which each party regarded the other as evil-doers to be suppressed, not as erring brothers to be argued with, would weigh lightly enough in the scale of European politics.

(Pg 78)

CHAPTER V. INTERVENTION OF THE KING OF DENMARK.

SECTION I.—Christian IV. and Gustavus Adolphus.

§ 1. Denmark and Sweden.

Whilst France was thus temporarily hindered from taking part in German affairs, and whilst James and his son were promising more than their poverty would allow them to perform, the rulers of Denmark and Sweden were watching with increasing interest the tide of war as it rolled northwards.

§ 2. Christian IV.

Christian IV. of Denmark had every reason to look with anxiety upon the future. As Duke of Holstein, he was a member of the Lower Saxon circle, and he had long been doing his best to extend his influence over the coasts of the North Sea. By his new fortifications at Glückstadt he aimed at intercepting the commerce of Hamburg, and his success in procuring for one of his sons the Bishopric of Verden and the coadjutorship and eventual succession to the archbishopric of Bremen was doubtless specially grateful to him on account of the position he thus acquired on the Elbe and the Weser. The question of the Protestant bishoprics was therefore a very important question to him personally, and he was well aware that a real national empire in Germany would make short work with his attempts to establish his dominion over the mouths of the German rivers.

§ 3. His early interest in the war.

His attention was not now called for the first time to the progress of the war. Like all the Lutheran princes, he had thoroughly disapproved of Frederick's Bohemian enterprise. But when Frederick was a fugitive he had seen that a(Pg 79) strong force was needed to stop the Emperor from a retaliation which would be ruinous to the Protestants, and he had in the beginning of 1621 given a willing ear to James's proposal for a joint armament in defence of the Palatinate. Had the war been undertaken then, with the character of moderation which James and Christian would have been certain to impress upon it, the world might perhaps have been spared the spectacle of Mansfeld's plunderings, with their unhappy results. But James came too soon to the conclusion that it was unnecessary to arm till mediation had failed; and Christian, auguring no good from such a course, drew back and left the Palatinate to its fate. But the events which followed had increased his anxiety, and in 1624 his mind was distracted between his desire to check the growth of the imperial power and his hesitation to act with allies so vacillating and helpless as the Lower Saxon princes were proving themselves to be. In his own lands he had shown himself a good administrator and able ruler. Whether he was possessed of sufficient military capacity to cope with Tilly remained to be seen.

§ 4. Gustavus Adolphus.

Gustavus Adolphus, King of Sweden, was a man of a higher stamp. His is the one of the few names which relieve the continental Protestantism of the seventeenth century from the charge of barrenness. Possessed of a high and brilliant imagination, and of a temperament restless and indefatigable, to which inaction was the sorest of trials, he was never happier than when he was infusing his own glowing spirit into the comrades of some perilous enterprise. Christian of Brunswick was not more ready than he to lead a charge or to conduct a storm. But he had, too, that of which no thought ever entered the mind of Christian for an instant—the power of seeing facts in their in(Pg 80)finite variety as they really were, and the self-restraint with which he curbed in his struggling spirit and his passionate longing for action whenever a calm survey of the conditions around showed him that action was inexpedient. In all the pages of history there is probably no man who leaves such an impression of that energy under restraint, which is the truest mark of greatness in human character as it is the source of all that is sublime or lovely in nature or in art.

§ 5. His conflict with Poland and Russia.

Such a man was certain not to be a mere enthusiast embarking heedlessly in a Protestant crusade. Neither would he be careful for mere temporal or political power, regardless of the higher interests of his time. His first duty, and he never forgot it, was to his country. When he came to the throne, in 1611, Sweden was overrun by Danish armies, and in an almost desperate condition. In two years he had wrested a peace from the invaders, under conditions hard indeed, but which at least secured the independence of Sweden. His next effort, an effort which to the day of his death he never relaxed, was to bring into his own hands the dominion of the Baltic. He drove the Russians from its coasts. 'Now,' he said triumphantly in 1617, 'this enemy cannot, without our permission launch a single boat upon the Baltic.' He had another enemy more dangerous than Russia. Sigismund, King of Poland, was his cousin, the son of his father's elder brother, who had been driven from the throne of Sweden for his attachment to the Catholic belief. And so Gustavus was involved in the great question which was agitating Europe. The bare legal right which gave the whole of the seventeen provinces of the Netherlands to Spain, which gave Bohemia to Ferdinand, and the Protestant bishoprics and the secularized(Pg 81) lands to the Catholic clergy, gave also Sweden to Sigismund. Was it strange if Gustavus stood forth to combat this doctrine to the death, or if in his mind the growth of the two branches of the House of Austria, by whom this doctrine was maintained, became inextricably blended with the creed which that doctrine was to favour? Was it strange, too, if Protestantism and the national right of each separate country to go its own way untrammelled by such a doctrine appeared in his eyes, as in his days for the most part they really were, but two forms of the same spirit?

§ 6. His visit to Germany.

The peace concluded by Gustavus with Russia in 1617 was accompanied by a fresh outbreak of the war with Poland; and this renewal of the contest with the old rival of his house naturally drew the king's attention to affairs in Germany; for Ferdinand, now rising into power, was the brother-in-law of Sigismund, and likely to give him what aid he could in his Swedish enterprise. And Gustavus, too, was not quite a foreigner in Germany. Through his mother German blood ran in his veins, and when, in the summer of 1618, he visited Berlin in secret, he was won by the lovely face of the daughter of that energetic Elector of Brandenburg who after boxing the ears of the rival candidate for the dukedom of Cleves had adopted the Calvinist creed and had entered the Union. The death of the Elector delayed the marriage, and it was not till 1620 that, on a second visit, Gustavus wrung a consent from the new Elector, George William, whose weakness and vacillation were to be a sore trial to the Swedish king in after years. In strict incognito, Gustavus travelled as far as Heidelberg, at a time when the Elector was far away, in the midst of his short-lived splendour at Prague. Gustavus learned something from that visit which(Pg 82) he never forgot. He saw the rich luxuriance of that fair Rhine valley, stretching away till the western hills are but dimly visible in the blue distance, and which, compared by Venetian travellers to the green Lombard plain, must have caused strange sensations of wonder in the wanderer from the cold and barren north. And he saw another sight, too, which he never forgot—the wealth and magnificence of the Rhenish prelates. 'If these priests were subjects to the king my master' (he spoke in the assumed character of a Swedish nobleman) 'he would long ago have taught them that modesty, humility, and obedience are the true characteristics of their profession.'

§ 7. His daring and prudence.

Plainly in this man there was something of Christian of Anhalt, something of the desire to overthrow existing institutions. But there was that in him which Christian of Anhalt was ignorant of—the long and calm preparation for the crisis, and the power of establishing a new order, if his life should be prolonged, to take the place of the old which was falling away.

§ 8. Renewed war with Poland.

Gustavus returned to carry on the war with Poland with renewed vigour. In 1621 Riga surrendered to him. The next year he concluded a truce which gave him leisure to look about him.

§ 9. His interest in the German war.

The year 1624 brought with it fresh alarm. The empire, hostile to Sweden and the religion of Sweden, was growing terribly strong. Unlike Christian of Denmark, Gustavus had sympathized with Frederick's Bohemian undertaking, although he had expected but little from an enterprise under Frederick's guidance. And now the tide of victory was running northward. An empire with a firm(Pg 83) grasp on the shores of Mecklenburg and Pomerania would soon call in question the Swedish dominion of the Baltic. If this was to be the end, Gustavus had gained but little by his victories over Russia and Poland.

§ 10. Character of his policy.

It all sounds like mere selfishness,—Christian alarmed for his family bishoprics, and his hold upon the Elbe and the Weser; Gustavus providing against an attack upon his lordship in the Baltic. But it does not follow that with both of them, and especially with Gustavus, the defence of the persecuted Gospel was not a very real thing. Historians coolly dissect a man's thoughts as they please, and label them like specimens in a naturalist's cabinet. Such a thing, they argue, was done for mere personal aggrandizement; such a thing for national objects; such a thing from high religious motives. In real life we may be sure it was not so. As with Ferdinand and Maximilian, the love of law and orderly government was indissolubly blended with the desire to propagate the faith on which their own spiritual life was based; so it was with Gustavus. To extend the power of Sweden, to support the princes of Germany against the Emperor's encroachments, to give a firm and unassailable standing ground to German Protestantism, were all to him parts of one great work, scarcely even in thought to be separated from one another. And, after all, let it never be forgotten that the unity which he attacked was the unity of the Jesuit and the soldier. It had no national standing ground at all. The Germany of a future day, the Germany of free intelligence and ordered discipline, would have far more in common with the destroyer than with the upholder of the hollow unity of the seventeenth century.

(Pg 84)

SECTION II.—English Diplomacy.

§ 1. English proposal to Sweden and Denmark.

In August 1624 two English ambassadors, Sir Robert Anstruther and Sir James Spens, set out from London; the first to the King of Denmark, the second to the King of Sweden. The object of the embassies was identical, to urge upon the two kings the necessity of stirring themselves up to take part in a war for the recovery of the Palatinate, and for the re-establishment of the old condition of things in Germany.

§ 2. The Danish answer.

Christian hesitated only so far as to wish to be quite sure that James was too much in earnest to turn back as he had turned back in 1621. Anstruther was to go around the circle of the princes of Lower Saxony, and as soon as a favorable report was received from them, and the impression made by that report was strengthened by the news of Mansfeld's preparations in England, Christian engaged to take part in the war.

§ 3. Foresight of Gustavus.

Gustavus was far more cautious. Never doubting for a moment that the task before him was one of enormous magnitude, he argued that it would not be too much if all who had reason to complain of the House of Austria, from Bethlen Gabor in the east to Lewis of France in the west, were to join heart and soul in the great enterprise. With this view he was already in close communication with his brother-in-law, George William, the Elector of Brandenburg, who for once in his life was eager for war, perhaps because he had hardly reached to a full conception of all that such a war implied.

§ 4. His answer.

Gustavus, too, had his own ideas about the way in which the war was to be carried on. In the first place there must be no divided command, and he himself(Pg 85) must have the whole military direction of the troops. A certain number of men must be actually levied, and a certain sum of money actually paid into his hands. To the mere promises which satisfied Christian he would not listen. And besides, two ports, one on the Baltic, the other on the North Sea, must be given over to him in order to secure his communications. Perhaps, however, the part of his scheme which gives the greatest evidence of his prescience is that which relates to France. Avoiding the rock upon which the English government was splitting, he made no attempt to force a Catholic sovereign like Lewis into over-close union with the Protestant powers. Help from France he would most willingly have if he could get it; but he argued that it would be better for the French forces to find a sphere of action for themselves in South Germany or Italy, far away from the regions in which Gustavus himself hoped to operate at the head of a purely Protestant army.

1625
§ 5. England adopts the Danish plan.

In January 1625 the answers of the two kings were known in England. Of the 50,000 men demanded by Gustavus, 17,000 were to be paid out of the English exchequer. Till four months' pay had been provided he would not stir. He, for his part, had no intention of being a second Mansfeld, the leader of an army driven by sheer necessity to exist upon pillage.

§ 6. Thinking it easier to satisfy Christian than Gustavus.

Christian's ideas were framed on a more moderate scale. He thought that 30,000 men would be sufficient altogether, and that 6,000 would be enough to fall to the share of England. Both James and Charles declared that if they must make a choice they preferred the Danish plan. Even 6,000 men would cost them 30,000*l*. a month, and,(Pg 86) though the French marriage was settled, Parliament had not yet been summoned to vote the subsidies on which alone such an expenditure could be based. But they did not yet understand that a choice was necessary. They thought that Gustavus might still come in as an auxiliary to the Danish armament. To this suggestion, however, Gustavus turned a deaf ear. He had no confidence in Christian, or in allies who had taken so scant a measure of the difficulties before them. It was true, he replied to a remonstrance from the English ambassador, that he had asked for hard conditions. 'But,' he added, 'if anyone thinks it easy to make war upon the most powerful potentate in Europe, and upon one, too, who has the support of Spain and of so many of the German princes, besides being supported, in a word, with the whole strength of the Roman Catholic alliance; and if he also thinks it easy to bring into common action so many minds, each having in view their own separate object and to regain for their own masters so many lands out of the power of those who tenaciously hold them, we shall be quite willing to leave to him the glory of his achievement, and all its accompanying advantages.'

§ 7. Gustavus attacks Poland.

With these words of bitter irony Gustavus turned away for a time from the German war to fight out his own quarrel with the King of Poland, a quarrel which he always held to be subservient to the general interests in so far as it hindered Sigismund from taking part in the larger conflict.

§ 8. Attempt of Charles to fulfil his engagements.

Christian's more sanguine ideas were soon to be put to the test. In March James of England died, and two months later Charles I. entered into an engagement to supply the king of Denmark with 30,000*l.* a month, and scraped together 46,000*l.* to make a beginning. Mansfeld, it was ar(Pg 87)ranged, should abandon his hopeless attempt to reach the Palatinate along the Rhine, and should convey the remnants of his force by the sea to the assistance of Christian.

§ 9. Commencement of the Danish war.

After all, however, the main point was the success or failure of the king to gain support in Germany itself. The circle of Lower Saxony, indeed, chose him for its military chief. But even then there was much division of opinion. With the commercial classes in the towns war against the Emperor was as yet decidedly unpopular. They were tolerably well assured that they would reap no benefit from any accession of strength to the princes, whilst the danger from the Emperor was still in the future. But they were not strong enough to carry the circle with them. A centre of resistance was formed, which must be broken down if the Emperor's pretensions were not to be abated. On July 18 Tilly crossed the Weser into Lower Saxony, and the Danish war began.

SECTION III.—**Wallenstein's Armament.**
§ 1. The Emperor's need of support.

Would Tilly's force be sufficient to overcome the King of Denmark and his foreign allies? Ferdinand and his ministers doubted it. In proportion as his power increased, the basis on which it rested grew narrower. Of his allies of 1620 the League alone supported him still. Spain, exhausted for the time with the siege of Breda, could do little for him, and contented herself with forming clever plans for cajoling the Elector of Saxony, and with urging the Pope to flatter the Lutherans by declaring them to be far better than the Calvinists. Of all such schemes as this nothing satisfactory was likely to come. John George of Saxony, indeed, refused to join in the King of Denmark's(Pg 88) movement. He thought that the Lower Saxony princes ought to have been content with the agreement of Mühlhausen, and that Frederick ought to have made his submission to the Emperor. But even in the eyes of John George the Lower Saxon war was very different from the Bohemian war. The Emperor's refusal to confirm permanently the Protestant bishoprics had made it impossible for any Protestant to give him more than a passive support.

§ 2. His numerous enemies.

And if the Emperor's friends were fewer, his enemies were more numerous. Christian IV. was more formidable than Frederick. Bethlen Gabor, who had made peace in 1622, was again threatening in the east; and no one could say how soon France might be drawn into the strife in the west. Ferdinand needed another army besides Tilly's. Yet his treasury was so empty that he could not afford to pay a single additional regiment.

§ 3. Wallenstein's offer.

Suddenly, in the midst of his difficulties, one of his own subjects offered to take the burden on his shoulders. Albert of Waldstein, commonly known as Wallenstein, sprang from an impoverished branch of one of the greatest of the families of the Bohemian aristocracy. His parents were Lutheran, but when, at the age of twelve, he was left an orphan, he was placed under the care of an uncle, who attempted to educate him in the strict school of the Bohemian Brotherhood, a body better known in later times under the name of Moravians, and distinguished, as they are now, for their severe moral training.

§ 4. His early life.

The discipline of the brethren seems to have had much the same influence upon the young nobleman that the long sermons of the Scotch Presbyterians had upon Charles II. The boy found his way to the Jesuits at Olmütz, and adopted their religion,(Pg 89) so far as he adopted any religion at all. His real faith was in himself and in the revelations of astrology, that mystic science which told him how the bright rulers of the sky had marked him out for fame. For a young Protestant of ability without wealth there was no room in Bohemia under the shadow of the great houses. With Ferdinand, as yet ruler only of his three hereditary duchies, he found a soldier's welcome, and was not long in displaying a soldier's capacity for war. To Wallenstein no path came amiss which led to fortune. A wealthy marriage made him the owner of large estates. When the revolution broke out he was colonel of one of the regiments in the service of the Estates of Moravia. The population and the soldiers were alike hostile to the Emperor. Seizing the cash-box of the estates he rode off, in spite of all opposition, to Vienna. Ferdinand refused to accept booty acquired after the fashion of a highwayman, and sent the money back to be used against himself. The Moravians said openly that Wallenstein was no gentleman. But the events which were hurrying on brought his name into prominence in connexion with more legitimate warfare, and he had become famous for many a deed of skill and daring before Frederick's banner sunk before the victors on the White Hill.

§ 5. Offers to raise an army.

Wallenstein was now in a position to profit by his master's victory. Ferdinand was not a man of business. In peace as in war he gladly left details to others, and there were good pickings to be had out of the ruin of the defeated aristocracy. Besides the lands which fell to Wallenstein's share as a reward for his merit, he contrived to purchase large estates at merely nominal prices. Before long he was the richest landowner in Bohemia. He became(Pg 90) Prince of Friedland. And now, when Ferdinand's difficulties were at their height, Wallenstein came forward offering to raise an army at his own cost. The Emperor needed not to trouble himself about its pay. Nor was it to be fed by mere casual plunder. Wherever it was cantoned the general would raise contributions from the constituted authorities. Discipline would thus be maintained, and the evils upon which Mansfeld's projects had been wrecked would be easily avoided.

§ 6. The larger the better.

Modern criticism has rejected the long accredited story of Wallenstein's assertion at this time that he could find means to support an army of 50,000 men, but not an army of 20,000. It is certain that his original request was for only 20,000. But the idea was sure to occur to him sooner or later. Government by military force was the essence of his proposal, and for that purpose the larger the number of his army the better.

§ 7. Ferdinand cannot refuse.

The connexion between two men whose characters differed so widely as those of Ferdinand and Wallenstein was from first to last of a nature to excite curiosity. Yet, after all, it was only the natural result of Ferdinand's own methods of government. The ruler who knows nothing beyond the duty of putting the law in execution, whilst he shuts his eyes to the real requirements of those for whom the law ought to have been made, must in the end have recourse to the sword to maintain him and his legality from destruction.

§ 8. Wallenstein's system.

The substitution of contributions for pillage may have seemed to Ferdinand a mode of having recourse to a legal, orderly way of making war. Unfortunately for him, it was not so. As the civil laws of the Empire gave him no right to raise(Pg 91) a penny for military purposes without the assent of the Diet, and as, in the distracted condition of Germany, the Diet was no longer available for the purpose, no one was likely to regard money so raised as legal in any sense at all. In fact, it could only be justified as Charles I. justified the forced loan of 1626, as an act done out of the plenitude of power inherent in the Crown, authorizing him to provide in cases of emergency for the good of his subjects. Ferdinand, in truth had brought himself into a position from which he could neither advance nor retreat with honour. If he did not accept Wallenstein's services he would almost certainly be beaten. If he did accept them, he would almost certainly raise a feeling in Germany which would provoke a still stronger opposition than that which he had for the present to deal with.

§ 9. Moderation impossible to Wallenstein.

For the contributions were to be raised by military authority, with no check or control whatever from civil officials. Even if the utmost moderation was used there was something utterly exasperating to the peasant or the townsman in having to pay over a greater or less share of his hoardings to a colonel who had no civil authority to produce, and who had no limit to his demands excepting in his own conscience. Those who expected that moderation would be used must have formed a very sanguine idea of the influence of the events of the war upon ordinary military character.

§ 10. Wallenstein's army.

In point of fact, neither Wallenstein nor his soldiers thought of moderation. With him there was just enough of regularity to preserve the discipline he needed; just enough order to wring the utmost possible amount of money out of the country. 'God help the land to which these men come,' was the natural exclamation of a frightened official who watched the troops march past him.

(Pg 92)

§ 11. Explanation of Wallenstein's success.

How was it then, if Wallenstein's system was no better than Mansfeld's system more thoroughly organized, that he did not meet with Mansfeld's misfortunes? The true explanation doubtless is that he was able to avoid the cause of Mansfeld's misfortunes. Mansfeld was a rolling stone from the beginning. With troops supporting themselves by plunder, he had to make head against armies in excellent condition, and commanded by such generals as Tilly and Cordova, before his own men had acquired the consistency of a disciplined army. Wallenstein made up his mind that it should not be so with him. He would lead his new troops where there was much to be gained and little to do. In due course of time they would learn to have confidence in him as their leader, and would be ready to march further under his orders.

§ 12. Wallenstein in the autumn of 1625.

In the autumn, Wallenstein entered the dioceses of Magdeburg and Halberstadt, levying the means of support for his army upon rich and poor. Nor were the requirements of himself and his men like the modest requirements of Tilly. With him every man was more highly paid. Splendid equipments and magnificence of every kind were necessaries of life to the general and his officers, and the example was quickly followed, so far as imitation was possible, in the lower ranks of the army. To Tilly's entreaties for aid Wallenstein turned a deaf ear, and left him to carry on the war against the Danes as best he could. He was doubtless wise in refusing to expose his recruits so early to the fierce trial of battle. With him everything was based on calculation. Even his luxury and splendour would serve to fix upon him the eyes of his soldiers, and to hold out to them another prospect than that of the endless hardships, varied by an occa(Pg 93)sional debauch at the storming of a town, which was the lot of those who followed Tilly. Yet Wallenstein never allowed this luxury and splendour to stand in the way of higher objects. He was himself a strategist of no mean order. He had a keen eye for military capacity. He never troubled himself to inquire what a man's religion was if he thought he could render good service as a soldier. There were generals in his army whose ancestry was as illustrious as that of any sovereign in Europe, and generals who had no other title to eminence than their skill and valour. High and low were equal before his military code. Honours and rewards were dispensed to the brave: his friendship was accorded to those who had been distinguished for special acts of daring.

§ 13. Wallenstein not a German.

It was a new power in Germany, a power which had no connexion with the princes of the Empire, scarcely more than a nominal connexion with the Emperor himself. And the man who wielded it was not even a German. By his birth he was a Bohemian, of Slavonian race. The foremost men of the war, Tilly, Wallenstein, Gustavus, were foreigners. Germany had failed to produce either a statesman or a warrior of the first rank.

1626
§ 14. Failure of peace negotiations.

During the winter, negotiations for peace were opened at Brunswick. But they foundered on the old rock. The Emperor and the League would grant the terms of Mühlhausen and nothing more. It was against their consciences to grant a permanent guarantee to the Protestant administrators, and to admit them to the full enjoyment of the privileges of princes of the Empire. With this the Lower Saxon princes refused to be contented. Amongst the means by which the chapters had secured their Protestant cha(Pg 94)racter were some acts of formal and even of technical illegality. Such acts might easily be made use of by the Emperor and his council to effect an alteration in the character of those bodies. The Emperor and his council might possibly intend to be just, but somehow or another they always contrived to decide disputed questions in favour of their own partisans. On behalf of the religious and political institutions of Protestant Germany, the King of Denmark and his allies refused to accept the terms which had been offered them, and demanded that Protestant territories should receive a legal and permanent confirmation of their right to continue Protestant.

Section IV.—Defeat of Mansfeld and Christian IV.

§ 1. Campaign of 1626.

When the campaign opened, in the spring of 1626, the numbers at the disposal of the two belligerents were not so very unequal. Wallenstein's forces had been swelling far beyond his original reckoning. He and Tilly together, it is said could command the services of 70,000 men, whilst 60,000 were ready to march against them. On Christian's side were fighting Mansfeld and Christian of Brunswick, and a nobler than either, John Ernest of Saxe-Weimar, on whom, first of German men, the idea had dawned of composing the distractions of his fatherland by proclaiming a general toleration. Bethlen Gabor was once more threatening Vienna from the side of Hungary. Even the Protestant peasants in Lower Austria had risen in defence of their religion and their homes against the Bavarian garrisons which guarded the land till their master's expenses had been paid.

§ 2. Christian IV. at a disadvantage.

In other respects than numbers, however, the conditions were most unequal. Tilly and Wallenstein both(Pg 95) quartered their troops on the enemy's country. In raising supplies they had no susceptibilities to consult, no friendly princes or cities to spare. Christian, on the other hand, was still amongst his allies, and was forced, on pain of driving them over to the Emperor, to show them every consideration. And in the midst of these difficulties one source of supply on which he had been justified in counting entirely failed him.

1625
§ 3. Failure of the English supplies.

Charles I. of England had engaged in the spring of 1625 to pay over to the King of Denmark 30,000*l*. a month, reckoning that Parliament would enable him to fulfil his promise. Parliament met in May, but it had no confidence either in Charles or in his favourite and adviser, the Duke of Buckingham. A war carried on in Germany with English money was most distasteful to the English feeling. The session came to an end after a vote of a bare 140,000*l*., to meet a war expenditure scarcely, if at all, short of 1,000,000*l*. a year. Still Charles persisted. In the winter Buckingham went over to Holland and negotiated the Treaty of the Hague, by which the Dutch were to pay 5,000*l*. a month, and the English renewed their obligation to pay the 30,000*l*. already promised to Christian IV. This time, it was thought, a fresh Parliament would be ready to take up the king's engagement. But the fresh Parliament proved more recalcitrant than its predecessor. The sum of 46,000*l*. which had been sent across the seas in May 1625 was the only representative of Charles' promised support.

1626
§ 4. Danger of the Danish army.

Christian of Denmark and his allies, therefore, were to some extent in the position in which Mansfeld had been in 1621 and 1622. If not utterly without resource, they were sadly(Pg 96) straitened, and were obliged to govern their movements by the necessity of finding supplies rather than by military calculations.

§ 5. Mansfeld in the north.

Mansfeld was the first to meet the enemy. For some time he had been quartered beyond the Elbe, making himself troublesome to the Lübeckers and the Elector of Brandenburg. But this could not go on for ever. Wallenstein was in front of him, and he must fight him, or leave him to join Tilly against the king.

§ 6. Battle of the bridge of Dessau.

Wallenstein never, in his whole career, exposed his men to a battle in the open field if he could help it; and least of all was he likely to do so whilst they were yet untried. He seized upon the bridge of Dessau over the Elbe, and, having fortified it strongly, waited for Mansfeld to do his work. On April 25 Mansfeld appeared. In vain he dashed his troops against the entrenchments. Then, watching a favourable opportunity, Wallenstein ordered a charge. The enemy fled in confusion and the victory was gained.

§ 7. Mansfeld's march towards Hungary.

Not long after Mansfeld's defeat at the bridge of Dessau, Christian of Brunswick died. The remaining chiefs of the Danish party had a desperate game to play. Mansfeld, reinforced by John Ernest of Weimar, was dispatched through Silesia, to hold out a hand to Bethlen Gabor. Wallenstein followed in pursuit, after sending some of his regiments to the assistance of Tilly.

§ 8. The battle of Lutter.

What could Christian do in the face of the danger? The English subsidies did not come. To remain on the defensive was to court starvation, with its inevitable accompaniment, mutiny. Elated by a slight success over the enemy, he made(Pg 97) a dash at Thuringia, hoping to slip through into Bohemia, and to combine with Bethlen Gabor and Mansfeld in raising the old Protestant flag in the heart of the Emperor's hereditary dominions. But Tilly was on the watch. On August 27 he came up with the Danish army at Lutter. The fight was fiercely contested. But before it was decided a cry arose from some of the men in the Danish ranks that they would fight no longer without pay. Christian was driven from the field. In after days he complained bitterly that if the King of England had fulfilled his promises the battle would have ended otherwise.

§ 9. Mansfeld's death.

The soldiers lent by Wallenstein to Tilly had borne them well in the fight. Wallenstein himself was far away. Mansfeld had been welcomed by the Protestants of Silesia, and when Wallenstein followed he found the principal towns garrisoned by the enemy. By the time he reached Hungary Mansfeld had joined Bethlen Gabor. Once more Wallenstein pursued his old tactics. Taking up a strong position, he left his opponents to do what they could. The events showed that his calculations were well founded. Bethlen Gabor had counted on help from the Turks. But the Turks gave him no adequate assistance, and he did not venture to repeat unaided the operation of the bridge of Dessau, and to attack Wallenstein in his entrenchments. He preferred making a truce, one of the conditions of which was that Mansfeld should be expelled from Hungary. On his way to Venice the great adventurer was seized by a mortal disease. The unconquerable man, like an old northern warrior, refused to die in a bed. 'Raise me up,' he said to his friends, 'I am dying now.' Propped up in an upright position in their arms, and gazing out upon the dawn, which was lighting up the hills(Pg 98) with the first rays of morning, he passed away. 'Be united, united,' he murmured with his last breath; 'hold out like men.' His own absence from the scene would perhaps remove one of the chief difficulties in the way of union.

CHAPTER VI. STRALSUND AND ROCHELLE.

Section I.—Fresh Successes of Wallenstein.

1626
§ 1. Confiscations in the north.

Differences had already arisen between Wallenstein and the League. It was understood that the defeat of the northern rebels would lead to confiscations in the north, as the defeat of Frederick had led to confiscations in the south. To part at least of the land of one of the defeated princes the Elector of Mentz laid claim. Wallenstein wished to have it all for George of Lüneburg, who, Lutheran as he was, had held high command in the imperial army.

§2. Wallenstein advocates religious equality.

The quarrel was more than a mere personal dispute. The League wished to pursue the old policy of pushing forward the interests of the Catholic clergy under cover of legality. Wallenstein wished Catholic and Protestant, already united in his army, to be equally united in the Empire. Rebellion would then be the only punishable crime; loyalty, and especially the loyalty of his own officers, the only virtue to be rewarded.

§ 3. Comes into collision with the League.

Another question between the two powers reached almost as deeply. The League demanded that Wallenstein should support his army upon supplies taken from the Protestants alone. Wallenstein asserted his right, as the Emperor's(Pg 99) general, to quarter his men where he would, and to levy contributions for their maintenance even on the territories of the League.

§ 4. Wallenstein could not found unity.

For the first time for many a long year, a friendly voice had been heard urging the Emperor in the only wise direction. Ferdinand, turning aside from the promotion of a sectional policy, was, if he would listen to Wallenstein, to place the unity of the Empire above the interests of the princes, by resting it on the basis of religious equality. Unhappily that advice was tendered to him by a man who could not offer him security for the realization of so wise a policy. To stand above parties it is necessary to obtain the confidence of a nation, and how could men have confidence in Wallenstein? Durable institutions may be guarded by the sword. They cannot be founded by the sword. All that was known of Wallenstein in Germany was that he was master of an army more numerous and more oppressive than that of Tilly. German unity, coming in the shape of boundless contributions and extortions, and enforced by the example of starving peasants and burning villages, was not likely to prove very attractive.

§ 5. Wallenstein's conference with Eggenberg.

It is strange that the better part of Wallenstein's programme did not repel Ferdinand at once. But Ferdinand never made up his mind in a hurry when there were difficulties on both sides, and he was accustomed to defer to the opinion of his chief minister, Eggenberg. In November Wallenstein held a conference with that minister. He unfolded all his scheme. He would increase his army, if it were necessary, to 70,000 men. With such a force he would be able to avoid a pitched battle, always dangerous to troops not thoroughly inured to campaigning. By the occupation of superior strategical points, he would(Pg 100) be able to out-manœuvre the enemy. And then Ferdinand would be master in Germany. The whole of the Empire would be brought under contribution. There would be submission at home, and abroad no power would be strong enough to lay a finger upon the re-established Empire.

1627
§ 6. Ferdinand supports Wallenstein.

Eggenberg was easily persuaded, and when Eggenberg was won, Ferdinand was won. In January, Wallenstein was created Duke of Friedland, a higher title than that of Prince of Friedland, which he already bore, in token of the Emperor's approbation. If only Wallenstein could have shown Ferdinand the way to win the hearts of Germans as readily as he showed him the way to overpower their resistance, the history of Germany and of Europe would have been changed.

§ 7. Preponderance of Wallenstein.

The resistance of the Protestants to the institutions of the Empire had hitherto failed. They had been weak because there had been something revolutionary in all their proceedings. And now those institutions, which up to this time had been working harmoniously, were giving signs of breaking-up. There was a little rift in them which might any day become wider. "Is the Emperor," asked Wallenstein, "to be a mere image which is never to move?" "It is not only the Empire," answered the representatives of the League, "which is bound to the Emperor. The Emperor is also bound to the Empire." There was nothing to reconcile the opposing theories. The Emperor who claimed to be something had been the tool of a few bishops; he would be, if Wallenstein had his way, the tool of a successful general. The Empire, in the mouth of the representatives of the League, meant not the populations of Germany, not even the true inter(Pg 101)est of the princes, but simply the interest of the bishops and their Church.

§ 8. The campaign of 1627.

The time had not yet come for an open quarrel. The enemy, though weakened, was still powerful. Charles I., by dint of a forced loan, which every Englishman except himself and his courtiers declared to be in violation of all constitutional precedents, contrived to get some money into his exchequer, and Sir Charles Morgan was sent over to the King of Denmark's aid with an army nominally of 6,000 men, but which in reality never reached two-thirds of that number. Thurn, the old hero of the revolution at Prague, and the Margrave of Baden-Durlach, brought their experience, such as it was, to Christian's aid, and a younger brother of John Ernest's, soon to be known to fame as Bernhard of Weimar, was also to be found fighting under his banners. Strong towns—Wolfenbüttel, Nordheim, and Nienburg—still held out on his side, and peasants and citizens were eager to free the land from the oppressions of the soldiery and the yoke of the priests.

§ 9. Submission of Bethlen Gabor.

Once more the Protestants of the north looked anxiously to the east. But Bethlen Gabor did not stir. Without Turkish help he could do nothing, and the Turks, involved in a war with Persia, resolved to negotiate a peace with the Emperor. When peace was agreed upon in September Bethlen Gabor was powerless.

§ 10. Wallenstein in Silesia.

Wallenstein's hands were freed as soon as these negotiations were opened. John Ernest of Weimar had died the year before, but his lieutenants were still in possession of Silesia. In May, Wallenstein sent Duke George of Lüneburg to cut off their retreat. In July, he was in Silesia himself. His men were three to one of the enemy. Place after place(Pg 102) surrendered. Only once did he meet with an attempt at resistance in the open field. Before the end of August the whole of Silesia was in his hands. Fifty-five standards were sent in triumph to Vienna. The Silesian towns were set to ransom, and the money of the citizens went to swell the military chest of the Emperor's general.

§ 11. Combat of Heiligenhafen.

When Silesia was lost Christian sought to avert destruction by offering terms of peace. But the two generals would accept nothing less than the surrender of Holstein, and to that Christian refused to accede. Wallenstein and Tilly joined their forces to drive him northwards before them. By this movement the Margrave of Baden was cut off from the rest of the Danish army. Making his way to the coast near Wismar, he had long to wait before transports arrived to carry him across the sea to join the King of Denmark. Scarcely had he landed at Heiligenhafen when a large body of imperialist troops arrived, and at once commenced the attack. He himself and a few of his principal officers escaped on ship-board. His men, seeing themselves deserted, took service under Wallenstein, and seven of the best regiments in the Danish army were lost to Christian.

§ 12. Conquest of Schleswig and Jutland.

Tilly found occupation for his men in the siege of the strong places in Lower Saxony. Wallenstein undertook to follow up the King of Denmark. Before the end of the year all Schleswig and Jutland, with the exception of two or three fortified towns, were in Wallenstein's hands.

§ 13. Wallenstein's schemes.

A few sieges, and all, it seemed, would be over. Wallenstein had begun to cherish the wildest plans. When(Pg 103) resistance had been put down in Germany, he would place himself at the head of 100,000 men and drive the Turks out of Constantinople. Such dreams, however, were to remain dreams. If Denmark had been beaten down, Tilly was still there, and Tilly represented forces with which the new military Empire was certain sooner or later to be brought into collision.

Section II.—Resistance to Wallenstein in the Empire.

§ 1. The Assembly of Mühlhausen.

In October, the electors in person, or by deputy, met at Mühlhausen to take into consideration the condition of the Empire. The Ecclesiastical electors urged that the engagement given in 1620 to the Protestant administrators was no longer valid. They had been told that they would not be dispossessed by force if they acted as loyal subjects. But they had not been loyal subjects. They had joined the King of Denmark in a war in which, with the aid of foreign powers, he had attempted to dismember the Empire. It was now time for justice to prevail, and for the Church, so far as the Peace of Augsburg allowed, to come by its own. To this reasoning the new Elector of Bavaria gave the whole weight of his authority, and even the two Protestant electors did not venture to meet the argument by an open denial. The circle of Lower Saxony had entered upon the war against the advice of John George, and he held that the administrators were only reaping the consequences of neglecting his counsel.

§ 2. The Catholic Electors complain of Wallenstein.

The Catholic electors felt themselves within reach of the settlement which they had long proclaimed as the object of their desires. They then proceeded to kick away the ladder by which they had climbed so high. It is not derogating from the merits of Tilly and his vete(Pg 104)rans to say that without Wallenstein they would have been unable to cope with the forces opposed to them. Wallenstein's army had driven Mansfeld back, had hemmed in Bethlen Gabor, had recovered Silesia, had contributed to the victory of Lutter. And yet that army threatened to establish itself upon the ruins of the authority of the princes and electors, and to set up a military despotism of the most intolerable kind. Everywhere Wallenstein's recruiting officers were beating their drums. Quiet episcopal cities in the south of Germany, which hoped to have seen the last of their troubles when Mansfeld vanished westward out of Alsace in 1622, found themselves suddenly selected as a trysting-place for some new regiment. Rough men poured in from every direction to be armed, clothed, lodged, and fed at their expense. The alarming doctrine that the army was to support itself, that men were to be raised for the purpose not of fighting the enemy, but of pressing contributions out of friends caused universal consternation. Wallenstein's officers, too, had been heard to talk with military frankness about pulling down princes and electors, and making a real sovereign of the Emperor.

§ 3. Yet they cannot do without him.

The voice of complaint swelled loudly. But those who raised it did not see that their own policy was at fault; that but for their refusal to yield on the question of the bishoprics, there would have been no need for Wallenstein's army at all. What they were doing required the aid of overpowering military force, and they were startled when he who wielded the sword insisted on being their master. For the present, therefore, the electors did not venture on anything more than a gentle remonstrance with Wallenstein, and a petition to the Emperor to remove the abuses which, as they well knew, were radically connected with the new system.

1628

§ 4. The commercial towns of the north.

The dislike of the rule of the sword which was felt amongst those for whom that sword had been drawn was sure to be felt far more strongly in the Protestant cities of North Germany. Up to Wallenstein's appearance the commercial oligarchies by which those cities were governed, had shown themselves at the best but lukewarm in the Protestant cause. The towns of the south had been the first to desert the Union. The towns of the north had been dragged half against their will into the Danish war. To them the imperial sway was connected by a tradition of centuries with support against the encroachments of the princes. But they had no traditions in favour of an army living at free quarters amongst them, of bullying colonels and hectoring soldiers. Magdeburg braved all the terrors of Wallenstein's anger rather than admit a single company within its walls. Hamburg declared itself ready to submit to the Emperor's authority, but closed its gates against his army. And though Magdeburg might be besieged when there was leisure, Hamburg and the other maritime towns were less easily to be gained. All-powerful on land, Wallenstein's authority ended at low-water mark. The King of Denmark had fled to his islands. The King of Sweden was master of the Baltic. If it was doubtful whether they could set an army in battle array in Germany, at least they could throw provisions and munitions of war into a besieged seaport town. If the Empire was to be secured, these seaports must be brought under the Emperor's authority.

§ 5. Wallenstein in possession of the Duchy of Mecklenburg.

Here, therefore, in the midst of the danger Wallenstein determined to plant himself firmly, with the instinctive conviction that the post of danger is the post of power. The two Dukes of Mecklenburg had steadily sup(Pg 106)ported the King of Denmark in his struggle against the Emperor. In 1627, when most of the other states ceased to pay any contributions towards the war, they had continued to fulfil their engagements, and though they now professed their readiness to make their submission, it was Wallenstein's interest to make the most of their treason, and the least of their repentance. In February, 1628, the Emperor, using the rights which he had claimed in the case of the Elector Palatine, declared them to have forfeited their lands and dignities, and placed the Duchies in Wallenstein's hands as a pledge for the payment of military expenses which still remained to be liquidated. It was significant of the change of feeling in Germany that the ecclesiastical electors, who had seen nothing amiss in the deprivation of Frederick, had not a good word to say for this concession to Wallenstein.

§ 6. Negotiation with the Hanse Towns.

In Mecklenburg the imperial general had gained a footing on the Baltic coast. But more than that was needed if he was to be safe from attack. All through the winter negotiations had been going on with the Hanse Towns, the maritime cities of the old commercial league, which had once taken up a dominant position in the north, and which, though shorn of its ancient glory, was still worth courting by a power which aspired to rule in Germany.

§ 7. Wallenstein's offers tempting.

Reasons were not wanting to induce the Hanse Towns to accept the Emperor's offers. There was something very tempting in the notion of having the power of the imperial armies to fall back upon in their conflicts for foreign states. Hamburg especially had been the object of the jealousy of these states, as the mart from whence the western nations supplied themselves with the materials used in ship-building. The King of Denmark had built Glück(Pg 107)stadt, lower down the Elbe, in the hope of intercepting so lucrative a trade. The King of England had blockaded the river, and carried off Hamburg vessels which he suspected of being freighted with timber and hemp for the use of his enemies in Spain.

§ 8. But they are repelled when they understand his plan.

From the growth of a national authority in Germany, therefore, the Hanse Towns would have had everything to gain. But Ferdinand was not, could not be really national. What he had to offer was a special agreement with Spain, which would have given them the monopoly of the trade between Germany and the Spanish dominions. Such a trade could only be supported by war. It was a privilege which would bring with it a deadly conflict with England and Holland, perhaps with Denmark and Sweden as well. And the prospect was none the more alluring because Wallenstein was to play the principal part in the design. The general of the imperial forces was appointed Admiral of the Baltic, and the Hanse Towns were expected to find him a fleet.

§ 9. They decline to accept his proposal.

What a prospect for a body of calculating traders. The Spanish monopoly, under such circumstances, was hardly to be recommended as a prudent investment. The Emperor's overtures were politely declined. Wallenstein, when he heard of their answer, rated them soundly. He had means, he said, to shut up their trade by land, and to seize goods which they might import either from England or the Netherlands. He would deal with them, in short, as Napoleon was to deal with them two centuries later.

§ 10. Wallenstein and the Baltic towns.

Wallenstein's thoughts, however, were more immediately directed to the towns on the Baltic. He had(Pg 108) long been alarmed at the danger which threatened him from Sweden. In November, 1627, he had entered into negotiations with an adventurer who offered to set fire to the ships in the Swedish harbours. But as the project had broken down there was nothing for it but to gain possession of the port towns on the Baltic coast, and to bar them against the enemy. For no man could expect that Gustavus would look on quietly, whilst a great military power was forming on the southern coast of the Baltic.

§ 11. Growth of his power.

Wismar was soon in Wallenstein's hands. The harbour of Rostock was blocked up by a line of sunken ships. Though Boguslav, the Duke of Pomerania, promised to keep his long line of coast safe from attack, he was compelled to admit a strong imperialist force within his territory. Everything seemed to be succeeding as Wallenstein wished.

Section III.—The Siege of Stralsund.

§ 1. Stralsund holds out.

One town alone held out. Stralsund was not a free city of the Empire. But though it was nominally dependent on the Duke of Pomerania it was practically its own mistress. The citizens had no wish to put themselves forward in opposition to the Emperor, far less to assist a foreign power to gain a footing in Germany. But they would never admit a garrison of such troops as Wallenstein's within their walls.

§ 2. He orders the siege to be commenced.

Wallenstein would have all or nothing. He ordered his commander in those parts, the Lutheran Arnim, to enforce submission. "I will never," he wrote, "allow them to keep anything back from me, lest others should be encouraged to do the like." Arnim, already master of Rügen, seized Dänholm, a smaller island commanding(Pg 109) the mouth of the harbour. In February hostilities were commenced. In March the citizens attacked the imperialists in Dänholm, and drove them out of the island.

§ 3. Wallenstein's first check.

It was Wallenstein's first check, and desperately did he struggle to wipe out the disgrace. Every day the spirit of the citizens was rising. There were old soldiers there, fugitives from the Danish war, and peasants who had fled from their desolated homes, and who had terrible tales to tell of the wretchedness which followed in the track of Wallenstein's soldiers. In April, all within the town bound themselves by a solemn oath to defend their religion and their liberty to the last drop of their blood, and to admit no garrison within their walls. In the midst of their resistance they still kept up some recollection of their nationality, so far as any tie of nationality could still be said to exist. The name of the Emperor was carefully avoided, but they professed attachment to the Empire and its laws.

§ 4. Succour from Denmark and Sweden.

Practically, however, the shape in which the Empire presented itself to them was that of Wallenstein's army, and if they were to resist that army, the Stralsunders must, whether they liked it or not, make common cause with those who were hostile to the Empire. In May a Danish embassy appeared amongst them, and the King of Sweden sent a present of gunpowder. When the siege was formally opened, these overtures were followed by a succour of armed men. Sweden and Denmark were working together to break up the new military Empire, and their forlorn hope was thrown into Stralsund.

§ 5. Wallenstein abandons the siege.

Wallenstein saw that the case was serious, and came in person to the help of his lieutenant. According to a doubtful story, he exclaimed, 'I will have(Pg 110) Stralsund, even if it be fastened by chains to heaven.' It is certain that when a deputation from the citizens pleaded with him that he would abandon his demand that they should admit a garrison within their walls, he drew his hand along the surface of a table before him, and answered sternly, 'Your town shall be made as flat as this.' But the problem of overcoming the resistance of a fortress open to unlimited succours by sea is one of the most difficult in the whole art of war. Still, however, there were fearful odds in favour of the besiegers. Without the walls Wallenstein had no enemy to fear. He was himself Duke of Mecklenburg. With the Elector of Brandenburg and the Duke of Pomerania he was on friendly terms, and he had received the support of the latter in his attempts upon the town. Within the walls there was no certainty of ultimate success. Those who had anything to lose placed their property on shipboard. Many sent their wives and daughters to seek a safe refuge in Sweden. But whatever doubts might arise the defenders of the town fought sturdily on.

Week after week passed away, and Stralsund was still untaken. Wallenstein lowered his terms. He ceased to demand entrance for a garrison of his own men. It would be enough, he now said, if the citizens would entrust their walls to troops of their own ruler, the Duke of Pomerania, and would in this manner tear themselves away from the connexion with foreign powers hostile to the Emperor. And to this offer the governing council of the town was ready to assent. But the general body of the citizens rejected it utterly. They deliberately preferred the alliance of the two foreign kings to submission, however indirect, to the Emperor's authority. Before this resolution, Wallenstein, with all his armies, was powerless. On August 3 he raised the siege.

(Pg 111)

§ 6. Character of the resistance.

Wallenstein's failure was an event of incalculable importance in the history of Germany. It was much that one, and that not one of the first, towns of the Empire should have beaten back the tide of conquest. But it was more that the resistance should have been attempted in a case which sooner or later would be the cause of the great majority of Germans. Ferdinand had floated to power because he personified order as opposed to anarchy. The Stralsunders fought for the Protestant religion and freedom from the presence of a garrison. Ferdinand's order meant the rule of the priest, and the rule of the soldiers. Slowly and unwillingly the citizens of Stralsund declared for the presence of foreigners as better than such order as this.

SECTION IV.—The Siege of Rochelle.

§ 1. Stralsund and Rochelle.

The tide was on the turn in Germany. But the tide was not on the turn in France. There, too, a maritime city, greater and wealthier than Stralsund, and supported by fleets and armies from beyond the sea, was defending the cause of Protestantism against the central government. Mainly because in France the central government represented something more than the rule of the priest and the soldier, the resistance which was successful in Germany was overpowered in France.

1625
§ 2. England and France.

During the year 1625 the coolness between England and France had been on the increase. The persecution of the English Catholics by Charles, in contravention of his promises, had greatly exasperated Lewis, and the seizure by the English cruisers of numerous French vessels charged with carrying on a contraband traffic with the Spanish(Pg 112)Netherlands had not contributed to calm his indignation. Charles, on the other hand, regarded himself as the natural protector of the French Protestants, and made demands in their favour which only served to make Lewis more resolved to refuse every concession.

§ 3. Richelieu would have made peace with the Huguenots if he could.

Richelieu had therefore a hard part to play. He knew perfectly well that the government had violated its engagements with the Huguenots, especially in keeping up the fortifications of Fort Louis, a work commanding the entrance to the harbour of Rochelle, which it had long ago promised to pull down. If Richelieu had had his way he would have pulled down the fort, and by generous concessions to the Huguenots would have carried them with him to the support of his foreign policy. But such a policy, in appearance so rash, in reality so wise, was not likely to be palatable to Lewis, and Richelieu had to steer his way between the danger of offending the king and the danger of lighting up still more vividly the flames of civil war. In the course of the winter all that could be done he did. Deputies of the Huguenot towns appeared to negotiate a peace, with the support of two English ambassadors. But they were instructed to demand the demolition of the fort, and to this the king steadily refused his consent.

1626
§ 4. An agreement effected.

The priests and the friends of the priests were delighted at the prospect of another civil war. The assembled clergy commissioned one of their number to offer to the king a considerable sum of money for the suppression of rebellion. The time was appointed for his audience, but Richelieu contrived to put it off for a few hours longer, and, by a representation of the dangers of the situation, induced the Huguenot deputies, with the support of the(Pg 113) English ambassadors, to be satisfied with a loose verbal promise from the king. When the clerical train swept into the royal presence it was too late. The king had already promised the Huguenot deputies that if they behaved as good subjects he would do for them more than they could possibly expect. His ministers had already assured them that these words pointed to the demolition of the fort.

§ 5. Intervention of Charles I.

If a peace thus made was to be enduring, it would be necessary to keep up for a long time the appearance of its being a submission and not a peace. Unhappily, the intervention of the King of England was not likely to help to keep up appearances. He urged Lewis to engage in the war in Germany in the exact way and to the exact extent that suited the English government, and he put himself ostentatiously forward as the protector of the Huguenots.

§ 6. Lewis indignant.

Such conduct awoke once more the susceptibilities of Lewis. It was bad enough to be bearded by his own subjects. But it was worse to be bearded by a foreign sovereign. A group of Huguenot communities in the south of France supported in practical independence by England would be as insupportable to him as the resistance of the Hanse Towns was two years later to Wallenstein.

1627
§ 7. War between France and England.

Fort Louis, therefore, was not demolished. A peace was patched up between France and Spain. Charles grew more and more angry with Lewis for deserting the common cause. Fresh seizures of French ships by English cruisers came to exasperate the quarrel, and in the early months of 1627 war existed between the two nations, in reality if not in name. In July a great English fleet, with a land army on board, appeared off Rochelle,(Pg 114) under the command of Charles' favourite, Buckingham. A landing was effected on the Isle of Rhé, and siege was laid to the principal fort of the island. At last the garrison was almost starved out, and the commander offered to come the next morning into the English quarters to treat for terms of surrender. That night a stiff easterly breeze sprung up, and a French flotilla, heavily laden with provisions, put off from the main land. Some of the boats were taken, but most of them made their way safely through the English guardships, and delivered their precious store under the guns of the fort.

Buckingham lingered for some weeks longer. Every day the besiegers swept the horizon in vain with their glasses, looking for succour from England. But Charles, without parliamentary support, was too poor to send off succours hurriedly, and when they were at last ready a long continuance of westerly winds prevented them from leaving the Channel. Before they could put to sea, a French force was landed on the island, and Buckingham, to save himself from defeat, was forced to break up the siege and to return home discomfited.

§ 8. Siege of Rochelle.

Richelieu and the king were now thoroughly of one mind. The French city which could enter into an understanding with the foreigner must be reduced to submission. An army of thirty thousand men gathered round the walls, and on the land side the town was as hopelessly blocked up as Stralsund. The only question was whether it would be possible to cut off the entrance of English supplies by sea. By the end of November a commencement was made of the mole which was to shut off Rochelle from all external help. Piles were driven in with stones between them. Heavily laden vessels were scuttled and sunk. Richelieu himself directed the operations, this time with the full support of(Pg 115) the clergy, who poured their money lavishly into the royal treasury. In May, 1628, the work, in spite of the storms of winter, was almost completed. An English fleet, which came up to the succour of the town, retired without accomplishing anything.

§ 9. Increasing despondency in the town.

Inside the town distress was rapidly growing unendurable. The mayor, Jean Guiton, was still the soul of the resistance. But he had to struggle against an increasing number who counselled surrender. He did not venture to appear in the streets without a pistol in his hand and half-a-dozen stout guardians around him.

§ 10. Failure of the English attempt to succour it.

The only hope for Rochelle lay in the great armament which was known to be prepared in England, and which was to be conducted by Buckingham in person. The House of Commons had purchased the Petition of Right with large subsidies, and Charles, for the first time in his reign, was enabled to make an effort worthy of his dignity. But the popular hatred found a representative in the murderer Felton, and a knife struck home to the favourite's heart put an end to his projects for ever. The dissatisfaction which arrayed the English people against its government had found its way into the naval service. When the fleet arrived in September, under a new commander, all was disorganization and confusion. It returned to England without accomplishing a single object for which it had been sent forth.

§ 11. Surrender of Rochelle.

The surrender of Rochelle followed as a matter of necessity. On November 1 the king entered the conquered town in triumph. The independence of French cities was at an end.

§ 12. Cause of Richelieu's success.

The different success of the two great sieges of the year may partly be accounted for by the difference of(Pg 116) vigour in the powers to which the threatened towns looked for succour. Charles was very far from being a Christian IV., much less a Gustavus Adolphus; and if England at unity with itself was stronger than Sweden, England distracted by civil broils was weaker than

Sweden. But there were more serious reasons than these for Richelieu's victory and Wallenstein's failure. Richelieu represented what Wallenstein did not—the authority of the state. His armies were under the control of discipline; and, even if the taxation needed to support them pressed hardly upon the poor, the pressure of the hardest taxation was easy to be borne in comparison with a far lighter contribution exacted at random by a hungry and rapacious soldiery. If Richelieu had thus an advantage over Wallenstein, he had a still greater advantage over Ferdinand and Maximilian. He had been able to isolate the Rochellese by making it clear to their fellow Huguenots in the rest of France that no question of religion was at stake. The Stralsunders fought with the knowledge that their cause was the cause of the whole of Protestant Germany. The Rochellese knew that their resistance had been tacitly repudiated by the whole of Protestant France.

§13. Religious liberty of the Huguenots.

When Lewis appeared within the walls of Rochelle he cancelled the privileges of the town, ordered its walls to be pulled down and its churches to be given over to the Catholic worship. But under Richelieu's guidance he announced his resolution to assure the Protestants a continuance of the religious liberties granted by his father. No towns in France should be garrisoned by troops other than the king's. No authorities in France should give orders independently of the king. But wherever a religion(Pg 117) which was not that of the king had succeeded in establishing its power over men's minds no attempt should be made to effect a change by force. Armed with such a principle as this, France would soon be far stronger than her neighbours. If Catholic and Huguenot could come to regard one another as Frenchmen and nothing else, what chance had foreign powers of resisting her? She had already beaten back the attack of a divided England. Would she not soon acquire a preponderance over a divided Germany? It is time for us now to ask what steps were being taken in Germany to meet or to increase the danger.

CHAPTER VII. THE EDICT OF RESTITUTION.

Section I.—*Oppression of the Protestants.*

1628
§ 1. Siege of Glückstadt.

It was not at Stralsund only that Wallenstein learned that he could be successfully resisted. Stade had surrendered with its English garrison to Tilly in April, but Glückstadt still held out. In vain Wallenstein came in person to Tilly's aid. The Danish cruisers kept the sea open. Wallenstein was obliged to retire. In January, 1629, the works of the besiegers were destroyed by a sally of the garrison.

1629
§ 2. The Peace of Lübeck.

Wallenstein, the great calculator, saw that peace with Denmark was necessary. The Swedes and the Danes were beginning to act together, and resistance to one nation, if there must be resistance, would be easier than resistance to two. Much to his satisfaction he found Christian not unwilling to listen to the voice of his charming. Just as the eagle eye of Gustavus descried(Pg 118) the first feeble beams of light on the horizon, the King of Denmark, weary of misfortune and vexed at the prospect of having to crave help from his old competitor of Sweden, laid down his arms. On May 22, 1629, a treaty of peace was signed at Lübeck. Christian received back the whole of his hereditary possessions. In return he resigned all claim to the bishoprics held by his family in the Empire, and engaged to meddle no further with the territorial arrangements of Lower Saxony.

§ 3. Necessity of healing measures.

If the Peace of Lübeck was really to be a source of strength to Ferdinand it must be accompanied by some such measures as those with which Richelieu was accompanying his victory at Rochelle. It was not enough to have got rid of a foreign enemy. Some means must be found to allay the fears of the Germans themselves, which had found expression in the resistance of Stralsund.

§ 4. Opposite views as to what measures are needed.

That there was much to be done in this direction was openly acknowledged by almost all who had been concerned in the imperialist successes. Maximilian and the League held that it was above all things necessary to restrain the excesses of Wallenstein and his soldiers. Wallenstein held that it was above all things necessary to restrain the excessive demands of Maximilian and the clergy. Ferdinand, the man in whose hands fortune had placed the decision of the great question, probably stood alone in thinking that it was possible to satisfy both the soldiers and the priests without weakening his hold on the Empire.

The first act of Ferdinand after the signature of the treaty was to invest Wallenstein formally with the Duchy of Mecklenburg. Offence was thus given to those who believed that the rights of territorial sovereignty had(Pg 119) been unduly invaded, and who were jealous of the right claimed by the Emperor to supersede by his own authority a prince of the Empire in favour of a successful soldier.

§ 5. Ill treatment of the Protestants.

On the other side offence was given still more widely to those who wished to maintain the rights of Protestantism. Without wishing to enter upon a general persecution, Ferdinand was resolved to allow no rights against his church to those who could not conclusively prove to his own satisfaction that those rights were under the guarantee of unassailable law. He had begun in his own hereditary dominions. It is true that in Bohemia and Austria no tortures were inflicted, no martyrs suffered either at the stake or on the scaffold. But it was found that the stern, relentless pressure of daily annoyance was sufficient for the purpose of producing at least external conformity. By 1627 the desired result had been obtained, and Protestantism existed only as a proscribed religion. Then came the turn of the Palatinate. For a time there had been no open persecution. In 1625 Maximilian had written to the governor of Heidelberg not to let any opportunity slip, if he could find an excuse for turning out a Protestant minister from his parish and replacing him by a Catholic priest. In February, 1628, the Jesuits were able to report that they had made 400 converts in Heidelberg itself, and 1,200 in the neighbouring country districts. Then came a further change. In March an agreement was drawn up between Maximilian and Ferdinand. The Emperor received back Upper Austria, and made over to the Elector of Bavaria, in its stead, the Upper Palatinate and that part of the Lower Palatinate which lies on the right bank of the Rhine. Maximilian held that by this transfer he had acquired the full rights of a territo(Pg 120)rial prince, and that amongst these rights was that of disposing of the religion of his new subjects. In June all noblemen residing in the country were told that they must either change their religion within two months or go into exile. In September the order was extended to the inhabitants generally.

§ 6. The cities of South Germany.

The year 1628 was a year of alarm over all Protestant South Germany. There at least Ferdinand was ready to carry out the wishes expressed by the Catholic electors at Mühlhausen the year before. Whilst Maximilian was threatening the Palatinate, imperial commissioners were passing through the other territories and cities, taking account of churches and church property which had come into Protestant possession since the Convention of Passau. To the wishes of the populations not the slightest attention was paid. In Nördlingen, for instance, not a single Catholic was to be found. Every church in the place was none the less marked down for re-delivery to the Catholic clergy. In some places to which the commissioners came, Shylock-like, to claim their pound of flesh, they demanded more even than the strict letter of the law allowed them. Not content with restoring to the Catholic worship churches which had with general consent been in the hands of Protestants for half a century, they proceeded to compel the inhabitants of the towns to attend the mass.

§ 7. The Edict of Restitution.

The success of these outrageous measures in the south encouraged Ferdinand to pursue the same course in the north. There he had to deal not merely with scattered towns, or a few abbeys, but with the great lay bishoprics, many of which were extensive enough to form the domain of a duke or a landgrave. On March 29, 1629, before the Peace of(Pg 121) Lübeck was actually signed, he issued the fatal Edict of Restitution. With a stroke of his pen, the two archbishoprics of Magdeburg and Bremen, the twelve bishoprics of Minden, Verden, Halberstadt, Lübeck, Ratzeburg, Misnia, Merseburg, Naumburg, Brandenburg, Havelberg, Lebus, and Camin, with about a hundred and twenty smaller ecclesiastical foundations, were restored to the Catholic clergy.

§ 8. Real weakness of the Emperor.

The wheel had come full circle round since the day when Christian of Anhalt had planned the great uprising to sweep away the Catholic bishops and the House of Austria. The House of Austria was firmer in its seat than ever. The Catholic bishops were triumphant. But in the midst of their triumph the enemies of the Empire were watching them keenly, and judging that both they and the Emperor were all the weaker for this grand vindication of legality.

Section II.—French Intervention in Italy.

§ 1. Gustavus and Richelieu.

In the north Gustavus had an eye not likely to be deceived for the joints of Ferdinand's harness. In the west Richelieu was preparing for the day when he too might aid in the overthrow of the Colossus. It is true that his first thought was of Spain and not of Germany. But he could hardly be brought into collision with one branch of the House of Austria without having sooner or later to deal with the other.

§ 2. The Mantuan War.

In Italy, the death of the Duke of Mantua and Montferrat without near heirs had given rise to war. The next heir was a very distant relation, the Duke of Nevers, whose family had long been naturalized in France. To Spain the presence of a dependent of France so near her possessions in the Milanese was in the highest degree undesi(Pg 122)rable, and she called upon Ferdinand to sequester the territory till another way of disposing it could be found. If in Germany before Ferdinand's election the rights of the Emperors had been but a shadow, those which they possessed in the old kingdom of Italy were but the shadow of a shade. But whatever they were, Ferdinand was the man to put them forth, and whilst Richelieu was engaged at Rochelle, Spanish troops had overrun Mantua, and in conjunction with the Duke of Savoy, ready now to seek his own interests by fighting for Spain, as in earlier days to seek his own interests by fighting against her, were besieging the Duke of Nevers in Casale, the only fortress which remained to him.

§ 3. Italian feeling against the Emperor.

This intervention of the Spaniards in the Emperor's name caused even greater indignation in Italy than their intervention in the Palatinate had caused in Germany. For in Germany the Emperor's name was in 1621 still connected with the ideas of law and order. In Italy it reminded men of nothing but foreign domination, a memory which was none the less vivid when the Emperor used his authority, whatever it might be, to support the real foreign domination of the immediate present, the Spanish domination in Milan. The Italian princes took alarm. Venice and the pope summoned France to their aid, and in March, 1629, Richelieu, taking Lewis with him across the snowy passes of the Alps, reduced the Duke of Savoy to submission, and forced the Spaniards to raise the siege of Casale.

§ 4. Check inflicted on him by Richelieu.

Casale was the Stralsund of Italy. A power which had ventured to clothe itself in the attributes of a national authority, with even less reason than in Germany, had found its limits. Richelieu had the general feeling on his side.

(Pg 123)

§ 5. The last Huguenot rebellion.

He did not venture to do more in Italy. The Duke of Rohan, the brother of that Soubise who had begun the war of Rochelle in 1625, had roused the Huguenots of Languedoc and the Cevennes to a fresh attempt at resistance, half Protestant, half aristocratic. As if the Rochellese had not sufficiently suffered for the mistake of calling in foreign aid, Rohan followed their example, and was foolish enough to ask for help from Spain. But the Spanish troops came not to his aid. Richelieu hurried back from Italy, made peace with England, and pitilessly crushed the rebellion in the south. Once more the victory was attended by the confirmation of the religious liberties of the Huguenots. They might worship as they pleased, but political independence they were not to have.

§ 6. Strength of France.

The French monarchy was stronger for external enterprise than ever. By crushing all resistance, it had no longer to fear occupation for its energies at home, and by its tolerance of religion it had rendered itself capable of accepting the service of all its subjects, and it could offer its alliance to Protestant states without fear of suffering a rebuff.

§ 7. Richelieu and the Imperialists in Italy.

Richelieu was again able to turn his attention to Italy. In the summer of 1629 an imperialist force of 20,000 men descended from the Alps and laid siege to Mantua. Ferdinand, having established peace in Germany, fancied that he could take up again in Italy the work which had been too great for Barbarossa. Spinola came to his aid with an army of equal force, and recommenced the attack upon Casale. In the spring of 1630 Richelieu was once more in Italy. Cardinal as he was, he was placed in command of the army. But instead of marching against the Spaniards, he turned first upon the Duke of Savoy.(Pg 124) Seizing Pignerol and Saluces, he gained possession of the Alpine passes. Then, with Piedmont at his feet, he passed on to relieve Casale, and forced the Spanish besiegers to retreat. But Richelieu was prudent as well as daring, and he left Mantua for the present in the hands of Spain and the Emperor.

§ 8. State of Germany.

It was a hard thing to attack the united forces of Spain and the Empire face to face. It might be easier to support their enemies abroad, and to favour dissensions at home. In the Netherlands, the Dutch, encouraged by the diversion of the Italian war, were at last taking the offensive, and entering upon that aggressive warfare which ended by bringing the whole of North Brabant under their authority. In the north, Gustavus had concluded a peace with Poland, and was making preparations for actual intervention in Germany. In all this Richelieu was deeply interested. An ambassador of Lewis was engaged in arranging with Gustavus the terms on which France should assist him in the attack upon the Empire which he already contemplated.

§ 9. Richelieu's expectations.

Not that even Richelieu foresaw the possibility of the magnificent results which were to follow from that enterprise. In 1630, as in 1624 and 1625, he would have preferred that a Protestant power should not be too successful. He would rather conquer with Sweden than not at all. But he would rather conquer with the help of the League than with the help of Sweden. Gustavus might be pushed on to do his best. He would effect a diversion, and that would be enough.

Section III.—Wallenstein deprived of his Command.

§ 1. Strong position of Wallenstein.

The long expected breach between the League and the Emperor's general had come at last. Instead of re(Pg 125)ducing his forces after the Peace of Lübeck, Wallenstein had increased them. He was now at the head of 100,000 men. From a military point of view no one could say it was too much. He had Mantua to defend, the coasts of the North Sea to watch, perhaps France to guard against, and that too with all the princes and peoples of Germany exasperated against him. Some efforts he made to curb the violence of his soldiers. But to restrain the monster he had created was beyond his power. And if his soldiers bore hard upon burgher and peasant, he himself treated the princes with contemptuous scorn. He asked why the electors and the other princes should not be treated as the Bohemian nobles had been treated. The Estates of the Empire had no more right to independence than the Estates of the kingdom. It was time for the Emperor to make himself master of Germany, as the kings of France and Spain were masters of their own dominions. All this made the electors above measure indignant. "A new domination," they told Ferdinand, "has arisen for the complete overthrow of the old and praiseworthy constitution of the Empire."

§ 2. What could he effect?

A reconstruction of that old rotten edifice would have done no harm. But its overthrow by military violence was another matter. A new form of government, to be exercised by a soldier with the help of soldiers, could never be found in justice,

For always formidable was the leagueAnd partnership of free power and free will.The way of ancient ordinances, though it winds,Is yet no devious path. Straight forward goesThe lightning's path, and straight the fearful pathOf the cannon-ball. Direct it flies, and rapid,Shattering that it may reach, and shattering what it reaches.

Schiller's *Piccolomini*, act i. scene 4.

(Pg 126)

§ 3. His partiality.

Even whilst he was defending the universality of oppression on the principle that it was but fair that all estates should contribute to the common defence, he was exhibiting in his own case an extraordinary instance of partiality. Whilst all Germany was subjected to contributions and exactions, not a soldier was allowed to set foot on Wallenstein's own duchy of Mecklenburg.

§ 4. The Edict of Restitution carried out.

And if the Catholic electors had good reason to complain of Wallenstein, Wallenstein had also good reason to complain of the electors. The process of carrying out the Edict of Restitution was increasing the number of his enemies. "The Emperor," he said, "needed recruits, not reforms." Ferdinand did not think so. He had persuaded the chapter of Halberstadt to elect a younger son of his own as their bishop. He induced the chapter of Magdeburg to depose their administrator, on the ground that he had taken part in the Danish war. But, in spite of the Edict of Restitution, the chapter of Magdeburg refused to choose a Catholic bishop in his place, and preferred a son of the Elector of Saxony. John George was thereby brought by his family interests into collision with the Edict of Restitution.

§ 5. Magdeburg refuses a garrison.

The city of Magdeburg had not been on good terms with the chapter. Wallenstein offered to support its resistance with the help of a garrison. But the city refused, and Wallenstein, in the face of the growing opposition, did not venture to force it to accept his offer.

§ 6. Growing opposition to Wallenstein.

Of the fact of the growing opposition no one could be doubtful. As to its causes there was much difference of opinion. The priests ascribed it to the barbarities of the soldiers. Wallenstein ascribed(Pg 127) it to the violence of the priests, and especially to the vigour with which they were attempting to reconvert the inhabitants of the archbishopric of Bremen, which they had recovered in virtue of the Edict of Restitution.

§ 7. He talks of attacking the Pope.

On every side the priests and their schemes were in the way of Wallenstein's dazzling visions of a grand imperialist restoration. The Pope, as an Italian prince, had sympathized with France. "It is a hundred years," said Wallenstein, "since Rome has been plundered, and it is richer now than ever."

§ 8. Assembly of Ratisbon.

On July 3, 1630, Ferdinand assembled round him the princes and electors at Ratisbon, in the hope of inducing them to elect his son, the King of Hungary, as King of the Romans, and therefore as his successor in the Empire. But to this project the electors refused even to listen. All who attended the assembly came with their minds full of the excesses of Wallenstein's soldiery. The commissioners of that very Duke of Pomerania who had served the imperial cause so well in the siege of Stralsund, had a tale of distress to pour out before the princes. His master's subjects, he said, had been driven to feed upon grass and the leaves of trees. Cases had occurred in which starving wretches had maintained life by devouring human flesh. A woman had even been known to feed upon her own child.

§ 9. The deprivation of Wallenstein demanded.

Other tales were told, bad enough, if not quite so bad as this, and the misery of the populations gave support to the political grievances of their rulers. Ferdinand was plainly told that the electors did not mean to be subjected to military despotism. He must choose between them and Wallenstein.

(Pg 128)

§ 10. Richelieu's intrigues.

Behind the Catholic Electors was Richelieu himself. Together with the recognized French ambassadors, the Capuchin Father Joseph, Richelieu's trusted confidant, had come to Ratisbon, encouraging the opposition to Wallenstein, and urging the electors to demand the neutrality of the Empire, if a war broke out between France and Spain.

§ 11. Policy of the Electors.

Unhappily for Germany, the policy of the electors was purely conservative. There was nothing constructive even in Maximilian, the greatest of them all. The old loose relationship between the princes and the Emperor was to be restored whether it was adequate to the emergency or not. At the very moment when he had every need of conciliating opposition, he and his brother electors were refusing the petition of the deputies of the Duke of Pomerania that their masters might be allowed to keep possession of the bishopric of Camin.

§ 12. Landing of Gustavus.

At the moment when the offence was given, it was known at Ratisbon that Gustavus Adolphus had landed on the coast of Pomerania.

§ 13. Gustavus comes without allies.

Five years before Gustavus had refused to stir against the Emperor without the aid of a powerful coalition. He now ventured to throw himself alone into the midst of Germany. He had no certainty even of French aid. The French ambassador had offered him money, but had accompanied the offer by conditions. Gustavus thrust aside both the money and the conditions. If he went at all, he would go on his own terms.

§ 14. His hopefulness.

He knew well enough that the task before him, apparently far harder than in 1625, was in reality far easier. He saw that between the ecclesiastical Electors on the one hand, and Wallenstein on(Pg 129) the other, the Protestant princes must cling to him for safety. To one who suggested that even if he were victorious the princes would seek to profit by his victory, he answered, with the assurance of genius, 'If I am victorious, they will be my prey.'

§ 15. Dismissal of Wallenstein.

Events were working for him at Ratisbon. Before the persistent demand of the electors for Wallenstein's dismissal Ferdinand was powerless. Even Wallenstein would not have been strong enough to contend against the League, backed by France, with a whole Protestant north bursting into insurrection in his rear. But, in truth, neither Ferdinand nor Wallenstein thought of resistance. The general, strong as his position was, at the head of the most numerous and well-appointed army in Europe, retired into private life without a murmur. He may, perhaps, have calculated that it would not be long before he would be again needed.

§ 16. Ferdinand's position.

That Ferdinand felt the blow keenly it is impossible to doubt. He thought much of the maintenance of the imperial dignity, and the uprising of the electors was in some sort an uprising against himself. But the system which had fallen was the system of Wallenstein rather than his own. He had sanctioned the contributions and exactions, feebly hoping that they were not so bad as they seemed, or that if anything was wrong a little more energy on Wallenstein's part would set things straight. As to Wallenstein's idea of a revolutionary empire founded on the ruins of the princes, Ferdinand would have been the first to regard it with horror. His policy was in the main far more in accordance with that of Maximilian than with that of Wallenstein.

§ 17. Concessions of Ferdinand in Italy.

Wallenstein's dismissal was not the only sacrifice to(Pg 130) which Ferdinand was obliged to consent. He agreed to invest the Duke of Nevers with the Duchy of Mantua, hoping in return to secure the neutrality of France in his conflict with Sweden.

§ 18. Tilly in command.

The result of that conflict depended mainly on the attitude taken by the Protestants of the north, whom Ferdinand, in combination with the Catholic electors, was doing his best to alienate. Tilly was placed in command of the army which had lately been Wallenstein's, as well as of his own. The variety of habits and of feeling in the two armies did not promise well for the future. But, numerically, Tilly was far superior to Gustavus.

Section IV.—The Swedes establish themselves on the Coast of the Baltic.

§ 1. The Swedish army.

Gustavus, on the other hand, commanded a force inferior only in numbers. Thoroughly disciplined, it was instinct with the spirit of its commander. It shared his religious enthusiasm and his devotion to the interests of his country. It had followed him in many a hardly-won fight, and had never known defeat under his orders. It believed with justice that his genius for war was far greater than that of any commander who was likely to be sent against him.

§ 2. The Duke of Pomerania submits to Gustavus.

The first attempt of Gustavus to win over a prince of the Empire to his side was made before Stettin, the capital of the Duke of Pomerania. He insisted on a personal interview with the aged Boguslav, the last of the old Wendish line. Boguslav had ever been on good terms with the Emperor. He had helped Wallenstein at Stralsund. But his deputies had pleaded in vain at Ratisbon for his right to retain(Pg 131) the bishopric of Camin and for some amelioration of the misery of his subjects. He now pleaded in person with Gustavus to be allowed to remain neutral. Gustavus, like Tilly in 1623, would hear nothing of neutrality. The old man could hold out no longer. "Be it as you wish, in God's name," he said. He begged the king to be a father to him. "Nay," replied Gustavus, "I would rather be your son." The inheritance of the childless man would make an excellent bulwark for the defence of the Baltic.

§ 3. The Elector of Brandenburg prefers neutrality.

For some time longer Gustavus was busy in securing a basis of operations along the coast by clearing Pomerania and Mecklenburg of imperialist garrisons. But, as yet, the northern princes were unwilling to support him. In vain Gustavus reasoned with the ambassador of his brother-in-law, the Elector of Brandenburg, who had come to announce his master's neutrality. "It is time," he said, "for his highness to open his eyes, and to rouse himself from his ease, that his highness may no longer be in his own land a lieutenant of the Emperor, nay, rather of the Emperor's servant. He who makes a sheep of himself is eaten by the wolf. His highness must be my friend or enemy, when I come to his frontier. He must be hot or cold. No third course will be allowed, be you sure of that." The words were thrown away for the present. There may have been something of mere cowardice in the Elector's resistance to the overtures made to him. Frederick had failed, and Christian had failed, and why not Gustavus? But there was something, too, of the old German feeling remaining, of unwillingness to join with the foreigner against the Empire. "To do so," said the Brandenburg ambassador, "would be both dishonourable and disloyal."

(Pg 132)

§ 4. Negotiations between Sweden and France.

Gustavus had but to wait till Ferdinand's repeated blunders made loyalty impossible even with the much-enduring George William. Fortunately for Gustavus, he was now in a position in which he was able to wait a little. An attempt had been made in France to overthrow Richelieu, in which the queen mother, Mary of Medici, had taken a leading part. Richelieu, she warned her son, was leading him to slight the interests of the Church. But Lewis was unconvinced, and Mary of Medici found that all political authority was in Richelieu's hands.

1631
§ 5. The Treaty of Bärwalde.

The complete success of the princes opposed to Wallenstein had perhaps exceeded Richelieu's expectations. A balance of power between Wallenstein and the League would have served his purpose better. But if Ferdinand was to be strong, it did not matter to France whether the army which gave him strength was commanded by Wallenstein or by Tilly. Richelieu, therefore, made up his mind to grant subsidies to Gustavus without asking for the conditions which had been refused in the preceding spring. On January 23 the Treaty of Bärwalde was signed between France and Sweden. A large payment of money was assured to Gustavus for five years. Gustavus, on his part, engaged to respect the constitutions of the Empire as they were before Ferdinand's victories, and to leave untouched the Catholic religion wherever he found it established. Out of the co-operation of Catholic and Protestant states, a milder way of treating religious differences was already arising, just as the final establishment of toleration in England grew out of the co-operation between the Episcopal Church and the Nonconformists.

Section V.—The Fall of Magdeburg.

§ 1. Hesitation of the Elector of Saxony.

Further successes marked the early months of 1631. But till the two Protestant Electors could make up their minds to throw in their lot with Gustavus, nothing serious could be effected. John George felt that something ought to be done. All over North Germany the Protestants were appealing to him to place himself at their head. To say that he was vacillating and irresolute, born to watch events rather than to control them, is only to say that he had not changed his nature. But it must never be forgotten that the decision before him was a very hard one. In no sense could it be regarded otherwise than as a choice between two evils. On the one side lay the preponderance of a hostile religion. On the other side lay the abandonment of all hope of German unity, a unity which was nothing to Gustavus, but which a German Elector could not venture to disregard. It might be, indeed, that a new and better system would arise on the ruins of the old. But if Saxony were victorious with the aid of Sweden, the destruction of the existing order was certain, the establishment of a new one was problematical.

§ 2. The Assembly at Leipzig.

A great Protestant assembly held at Leipzig in March, determined to make one more appeal to the Emperor. If only he would withdraw that fatal Edict of Restitution, the Protestants of the north would willingly take their places as obedient estates of the Empire. No foreign king should win them from their allegiance, or induce them to break asunder the last ties which bound them together to their head. But this time the appeal was accompanied by a step in the direction of active resistance. The Protestant estates represented at Leipzig agreed to levy soldiers, in order to be prepared for whatever might happen.

§ 3. Tilly in the north.

Time was pressing. The Treaty of Bärwalde had opened the eyes of Maximilian and the League to the danger of procrastination. If they had entertained any hope that France would leave them to contend with Gustavus alone, that hope was now at an end. Tilly was despatched into the north to combat the Swedish king.

§ 4. Tilly's advance and retreat.

Ferdinand had despised the danger from Gustavus. "We have got a new little enemy," he said, laughing, when he heard of the disembarkation of the Swedes. Tilly knew better. He pressed rapidly forward, hoping to thrust himself between Gustavus in Pomerania and his lieutenant, Horn, in Mecklenburg. If he succeeded, the invading army would be cut in two, and liable to be defeated in detail. Success at first attended his effort. On March 29, whilst the princes were debating at Leipzig, he took New Brandenburg, cutting down the whole Swedish garrison of 2,000 men. But Gustavus was too rapid for him. Uniting his forces with those of Horn, he presented a bold front to the enemy. Tilly was driven back upon the Elbe. The remaining fortresses on the Baltic, and the important post of Frankfort on the Oder, garrisoned with eight imperialist regiments, fell into the power of the conqueror.

§ 5. Magdeburg.

A greater and more important city than Frankfort was at stake. The citizens of Magdeburg had raised the standard of independence without waiting for leave from John George of Saxony. Gustavus had sent a Swedish officer to conduct their defence. But without the support of the Electors of Saxony and Brandenburg, he durst not bring his army to their assistance.

§ 6. Treaty of Cherasco.

The imperialists were gathering thickly round Mag(Pg 135)deburg. On April 26 a treaty was signed at Cherasco, between France and the Empire, which restored peace in Italy, and set free the Emperor's troops beyond the Alps for service in Germany. If Tilly saw matters still in a gloomy light, his fiery lieutenant, Pappenheim, thought there was no reason to despair. "This summer," he wrote, "we can sweep our enemies before us. God give us grace thereto."

§ 7. Convention with the Elector of Brandenburg.

As the siege went on, Gustavus, writing under his enforced inaction, pleaded hard with the two Electors. From the Elector of Brandenburg he demanded the right to occupy the two fortresses of Küstrin and Spandau. Hopes were held out to him of the surrender of Küstrin, but he was assured that Spandau should never be his. Accompanied by a picked body of troops, he marched straight upon Berlin. On May 13, outside the city gates, he held a long conference with his brother-in-law, the Elector. He argued in vain. To one of the Dukes of Mecklenburg, who had accompanied him, he spoke in bitter words. "I am marching," he said, "upon Magdeburg, to deliver the city. If no one will assist me, I will retreat at once. I will offer peace to the Emperor, and go home to Stockholm. I know that the Emperor will agree to my terms. But you Protestants will have to answer at the day of judgment that you would do nothing for the cause of God. In this world, too, you will be punished. Magdeburg will be taken, and, if I retire, you will have to look to yourselves." The next day the conference was resumed. From early morning till nine at night the Elector persisted in his refusal. But the armed men who stood behind Gustavus were the most powerful of arguments.(Pg 136) At last the Swedish king had his way. On the 15th the gates of Spandau were thrown open to his troops.

§ 8. Resistance of the Elector of Saxony.

But, if the Elector of Brandenburg had given way, the Elector of Saxony was not to be moved. He had not yet received an answer to his appeal to the Emperor; and till that arrived he would enter into no alliance with a foreigner. Further advance was impossible. Cut to the heart by the refusal, Gustavus withdrew, leaving Magdeburg to its fate.

§ 9. Storming of Magdeburg.

That fate was not long in coming. The city was hardly in a state to make a desperate resistance. The council had levied men to fight their battle. But amongst the body of the townsmen there were some who counselled submission, and others who preferred taking their ease whilst the hired soldiers were manning the walls. On May 20, Pappenheim stormed the city. In those days the sack of a town taken by storm was claimed as a right by the soldiers, as firmly by those of Gustavus as by those of Tilly and Wallenstein. But a few weeks before, the Protestant population of Frankfort had been exposed to the violence and greed of the Swedish army, simply because they had been unable to prevent the imperialists from defending the place. But the sack of Magdeburg was accompanied by circumstances of peculiar horror. Scarcely had the first rush taken place over the walls when, either intentionally or by accident, some of the houses were set on fire. In the excitement of plunder or of terror no one thought of stopping the progress of the flames. The conquerors, angered by the thought that their booty was being snatched away from before their eyes by an enemy more irresistible than themselves, were inflamed almost to madness. Few could meet that infuriated soldiery(Pg 137) and live. Whilst every form of death, and of outrage worse than death, was encountered in the streets, the shrieks of the wretched victims were overpowered by the roaring of the flames. In a few hours the great city, the virgin fortress which had resisted Charles V. and Wallenstein, with the exception of the Cathedral and a few houses around it, was reduced to a blackened ruin, beneath which lay the calcined bones of men, of tender women, and of innocent babes.

§ 10. Tilly's part in the matter.

For the horrors of that day Tilly was not personally responsible. He would have hindered the storm if he had been able. The tales which carried through all Protestant Germany the evil deeds of the old warrior, and represented him as hounding on his men to the wretched work, were pure inventions. He had nothing to gain by the destruction of Magdeburg. He had everything to gain by saving it as a basis of operations for his army.

§ 11. False policy which led to the disaster.

But if Tilly was not responsible for the consequences of the siege, he and his masters were responsible for the policy which had made the siege possible. That cathedral standing out from amidst the ruins of Magdeburg was but too apt a symbol of the work which he and the League had set themselves to do. That the rights of the clergy and the church might be maintained, all the homes and dwellings of men in Germany were to be laid waste, all the social and political arrangements to which they had attached themselves were to be dashed into ruin.

§ 12. Ferdinand refuses to cancel the Edict of Restitution.

Even now Ferdinand was preparing his answer to the last appeal of the faithful Protestant estates. The Edict of Restitution he would maintain to the uttermost. Of the armament of the princes he spoke in terms of contemptuous(Pg 138) arrogance. Let John George and his companions in ill-doing dismiss their soldiers, and not presume to dictate terms by force to the head of the Empire. Ferdinand had declared the law as it was, and by the law he meant to abide.

CHAPTER VIII. THE VICTORIES OF GUSTAVUS ADOLPHUS.

Section I.—Alliance between the Swedes and the Saxons.

1631

§ 1. The camp of Werben.

A great fear fell upon the minds of all Protestant men. The cities of the south, Augsburg and Nüremberg, which had begun to protest against the execution of the edict, fell back into silence. In the north, Gustavus, using terror to counteract terror, planted his cannon before the walls of Berlin, and wrung from his reluctant brother-in-law the renunciation of his neutrality. But such friendship could last no longer than the force which imposed it, and John George could not be won so easily. William of Hesse Cassel was the first of the German princes to come voluntarily into the camp of Gustavus. Bernhard of Saxe-Weimar came too, young as he was, full of military experience, and full too of memories of his forefathers, the heroes of that old Saxon line which had forfeited the Saxon Electorate for the sake of the Gospel. But neither William nor Bernhard could bring much more than their own swords. Gustavus dared not take the offensive. Throwing up an entrenched camp at Werben, where the Havel joins the Elbe, he waited for Tilly, and repulsed an attack made upon him. But what was such a victory worth? Hardships and disease were thinning his ranks, and unless aid came, the end would be very near.

(Pg 139)

§ 2. Tilly reinforced.

The aid which he needed was brought to him by the blindness of Ferdinand. At last the results of the treaty of Cherasco were making themselves felt. The troops from Italy had reached the north, and, in August, Tilly was at the head of 40,000 men. With the reinforcements came orders from the Emperor. The tame deflection of John George from the line of strict obedience was no longer to be borne. Tilly must compel him to lay down his arms, or to join in the war against the foreign invasion.

§ 3. Summons John George to disarm.

These orders reached Tilly on August 18. On the 24th he sent a message to the Elector, asking him by what right he was in arms against the laws of the Empire. John George had some difficulty in finding an answer, but he refused to dismiss his troops.

§ 4. Attacks Saxony.

If Tilly had only let the Elector alone, he would probably have had nothing to fear from him for some time to come. But Tilly knew no policy beyond the letter of his instructions. He at once crossed the Saxon frontier. Pappenheim seized Merseburg. Tilly reduced Leipzig to surrender by the threat that he would deal with the city worse than with Magdeburg. The Elector, so long unwilling to draw the sword, was beyond measure angry. He sent speedy couriers to Gustavus, offering his alliance on any terms.

§ 5. Union of the Swedes and the Saxons.

Gustavus did not wait for a second bidding. The wish of his heart was at last accomplished. He put his forces at once in motion, bringing the Elector of Brandenburg with him. The Saxon commander was the Lutheran Arnim, the very man who had led Wallenstein's troops to the siege of Stralsund. The Edict of Restitution had taught him that Wallenstein's idea of a Germany united without respect(Pg 140) for differences of religion was not to be realized under Ferdinand. He had thrown up his post, and had sought service with John George. Without being in any way a man of commanding ability, he had much experience in war.

§ 6. The Saxon troops.

The Saxon soldiers were a splendid sight. New clothed and new armed, they had with them all the pomp and circumstance of glorious war. But they had had no experience of fighting. They were as raw as Wallenstein's troops had been when he first entered the diocese of Halberstadt in 1625.

§ 7. The Swedish troops.

The Swedes were a rabble rout to look upon, at least in the eyes of the inexperienced Saxons. Their new allies laughed heartily at their uniforms, ragged with long service and soiled with the dust of the camp and the bivouac. But the war-worn men had confidence in their general, and their general had confidence in them.

§ 8. Gustavus as a commander.

Such confidence was based on even better grounds than the confidence of the veterans of the League in Tilly. Tilly was simply an excellent commander of the old Spanish school. He had won his battles by his power of waiting till he was superior in numbers. When the battles came they were what are generally called soldiers' battles. The close-packed columns won their way to victory by sheer push of pike. But Gustavus, like all great commanders, was an innovator in the art of war. To the heavy masses of the enemy he opposed lightness and flexibility. His cannon were more easily moved, his muskets more easily handled. In rapidity of fire he was as superior to the enemy as Frederick the Great with his iron ramrods at Mollwitz, or Moltke with his needle-guns at Sadowa. He had, too, a new method of drill. His troops were(Pg 141) drawn up three deep, and were capable of manœuvering with a precision which might be looked for in vain from the solid columns of the imperialists.

SECTION II.—The Battle of Breitenfeld.

§ 1. Battle of Breitenfeld.

On the morning of September 17 Swede and Saxon were drawn up opposite Tilly's army, close to the village of Breitenfeld, some five miles distant from Leipzig. Gustavus had need of all his skill. Before long the mocking Saxons were flying in headlong rout. The victors, unlike Rupert at Marston Moor, checked themselves to take the Swedes in the flanks. Then Gustavus coolly drew back two brigades and presented a second front to the enemy. Outnumbered though he was, the result was never for a moment doubtful. Cannon shot and musket ball tore asunder the dense ranks of the imperialist army. Tilly's own guns were wrenched from him and turned upon his infantry. The unwieldy host staggered before the deft blows of a more active antagonist. Leaving six thousand of their number dying or dead upon the field, Tilly's veterans, gathering round their aged leader, retreated slowly from their first defeat, extorting the admiration of their opponents by their steadiness and intrepidity.

§ 2. Political importance of the victory.

The victory of Breitenfeld, or Leipzig—the battle bears both names—was no common victory. It was the grave of the Edict of Restitution, and of an effort to establish a sectarian domination in the guise of national unity. The bow, stretched beyond endurance, had broken at last. Since the battle on the White Hill, the Emperor, the Imperial Council, the Imperial Diet, had declared themselves the only accredited organs of the national life. Then had come a coolness between the Emperor and(Pg 142) the leaders of the Diet. A good understanding had been re-established by the dismissal of Wallenstein. But neither Emperor nor Diet had seen fit to take account of the feelings or wants of more than half the nation. They, and they alone, represented legal authority. The falsehood had now been dashed to the ground by Gustavus. Breitenfeld was the Naseby of Germany.

§ 3. Victory of intelligence over routine.

Like Naseby, too, Breitenfeld had in it something of more universal import. Naseby was the victory of disciplined intelligence over disorderly bravery. Breitenfeld was the victory of disciplined intelligence over the stiff routine of the Spanish tactics. Those tactics were, after all, but the military expression of the religious and political system in defence of which they were used. Those solid columns just defeated were the types of what human nature was to become under the Jesuit organization. The individual was swallowed up in the mass. As Tilly had borne down by the sheer weight of his veterans adventurers like Mansfeld and Christian of Brunswick, so the renewed Catholic discipline had borne down the wrangling theologians who had stepped into the places of Luther and Melanchthon. But now an army had arisen to prove that order and obedience were weak unless they were supported by individual intelligence. The success of the principle upon which its operations were based could not be confined to mere fighting. It would make its way in morals and politics, in literature and science.

§ 4. Wallenstein's intrigues with Gustavus.

Great was the joy in Protestant Germany when the news was told. The cities of the south prepared once more to resist their oppressors. All that was noblest in France hailed the tidings with acclamation. English Eliot, writing from(Pg 143) his prison in the Tower, could speak of Gustavus as that person whom fortune and virtue had reserved for the wonder of the world! Even Wallenstein, from his Bohemian retreat, uttered a cry of satisfaction. For Wallenstein was already in communication with Gustavus, who, Protestant as he was, was avenging him upon the League which had assailed him and the Emperor who had abandoned him. He had offered to do great things, if he could be trusted with a Swedish force of 12,000 men. He was well pleased to hear of Tilly's defeat. "If such a thing had happened to me," he said to an emissary of Gustavus, "I would kill myself. But it is a good thing for us." If only the King of Sweden would trust him with men, he would soon bring together the officers of his old army. He would divide the goods of the Jesuits and their followers amongst the soldiers. The greatest folly the Bohemians had committed, he said, had been to throw Martinitz and Slawata out of window instead of thrusting a sword through their bodies. If his plan were accepted he would chase the Emperor and the House of Austria over the Alps. But he hoped Gustavus would not allow himself to be entangled too far in the French alliances.

§ 5. His designs.

Wallenstein's whole character was expressed in these proposals, whether they were meant seriously or not. Cut off from German ideas by his Bohemian birth, he had no roots in Germany. The reverence which others felt for religious or political institutions had no echo in his mind. As he had been ready to overthrow princes and electors in the Emperor's name, so he was now ready to overthrow the Emperor in the name of the King of Sweden. Yet there was withal a greatness about him which raised him above such mere adventurers as Mansfeld. At the head(Pg 144) of soldiers as uprooted as himself from all ties of home or nationality, he alone, amongst the leaders of the war, had embraced the two ideas which, if they had been welcomed by the statesmen of the Empire, would have saved Germany from intolerable evil. He wished for union and strength against foreign invasion, and he wished to found that union upon religious liberty. He would have kept out Gustavus if he could. But if that could not be done, he would join Gustavus in keeping out the French.

§ 6. Impossibility of an understanding between Wallenstein and Gustavus.

Yet between Wallenstein and Gustavus it was impossible that there should be anything really in common. Wallenstein was large-minded because he was far removed from the ordinary prejudices of men. He was no more affected by their habits and thoughts than the course of a balloon is affected by the precipices and rivers below. Gustavus trod firmly upon his mother earth. His Swedish country, his Lutheran religion, his opposition to the House of Austria, were all very real to him. His greatness was the greatness which rules the world, the greatness of a man who, sharing the thoughts and feelings of men, rises above them just far enough to direct them, not too far to carry their sympathies with him.

§ 7. Political plans of Gustavus.

Such a man was not likely to be content with mere military success. The vision of a soldier sovereignty to be shared with Wallenstein had no charms for him. If the Empire had fallen, it must be replaced not by an army but by fresh institutions; and those institutions, if they were to endure at all, must be based as far as possible on institutions already existing. Protestant Germany must be freed from oppression. It must be organized apart sufficiently(Pg 145) for its own defence. Such an organization, the *Corpus Evangelicorum*, as he called it, like the North German Confederation of 1866, might or might not spread into a greater Germany of the future. It would need the support of Sweden and of France. It would not, indeed, satisfy Wallenstein's military ambition, or the more legitimate national longings of German patriots. But it had the advantage of being attainable if anything was attainable. It would form a certain bulwark against the aggression of the Catholic states without necessitating any violent change in the existing territorial institutions.

§ 8. His military schemes.

If these were the views of Gustavus—and though he never formally announced them to the world his whole subsequent conduct gives reason to believe that he had already entertained them—it becomes not so very hard to understand why he decided upon marching upon the Rhine, and despatching the Elector of Saxony to rouse Bohemia. It is true that Oxenstjerna, the prudent Chancellor of Sweden, wise after the event, used to declare that his master had made a mistake, and later military historians, fancying that Vienna was in the days of Gustavus what it was in the days of Napoleon, have held that a march upon Ferdinand's capital would have been as decisive as a march upon the same capital in 1805 or 1809. But the opinion of Gustavus is at least as good as that of Oxenstjerna, and it is certain that in 1631 Vienna was not, in the modern sense of the word, a capital city. If we are to seek for a parallel at all, it was rather like Madrid in the Peninsular War. The King had resided at Madrid. The Emperor had resided at Vienna. But neither Madrid in 1808 nor Vienna in 1631 formed the centre of force. No administrative threads controlling the military system stretched out from either. In the(Pg 146) nineteenth century Napoleon or Wellington might be in possession of Madrid and have no real hold of Spain. In the seventeenth century, Ferdinand and Gustavus might be in possession of Vienna and have no real hold on Austria or Bohemia. Where an army was, there was power; and there would be an army wherever Wallenstein, or some imitator of Wallenstein, might choose to beat his drums. If Gustavus had penetrated to Vienna, there was nothing to prevent a fresh army springing up in his rear.

§ 9. Necessity of finding a basis for his operations.

The real danger to be coped with was the military system which Wallenstein had carried to perfection. And, in turning to the Rhine, Gustavus showed his resolution not to imitate Wallenstein's example. His army was to be anchored firmly to the enthusiasm of the Protestant populations. There lay the Palatinate, to be freed from the oppressor. There lay the commercial cities Augsburg, Nüremberg, Ulm, and Strassburg, ready to welcome enthusiastically the liberator who had set his foot upon the Edict of Restitution; and if in Bohemia too there were Protestants to set free, they were not Protestants on whom much dependence could be placed. If past experience was to be trusted, the chances of organizing resistance would be greater amongst Germans on the Rhine than amongst Slavonians on the Moldau.

§ 10. He resolves to march to the south-west.

For purposes of offence, too, there was much to induce Gustavus to prefer the westward march. Thither Tilly had retreated with only the semblance of an army still in the field. There, too, were the long string of ecclesiastical territories, the Priest's Lane, as men called it, Würzburg, Bamberg, Fulda, Cologne, Treves, Mentz, Worms, Spires, the richest district in Germany, which had fur(Pg 147)nished men and money to the armies of the League, and which were now to furnish at least money to Gustavus. There Spain, with its garrisons on the left bank of the Rhine, was to be driven back, and France to be conciliated, whilst the foundations were laid of a policy which would provide for order in Protestant Germany, so as to enable Gustavus to fulfil in a new and better spirit the work left undone by Christian of Anhalt. Was it strange if the Swedish king thought that such work as this would be better in his own hands than in those of John George of Saxony?

SECTION III.—March of Gustavus into South Germany.

§ 1. March of Gustavus upon the Rhine.

The march of the victorious army was a triumphal progress. On October 2, Gustavus was at Erfurt. On the 10th he entered Würzburg: eight days later, the castle on its height beyond the Main was stormed after a fierce defence. Through all the north the priests were expelled from the districts which had been assigned them by the Edict of Restitution. Gustavus was bent upon carrying on reprisals upon them in their own homes. On December 16, Oppenheim was stormed and its Spanish garrison put to the sword. The Priest's Lane was defenceless. Gustavus kept his Christmas at Mentz. His men, fresh from the rough fare and hard quarters of the north, revelled in the luxuries of the southern land, and drank deep draughts of Rhenish wine from their helmets.

§ 2. Gustavus at Mentz.

There is always a difficulty in conjecturing the intentions of Gustavus. He did not, like Ferdinand, form plans which were never to be changed. He did not, like Wallenstein, form plans which he was ready to give up at a moment's notice for others entirely different. The essence of his(Pg 148) policy was doubtless the formation, under his own leadership, of the *Corpus Evangelicorum*. What was to be done with the ecclesiastical territories which broke up the territorial continuity of South German Protestantism he had, perhaps, not definitely decided. But everything points to the conclusion that he wished to deal with them as Wallenstein would have dealt with them, to parcel them out amongst his officers and amongst the German princes who had followed his banner. In doing so, he would have given every security to the Catholic population. Gustavus, at least in Germany, meddled with no man's religion. In Sweden it was otherwise. There, according to the popular saying, there was one king, one religion, and one physician.

§ 3. The French startled at his victories.

He placed the conquered territories in sure hands. Mentz itself was committed to the Chancellor Oxenstjerna. French ambassadors remonstrated with him roundly. Richelieu had hoped that, if the House of Austria were humbled, the German ecclesiastics would have been left to enjoy their dignities. The sudden uprising of a new power in Europe had taken the French politicians as completely by surprise as the Prussian victories took their successors by surprise in 1866. "It is high time," said Lewis, "to place a limit to the progress of this Goth." Gustavus, unable to refuse the French demands directly, laid down conditions of peace with the League which made negotiation hopeless. But the doubtful attitude of France made it all the more necessary that he should place himself in even a stronger position than he was in already.

§ 4. Campaign in South Germany.

On March 31 he entered Nüremberg. As he rode through the streets he was greeted with heartfelt acclamations. Tears of joy streamed down the cheeks of bearded men as they welcomed(Pg 149) the deliverer from the north, whose ready jest and beaming smile would have gone straight to the popular heart even if his deserts had been less. The picture of Gustavus was soon in every house, and a learned citizen set to work at once to compose a pedigree by which he proved to his own satisfaction that the Swedish king was descended from the old hereditary Burggraves of the town. In all that dreary war, Gustavus was the one man who had reached the heart of the nation, who had shown a capacity for giving them that for which they looked to their Emperor and their princes, their clergy and their soldiers, in vain.

§ 5. Gustavus at Donauwörth.

Gustavus did not tarry long with his enthusiastic hosts. On April 5 he was before Donauwörth. After a stout resistance the imperialists were driven out. Once more a Protestant Easter was kept within the walls, and the ancient wrong was redressed.

§ 6. The passage of the Lech and the death of Tilly.

On the 14th the Swedes found the passage of the Lech guarded by Tilly. Every advantage appeared to be on the side of the defenders. But Gustavus knew how to sweep their positions with a terrible fire of artillery, and to cross the river in the very teeth of the enemy. In the course of the battle Tilly was struck down, wounded by a cannon shot above the knee. His friends mournfully carried him away to Ingolstadt to die. His life's work was at an end. If simplicity of character and readiness to sacrifice his own personal interests be a title to esteem, that esteem is but Tilly's due. To the higher capacity of a statesman he laid no claim. Nor has he any place amongst the masters of the art of war. He was an excellent officer, knowing no other rule than the orders of constituted authorities, no virtue higher than(Pg 150) obedience. The order which he reverenced was an impossible one, and there was nothing left him but to die for it.

§ 7. Gustavus at Augsburg and Munich.

The conqueror pushed on. In Augsburg he found a city which had suffered much from the Commissions of Resumption which had, in the south, preceded the Edict of Restitution. The Lutheran clergy had been driven from their pulpits; the Lutheran councillors had been expelled from the town hall. In the midst of the jubilant throng Gustavus felt himself more strongly seated in the saddle. Hitherto he had asked the magistrates of the recovered cities to swear fidelity to him as long as the war lasted. At Augsburg he demanded the oath of obedience as from subjects to a sovereign. Gustavus was beginning to fancy that he could do without France.

Then came the turn of Bavaria. As Gustavus rode into Munich, Frederick, the exiled Elector Palatine, was by his side, triumphing over the flight of his old enemy. It was not the fault of Gustavus if Frederick was not again ruling at Heidelberg. Gustavus had offered him his ancestral territories on the condition that he would allow Swedish garrisons to occupy his fortresses during the war, and would give equal liberty to the Lutheran and the Calvinist forms of worship. Against this latter demand Frederick's narrow-hearted Calvinism steeled itself, and when, not many months later, he was carried off by a fever at Bacharach, he was still, through his own fault, a homeless wanderer on the face of the earth.

§ 8. Gustavus at Munich.

At Munich Gustavus demanded a high contribution. Discovering that Maximilian had buried a large number of guns in the arsenal, he had them dug up again by the Bavarian peasants, who were glad enough to earn the money with which the foreign(Pg 151) invader paid them for their labours. When this process was over—waking up the dead, he merrily called it—he prepared to leave the city with his booty. During his stay he had kept good discipline, and took especial care to prohibit any insult to the religion of the inhabitants. If, as may well have been the case, he was looking beyond the *Corpus Evangelicorum* to the Empire itself, if he thought it possible that the golden crown of Ferdinand might rest next upon a Lutheran head, he was resolved that religious liberty, not narrow orthodoxy, should be the corner-stone on which that Empire should be built.

§ 9. Strong position of Gustavus.

All Germany, except the hereditary dominions of the House of Austria, was at his feet. And he knew well that, as far as those dominions were concerned, there was no strength to resist him. Ferdinand had done enough to repress the manifestation of feeling, nothing to organize it. He would have been even more helpless to resist a serious attack than he had been in 1619, and this time Bavaria was as helpless as himself. Even John George, who had fled hastily from the field of Breitenfeld, marched through Bohemia without finding the slightest resistance. His army entered Prague amidst almost universal enthusiasm.

SECTION IV.—Wallenstein's Restoration to Command.

§ 1. Ferdinand looks about for help.

Unless Ferdinand could find help elsewhere than in his own subjects he was lost. Abroad he could look to Spain. But Spain could not do very much under the eyes of Richelieu. Some amount of money it could send, and some advice. But that was all.

1631
§ 2. The Spaniards recommend the recall of Wallenstein.

What that advice would be could hardly be doubted. The dismissal of Wallenstein had been a check for(Pg 152) Spain. He had been willing to join Spain in a war with France. The electors had prevailed against him with French support, and the treaty of Cherasco, by which the German troops had been withdrawn from fighting in support of the Spanish domination in Italy, had been the result. Even before the battle of Breitenfeld had been fought, the Spanish government had recommended the reinstatement of Wallenstein, and the Spaniards found a support in Eggenberg, Wallenstein's old protector at court.

§ 3. Wallenstein as the rival of Gustavus.

Soon after the battle of Breitenfeld, Wallenstein broke off his intercourse with Gustavus. By that time it was evident that in any alliance which Gustavus might make he meant to occupy the first place himself. Even if this had been otherwise, the moral character and the political instincts of the two men were too diverse to make co-operation possible between them. Gustavus was a king as well as a soldier, and he hoped to base his military power upon the political reconstruction of Protestant Germany, perhaps even of the whole Empire. Wallenstein owed everything to the sword, and he wished to bring all Germany under the empire of the sword.

§ 4. His plan of a reconciliation with John George.

The arrival of the Saxons in Bohemia inspired Wallenstein with the hope of a new combination, which would place the destinies of Germany in his hands. The reluctance with which John George had abandoned the Emperor was well known. If only Ferdinand, taught by experience, could be induced to sacrifice the Edict of Restitution, might not the Saxons be won over from their new allies? Wallenstein's former plans would be realized, and united Germany, nominally under Ferdinand,(Pg 153) in reality under his general, would rise to expel the foreigner and to bar the door against the Frenchman and the Swede.

§ 5. He is reinstated in the command.

In November, 1631, Wallenstein met his old lieutenant, Arnim, now the Saxon commander, to discuss the chances of the future. In December, just as Gustavus was approaching the Rhine, he received a visit from Eggenberg, at Znaim. Eggenberg had come expressly to persuade him to accept the command once more. Wallenstein gave his consent, on condition that the ecclesiastical lands should be left as they were before the Edict of Restitution. And besides this he was to wield an authority such as no general had ever claimed before. No army could be introduced into the Empire excepting under his command. To him alone was to belong the right of confiscation and of pardon. As Gustavus was proposing to deal with the ecclesiastical territories, so would Wallenstein deal with the princes who refused to renounce their alliance with the Swede. A new class of princes would arise, owing their existence to him alone. As for his own claims, if Mecklenburg could not be recovered, a princely territory was to be found for him elsewhere.

§ 6. Wallenstein's army.

After all it was not upon written documents that Wallenstein's power was founded. The army which he gathered round him was no Austrian army in any real sense of the word. It was the army of Wallenstein—of the Duke of Friedland, as the soldiers loved to call him, thinking perhaps that his duchy of Mecklenburg would prove but a transitory possession. Its first expenses were met with the help of Spanish subsidies. But after that it had to depend on itself. Nor was it more than an accident that it was levied and equipped in Bohemia. If Gustavus(Pg 154) had been at Vienna instead of at Munich, the thousands of stalwart men who trooped in at Wallenstein's bare word would have gathered to any place where he had set up his standards. Gustavus had to face the old evil of the war, which had grown worse and worse from the days of Mansfeld to those of Wallenstein, the evil of a military force existing by itself and for itself. From far distant shores men practised in arms came eagerly to the summons; from sunny Italy, from hardy Scotland, from every German land between the Baltic and the Alps. Protestant and Catholic were alike welcome there. The great German poet has breathed the spirit of this heterogeneous force into one of its officers, himself a wanderer from distant Ireland, ever prodigal of her blood in the quarrels of others. "This vast and mighty host," he says (Schiller, *The Piccolomini*, act i. sc. 2),

is all obedientTo Friedland's captains; and its brave commanders.Bred in one school, and nurtured with one milk,Are all excited by one heart and soul.They are strangers on the soil they tread.The service is their only house and home.No zeal inspires them for their country's cause,For thousands like myself, were born abroad;Nor care they for the Emperor, for one half,Deserting other service, fled to ours,Indifferent what their banner, whether 'twereThe Double Eagle, Lily, or the Lion;[(A)]Yet one sole man can rein this fiery host,By equal rule, by equal love and fear,Blending the many-nationed whole in one.
Was it, forsooth, the Emperor's majesty(Pg 155)That gave the army ready to his hand,And only sought a leader for it? No!The army then had no existence. He,Friedland, it was who called it into being,And gave it to his sovereign—but receivingNo army at his hand;—nor did the EmperorGive Wallenstein to us as General. No,It was from Wallenstein we first receivedThe Emperor as our master and our sovereign;And he, he only, binds us to our banner.

(A)That is to say, the standard of the Emperor, of France, or of Sweden.

1632
§ 7. He receives full powers.

Wallenstein at first accepted the command for three months only. In April it was permanently conferred on him. The Emperor was practically set aside in favour of a dictator.

§ 8. The Saxons driven out of Bohemia.

Wallenstein turned first upon the Saxons. In one hand he held the olive branch, in the other the sword. On May 21st his emissary was offering peace on the terms of the retractation of the Edict of Restitution. On the 22d Wallenstein himself fell upon the Saxon garrison of Prague, and forced it to surrender. It was a plain hint to John George to make his mind up quickly. Before long the Saxons had been driven out of the whole of Bohemia.

§ 9. But John George will not treat alone.

John George loved peace dearly, and he had joined Sweden sorely against his will. But he was a man of his word, and he had promised Gustavus not to come to terms with the enemy without his consent. He forwarded Wallenstein's propositions to Gustavus.

§ 10. Demands of Gustavus.

No man was so ready as Gustavus to change his plans in all matters of secondary importance, as circumstances might require. In the face of Wallenstein's armament and of the hesitations of the Saxon court, he at once aban(Pg 156)doned all thought of asking that the Rhine bishoprics should remain in his hands. He was ready to assent to the solution of religious questions which satisfied Wallenstein and John George. For himself, he expected the cession of at least part of Pomerania, in order to protect himself from a future naval attack proceeding from the Baltic ports. The Elector of Brandenburg had claims upon Pomerania; but he might be satisfied with some of the bishoprics which it had been agreed to leave in Protestant hands.

§ 11. Impossibility of reconciling Gustavus and Wallenstein.

Such terms would probably have met with opposition. But the real point of difference lay elsewhere. Wallenstein would have restored the old unity of the Empire, of which he hoped to be the inspiring genius. Gustavus pressed for the formation of a separate Protestant league, if not under his own guidance, at least in close alliance with Sweden. Wallenstein asked for confidence in himself and the Emperor. Gustavus had no confidence in either.

§ 12. Hesitation of John George.

John George wavered between the two. He, too, distrusted Wallenstein. But he did not see that he must either accept the Empire, or help on its dissolution, unless he wished to leave the future of Germany to chance. The imperial unity of Wallenstein was something. The *Corpus Evangelicorum* of Gustavus was something. The Protestant states, loosely combined, were doomed to defeat and ruin.

SECTION V.—The Struggle between Gustavus and Wallenstein.

§ 1. Gustavus proposes a league of cities.

Long before John George's answer could reach Gustavus the war had blazed out afresh. The Swedish king(Pg 157) did not yet know how little reliance he could place on the Elector for the realization of his grand plan, when Wallenstein broke up from Bohemia, and directed his whole force upon Nüremberg. Gustavus threw himself into the town to defend it. Here, too, his head was busy with the *Corpus Evangelicorum*. Whilst he was offering to Saxony to abandon the ecclesiastical territories, he proposed to the citizens of Nüremberg to lay the foundations of a league in which the citizens alone should ally themselves with him, leaving the princes to come in afterwards if they would, whilst the ecclesiastical territories should remain in his own hands. There is nothing really discrepant in the two schemes. The one was a plan to be adopted only on condition of a final and permanent peace. The other was a plan for use as a weapon of war. The noticeable thing is the persistent way in which Gustavus returned again and again to the idea of founding a political union as the basis of military strength.

§ 2. His proposal unacceptable.

He was no more successful with the citizens of Nüremberg than with the Elector of Saxony. They replied that a matter of such importance should be treated in common by all the cities and princes interested. "In that case," he replied, bitterly, "the Elector of Saxony will dispute for half a year in whose name the summons to the meeting ought to be issued. When the cities, too, send deputies, they usually separate as they meet, discovering that there is a defect in their instructions, and so refer everything home again for further consideration, without coming to any conclusion whatever." Can it be doubted that the political incompetence of the Germans, caused by their internal divisions and their long disuse of such(Pg 158) institutions as would have enabled them to act in common, was a thorn in the side of Gustavus, felt by him more deeply than the appearance in the field, however unexpected, of Wallenstein and his army?

§ 3. Gustavus and Wallenstein at Nüremberg.

That army, however, must be met. Wallenstein had 60,000 men with him; Gustavus but a third of the number. The war had blazed up along the Rhine from Alsace to Coblentz. Pappenheim was fighting there, and the Spaniards had sent troops of their own, and had summoned the Duke of Lorraine to their aid. By-and-by it was seen how rightly Gustavus had judged that France could not afford to quarrel with him. Though he had dashed aside Richelieu's favourite scheme of leaving the ecclesiastical territories untouched, and had refused to single out the House of Austria as the sole object of the war, Richelieu could not fail to support him against Spanish troops. In a few weeks the danger in his rear was at an end, and the scattered detachments of the Swedish army were hurrying to join their king at Nüremberg.

§ 4. Wallenstein entrenches himself.

Gustavus was now ready for a battle. But a battle he could not have. Wallenstein fell back upon his old tactics of refusing battle, except when he had a manifest superiority of numbers. He entrenched himself near Fürth, to the north of Nüremberg, on a commanding eminence overlooking the whole plain around. For twelve miles his works protected his newly-levied army. House, villages, advantages of the ground were everywhere utilized for defence.

§ 5. Wants of the Swedish army.

In the meanwhile, scarcity and pestilence were doing their terrible work at Nüremberg. The country people had flocked in for refuge, and the population was too great to be easily supplied with food. Even in the army(Pg 159) want began to be felt. And with want came the relaxation of that discipline upon which Gustavus prided himself. He had large numbers of German troops in his army now, and a long evil experience had taught Germans the habits of marauders.

§ 6. Gustavus remonstrates.

Gustavus was deeply irritated. Sending for the chief Germans in his service, he rated them soundly. "His Majesty," says one who described the scene, "was never before seen in such a rage."

§ 7. His speech to the officers.

"You princes, counts, lords, and noblemen," he said, "you are showing your disloyalty and wickedness on your own fatherland, which you are ruining. You colonels, and officers from the highest to the lowest, it is you who steal and rob every one, without making any exceptions. You plunder your own brothers in the faith. You make me disgusted with you; and God my Creator be my witness that my heart is filled with gall when I see any one of you behaving so villanously. For you cause men to say openly, 'The king, our friend, does us more harm than our enemies.' If you were real Christians you would consider what I am doing for you, how I am spending my life in your service. I have given up the treasures of my crown for your sake, and have not had from your German Empire enough to buy myself a bad suit of clothes with."

§ 8. Complains bitterly of them.

After this strain he went on: "Enter into your hearts," he said, "and think how sad you are making me, so that the tears stand in my eyes. You treat me ill with your evil discipline; I do not say with your evil fighting, for in that you have behaved like honourable gentlemen, and for that I am much obliged to you. I am so grieved for you that I am(Pg 160) vexed that I ever had anything to do with so stiff-necked a nation. Well, then, take my warning to heart; we will soon show our enemies that we are honest men and honourable gentlemen."

§ 9. Punishes plunderers.

One day the king caught a corporal stealing cows. "My son," he said, as he delivered him over to the provost marshal, "it is better that I should punish you, than that God should punish not only you, but me and all of us for your sake."

§ 10. Fails to storm Wallenstein's lines.

Such a state of things could not last long. On September 3 Gustavus led his army to the shores of Wallenstein's entrenchments; but though he made some impression, the lines were too skilfully drawn, and too well defended, to be broken through. On the other hand, Gustavus was not a Mansfeld, and Wallenstein did not venture, as at the Bridge of Dessau, to follow up his successful defence by an offensive movement.

§ 11. Is obliged to march away.

Want of supplies made it impossible for Gustavus to remain longer at Nüremberg. For the first time since he landed in Germany he had failed in securing a victory. With drums beating and banners flying, he marched away past Wallenstein's encampment; but the wary man was not to be enticed to a combat. As soon as he was gone, Wallenstein broke up his camp. But he knew too well where his opponent's weakness lay to go in pursuit of Gustavus. Throwing himself northwards, he established himself firmly in Saxony, plundering and burning on every side. If only he could work ruin enough, he might hope to detach the Elector from his alliance with the Swedes.

§ 12. Wallenstein and Gustavus in Saxony.

Gustavus could not choose but follow. Wallenstein had hoped to establish himself as firmly in Saxony as he had established(Pg 161) himself at Fürth. He would seize Torgau and Halle, to make himself master of the passages over the Elbe and Saale, whilst Erfurt and Naumburg would complete the strength of his position. Gustavus might dash his head against it as he pleased. Like Wellington at Torres Vedras, or Gustavus himself at Werben, he would meet the attack of the enemy by establishing himself in a carefully selected position of defence.

SECTION VI.—The Battle of Lützen.

§ 1. Gustavus in Saxony.

Wallenstein had succeeded at Nüremberg, but he was not to succeed in Saxony. Gustavus was upon him before he had gained the positions he needed. Erfurt was saved from the imperialists. Gustavus entered Naumburg to be adored as a saviour by men flying from Wallenstein's barbarities. As he passed through the streets the poor fugitives bent down to kiss the hem of his garments. He would have resisted them if he could. He feared lest God should punish him for receiving honour above that which befitted a mortal man.

§ 2. Wallenstein believes himself safe.

The Saxon army was at Torgau, and that important post was still guarded. Wallenstein lay at Lützen. Even there, shorn as he was of his expected strength, he threw up entrenchments, and believed himself safe from attack. It was now November, and he fancied that Gustavus, satisfied with his success, would go, after the fashion of the time, into winter quarters.

§ 3. Pappenheim leaves him.

In Wallenstein's army, Pappenheim's dashing bravery made him the idol of the soldiers, and gave him an almost independent position. He begged to be allowed to attempt a diversion on the Rhenish bishoprics. Wallenstein gave the re(Pg 162)quired permission, ordering him to seize Halle on the way.

§ 4. Attack of the Swedes. Gustavus before the battle.

It was a serious blunder to divide an army under the eyes of Gustavus. Early on the morning of November 16 the Swedish king was in front of Wallenstein's position at Lützen. He knew well that, if there was to be a battle at all, he must be the assailant. Wallenstein would not stir. Behind ditches and entrenchments, ready armed, his heavy squares lay immovably, waiting for the enemy, like the Russians at the Alma or the English at Waterloo. A fog lay thick upon the ground. The Swedish army gathered early to their morning prayer, summoned by the sounds of Luther's hymn tune, "God is a strong tower," floating on the heavy air from the brazen lips of a trumpet. The king himself joined in the morning hymn, "Fear not, little flock." Then, as if with forebodings of the coming slaughter, others sung of "Jesus the Saviour, who was the conqueror of death." Gustavus thrust aside the armour which was offered him. Since he had received a wound, not long before, he felt uncomfortable in it. Unprotected, he mounted on his horse, and rode about the ranks encouraging the men.

§ 5. Attack of the Swedes, and death of the king.

At eleven the mist cleared away, and the sun shone out. The king gave his last orders to his generals. Then, looking to heaven, "Now," he said, "in God's name, Jesus, give us to-day to fight for the honour of thy holy name." Then, waving his sword over his head, he cried out, "Forwards!" The whole line advanced, Gustavus riding at the head of the cavalry at the right. After a fierce struggle, the enemy's lines were broken through everywhere. But Wallenstein was not(Pg 163) yet mastered. Bringing up his reserves, he drove back the Swedish infantry in the centre. Gustavus, when he heard the news, flew to the rescue. In all other affairs of life he knew better than most men how to temper daring with discretion. In the battle-field he flung prudence to the winds. The horsemen, whom he had ordered to follow him, struggled in vain to keep up with the long strides of their master's horse. The fog came down thickly once more, and the king, left almost alone in the darkness, dashed unawares into a regiment of the enemy's cuirassiers. One shot passed through his horse's neck. A second shattered his left arm. Turning round to ask one of those who still followed him to help him out of the fight, a third shot struck him in the back, and he fell heavily to the ground. A youth of eighteen, who alone was left by his side, strove to lift him up and to bear him off. But the wounded man was too heavy for him. The cuirassiers rode up and asked who was there. "I was the King of Sweden," murmured the king, as the young man returned no answer, and the horseman shot him through the head, and put an end to his pain.

§ 6. Defeat of Wallenstein.

Bernard of Weimar took up the command. On the other side Pappenheim, having received orders to return, hurried back from Halle. But he brought only his cavalry with him. It would be many hours before his foot could retrace their weary steps. The Swedes, when they heard that their beloved king had fallen, burnt with ardour to revenge him. A terrible struggle ensued. Hour after hour the battle swayed backwards and forwards. In one of the Swedish regiments only one man out of six left the fight unhurt. Pappenheim, the dashing and the brave, whose word was ever for fight, the Blücher of the seventeenth cen(Pg 164)tury, was struck down. At the battle of the White Hill he had lain long upon the field senseless from his wounds, and had told those who were around him when he awakened that he had come back from Purgatory. This time there was no awakening for him. The infantry which in his lifetime he had commanded so gallantly, came up as the winter sun was setting. But they came too late to retrieve the fight. Wallenstein, defeated at last, gave orders for retreat.

§ 7. The loss of Gustavus irreparable.

The hand which alone could gather the results of victory was lying powerless. The work of destruction was practically complete. The Edict of Restitution was dead, and the Protestant administrators were again ruling in the northern bishoprics. The Empire was practically dead, and the princes and people of Germany, if they were looking for order at all, must seek it under other forms than those which had been imposed upon them in consequence of the victories of Tilly and Wallenstein. It is in vain to speculate whether Gustavus could have done anything towards the work of reconstruction. Like Cromwell, to whom, in many respects, he bore a close resemblance, he had begun to discover that it was harder to build than to destroy, and that it was easier to keep sheep than to govern men. Perhaps even to him the difficulties would have been insuperable. The centrifugal force was too strong amongst the German princes to make it easy to bind them together. He had experienced this in Saxony. He had experienced it at Nüremberg. To build up a *Corpus Evangelicorum* was like weaving ropes of sand.

§ 8. What were his purposes?

And Gustavus was not even more than half a German by birth; politically he was not a German at all. In his own mind he could not help thinking first of Sweden. In(Pg 165) the minds of others the suspicion that he was so thinking was certain to arise. He clung firmly to his demand for Pomerania as a bulwark for Sweden's interests in the Baltic. Next to that came the *Corpus Evangelicorum*, the league of German Protestant cities and princes to stand up against the renewal of the overpowering tyranny of the Emperor. If his scheme had been carried out Gustavus would have been a nobler Napoleon, with a confederation, not of the Rhine, but of the Baltic, around him. For, stranger as he was, he was bound by his religious sympathies to his Protestant brethren in Germany. The words which he spoke at Nüremberg to the princes, telling them how well off he might be at home, were conceived in the very spirit of the Homeric Achilles, when the hardness of the work he had undertaken and the ingratitude of men revealed itself to him. Like Achilles, he dearly loved war, with its excitement and danger, for its own sake. But he desired more than the glory of a conqueror. The establishment of Protestantism in Europe as a power safe from attack by reason of its own strength was the cause for which he found it worth while to live, and for which, besides and beyond the greatness of his own Swedish nation, he was ready to die. It may be that, after all, he was "happy in the opportunity of his death."

(Pg 166)

CHAPTER IX. THE DEATH OF WALLENSTEIN AND THE TREATY OF PRAGUE.

SECTION I.—French Influence in Germany.

1631
§ 1. Bernhard of Saxe Weimar.

In Germany, after the death of Gustavus at Lützen, it was as it was in Greece after the death of Epaminondas at Mantinea. "There was more disturbance and more dispute after the battle than before it." In Sweden, Christina, the infant daughter of Gustavus, succeeded peaceably to her father's throne, and authority was exercised without contradiction by the Chancellor Oxenstjerna. But, wise and prudent as Oxenstjerna was, it was not in the nature of things that he should be listened to as Gustavus had been listened to. The chiefs of the army, no longer held in by a soldier's hand, threatened to assume an almost independent position. Foremost of these was the young Bernhard of Weimar, demanding, like Wallenstein, a place among the princely houses of Germany. In his person he hoped the glories of the elder branch of the Saxon House would revive, and the disgrace inflicted upon it by Charles V. for its attachment to the Protestant cause would be repaired. He claimed the rewards of victory for those whose swords had gained it, and payment for the soldiers, who during the winter months following the victory at Lützen had received little or nothing. His own share was to be a new(Pg 167) duchy of Franconia, formed out of the united bishoprics of Würzburg and Bamberg. Oxenstjerna was compelled to admit his pretensions, and to confirm him in his duchy.

§ 2. The League of Heilbronn.

The step was thus taken which Gustavus had undoubtedly contemplated, but which he had prudently refrained from carrying into action. The seizure of ecclesiastical lands in which the population was Catholic was as great a barrier to peace on the one side as the seizure of the Protestant bishoprics in the north had been on the other. There was, therefore, all the more necessity to be ready for war. If a complete junction of all the Protestant forces was not to be had, something at least was attainable. On April 23, 1633, the League of Heilbronn was signed. The four circles of Swabia, Franconia, and the Upper and Lower Rhine formed a union with Sweden for mutual support.

§ 3. Defection of Saxony.

It is not difficult to explain the defection of the Elector of Saxony. The seizure of a territory by military violence had always been most obnoxious to him. He had resisted it openly in the case of Frederick in Bohemia. He had resisted it, as far as he dared, in the case of Wallenstein in Mecklenburg. He was not inclined to put up with it in the case of Bernhard in Franconia. Nor could he fail to see that with the prolongation of the war, the chances of French intervention were considerably increasing.

1631
§ 4. French politics.

In 1631 there had been a great effervescence of the French feudal aristocracy against the royal authority. But Richelieu stood firm. In March the king's brother, Gaston Duke of Orleans, fled from the country. In July his mother,(Pg 168) Mary of Medici, followed his example. But they had no intention of abandoning their position. From their exile in the Spanish Netherlands they formed a close alliance with Spain, and carried on a thousand intrigues with the nobility at home. The Cardinal smote right and left with a heavy hand. Amongst his enemies were the noblest names in France. The Duke of Guise shrank from the conflict and retired to Italy to die far from his native land. The keeper of the seals died in prison. His kinsman, a marshal of France, perished on the scaffold. In the summer of the year 1632, whilst Gustavus was conducting his last campaign, there was a great rising in the south of France. Gaston himself came to share in the glory or the disgrace of the rebellion. The Duke of Montmorenci was the real leader of the enterprise. He was a bold and vigorous commander, the Rupert of the French cavaliers. But his gay horsemen dashed in vain against the serried ranks of the royal infantry, and he expiated his fault upon the scaffold. Gaston, helpless and low-minded as he was, could live on, secure under an ignominious pardon.

§ 5. Richelieu did for France all that could be done.

It was not the highest form of political life which Richelieu was establishing. For the free expression of opinion, as a foundation of government, France, in that day, was not prepared. But within the limits of possibility, Richelieu's method of ruling was a magnificent spectacle. He struck down a hundred petty despotisms that he might exalt a single despotism in their place. And if the despotism of the Crown was subject to all the dangers and weaknesses by which sooner or later the strength of all despotisms is eaten away, Richelieu succeeded for the time in gaining the co-operation of those classes whose good will was worth conciliating. Under(Pg 169) him commerce and industry lifted up their heads, knowledge and literature smiled at last. Whilst Corneille was creating the French drama, Descartes was seizing the sceptre of the world of science. The first play of the former appeared on the stage in 1629. Year by year he rose in excellence, till in 1636 he produced the 'Cid;' and from that time one masterpiece followed another in rapid succession. Descartes published his first work in Holland in 1637, in which he laid down those principles of metaphysics which were to make his name famous in Europe.

§ 6. Richelieu and Germany.

All this, however welcome to France, boded no good to Germany. In the old struggles of the sixteenth century, Catholic and Protestant each believed himself to be doing the best, not merely for his own country, but for the world in general. Alva, with his countless executions in the Netherlands, honestly believed that the Netherlands as well as Spain would be the better for the rude surgery. The English volunteers, who charged home on a hundred battle-fields in Europe, believed that they were benefiting Europe, not England alone. It was time that all this should cease, and that the long religious strife should have its end. It was well that Richelieu should stand forth to teach the world that there were objects for a Catholic state to pursue better than slaughtering Protestants. But the world was a long way, in the seventeenth century, from the knowledge that the good of one nation is the good of all, and in putting off its religious partisanship France became terribly hard and selfish in its foreign policy. Gustavus had been half a German, and had sympathized deeply with Protestant Germany. Richelieu had no sympathy with Protestantism, no sympathy with German nationality. He doubtless had a(Pg 170) general belief that the predominance of the House of Austria was a common evil for all, but he cared chiefly to see Germany too weak to support Spain. He accepted the alliance of the League of Heilbronn, but he would have been equally ready to accept the alliance of the Elector of Bavaria if it would have served him as well in his purpose of dividing Germany.

§ 7. His policy French, not European.

The plan of Gustavus might seem unsatisfactory to a patriotic German, but it was undoubtedly conceived with the intention of benefiting Germany. Richelieu had no thought of constituting any new organization in Germany. He was already aiming at the left bank of the Rhine. The Elector of Treves, fearing Gustavus, and doubtful of the power of Spain to protect him, had called in the French, and had established them in his new fortress of Ehrenbreitstein, which looked down from its height upon the low-lying buildings of Coblentz, and guarded the junction of the Rhine and the Moselle. The Duke of Lorraine had joined Spain, and had intrigued with Gaston. In the summer of 1632 he had been compelled by a French army to make his submission. The next year he moved again, and the French again interfered, and wrested from him his capital of Nancy. Richelieu treated the old German frontier-land as having no rights against the King of France.

Section II.—Wallenstein's Attempt to dictate Peace.

§ 1. Saxon negotiations with Wallenstein.

Already, before the League of Heilbronn was signed, the Elector of Saxony was in negotiation with Wallenstein. In June peace was all but concluded between them. The Edict of Restitution was to be cancelled. A few places on the Baltic coast were to be ceded to Sweden,(Pg 171) and a portion at least of the Palatinate was to be restored to the son of the Elector Frederick, whose death in the preceding winter had removed one of the difficulties in the way of an agreement. The precise form in which the restitution should take place, however, still remained to be settled.

Such a peace would doubtless have been highly disagreeable to adventurers like Bernhard of Weimar, but it would have given the Protestants of Germany all that they could reasonably expect to gain, and would have given the House of Austria one last chance of taking up the championship of national interests against foreign aggression.

§ 2. Opposition to Wallenstein.

Such last chances, in real life, are seldom taken hold of for any useful purpose. If Ferdinand had had it in him to rise up in the position of a national ruler, he would have been in that position long before. His confessor, Father Lamormain, declared against the concessions which Wallenstein advised, and the word of Father Lamormain had always great weight with Ferdinand.

§ 3. General disapprobation of his proceedings.

Even if Wallenstein had been single-minded he would have had difficulty in meeting such opposition. But Wallenstein was not single-minded. He proposed to meet the difficulties which were made to the restitution of the Palatinate by giving the Palatinate, largely increased by neighbouring territories, to himself. He would thus have a fair recompense for the loss of Mecklenburg, which he could no longer hope to regain. He fancied that the solution would satisfy everybody. In fact, it displeased everybody. Even the Spaniards, who had been on his side in 1632 were alienated by it. They were especially jealous of the rise of any strong power near the line of march between Italy and the Spanish Netherlands.

(Pg 172)

§ 4. Wallenstein and the Swedes.

The greater the difficulties in Wallenstein's way the more determined he was to overcome them. Regarding himself, with some justification, as a power in Germany, he fancied himself able to act at the head of his army as if he were himself the ruler of an independent state. If the Emperor listened to Spain and his confessor in 1633 as he had listened to Maximilian and his confessor in 1630, Wallenstein might step forward and force upon him a wiser policy. Before the end of August he had opened a communication with Oxenstjerna, asking for his assistance in effecting a reasonable compromise, whether the Emperor liked it or not. But he had forgotten that such a proposal as this can only be accepted where there is confidence in him who makes it. In Wallenstein—the man of many schemes and many intrigues—no man had any confidence whatever. Oxenstjerna cautiously replied that if Wallenstein meant to join him against the Emperor he had better be the first to begin the attack.

§ 5. Was he in earnest?

Whether Wallenstein seriously meant at this time to move against the emperor it is impossible to say. He loved to enter upon plots in every direction without binding himself to any; but he was plainly in a dangerous position. How could he impose peace upon all parties when no single party trusted him?

§ 6. He attacks the Saxons.

If he was not trusted, however, he might still make himself feared. Throwing himself vigorously upon Silesia, he forced the Swedish garrisons to surrender, and, presenting himself upon the frontiers of Saxony, again offered peace to the two northern electors.

§ 7. Bernhard at Ratisbon.

But Wallenstein could not be everywhere. Whilst the electors were still hesitating, Bernhard made a dash(Pg 173) at Ratisbon, and firmly established himself in the city, within a little distance of the Austrian frontier. Wallenstein, turning sharply southward, stood in the way of his further advance, but he did nothing to recover the ground which had been lost. He was himself weary of the war. In his first command he had aimed at crushing out all opposition in the name of the imperial authority. His judgment was too clear to allow him to run the old course. He saw plainly that strength was now to be gained only by allowing each of the opposing forces their full weight. 'If the Emperor,' he said, 'were to gain ten victories it would do him no good. A single defeat would ruin him.' In December he was back again in Bohemia.

§ 8. Wallenstein's difficulties.

It was a strange, Cassandra-like position, to be wiser than all the world, and to be listened to by no one; to suffer the fate of supreme intelligence which touches no moral chord and awakens no human sympathy. For many months the hostile influences had been gaining strength at Vienna. There were War-Office officials whose wishes Wallenstein systematically disregarded; Jesuits who objected to peace with heretics at all; friends of the Bavarian Maximilian who thought that the country round Ratisbon should have been better defended against the enemy; and Spaniards who were tired of hearing that all matters of importance were to be settled by Wallenstein alone.

§ 9. Opposition of Spain.

The Spanish opposition was growing daily. Spain now looked to the German branch of the House of Austria to make a fitting return for the aid which she had rendered in 1620. Richelieu, having mastered Lorraine, was pushing on towards Alsace, and if Spain had good reasons for objecting to see Wallenstein established in the(Pg 174) Palatinate, she had far better reasons for objecting to see France established in Alsace. Yet for all these special Spanish interests Wallenstein cared nothing. His aim was to place himself at the head of a German national force, and to regard all questions simply from his own point of view. If he wished to see the French out of Alsace and Lorraine, he wished to see the Spaniards out of Alsace and Lorraine as well.

§ 10. The Cardinal Infant.

And, as was often the case with Wallenstein, a personal difference arose by the side of the political difference. The Emperor's eldest son, Ferdinand, the King of Hungary, was married to a Spanish Infanta, the sister of Philip IV., who had once been the promised bride of Charles I. of England. Her brother, another Ferdinand, usually known from his rank in Church and State as the Cardinal-Infant, had recently been appointed Governor of the Spanish Netherlands, and was waiting in Italy for assistance to enable him to conduct an army through Germany to Brussels.

That assistance Wallenstein refused to give. The military reasons which he alleged for his refusal may have been good enough, but they had a dubious sound in Spanish ears. It looked as if he was simply jealous of Spanish influence in Western Germany.

§ 11. The Emperor's hesitation.

Such were the influences which were brought to bear upon the Emperor after Wallenstein's return from Ratisbon in December. Ferdinand, as usual, was distracted between the two courses proposed. Was he to make the enormous concessions to the Protestants involved in the plan of Wallenstein; or was he to fight it out with France and the Protestants together according to the plan of Spain? To Wallenstein by this time the Emperor's resolutions(Pg 175) had become almost a matter of indifference. He had resolved to force a reasonable peace upon Germany, with the Emperor, if it might be so; without him, if he refused his support.

1634
§ 12. Wallenstein and the army.

Wallenstein was well aware that his whole plan depended on his hold over the army. In January he received assurances from three of his principal generals, Piccolomini, Gallas, and Aldringer, that they were ready to follow him wheresoever he might lead them, and he was sanguine enough to take these assurances for far more than they were worth. Neither they nor he himself were aware to what lengths he would go in the end. For the present it was a mere question of putting pressure upon the Emperor to induce him to accept a wise and beneficent peace.

SECTION III.—Resistance to Wallenstein's Plans.

§ 1. Oñate's movements.

The Spanish ambassador, Oñate, was ill at ease. Wallenstein, he was convinced, was planning something desperate. What it was he could hardly guess; but he was sure that it was something most prejudicial to the Catholic religion and the united House of Austria. The worst was that Ferdinand could not be persuaded that there was cause for suspicion. "The sick man," said Oñate, speaking of the Emperor, "will die in my arms without my being able to help him."

§ 2. Belief at Vienna that Wallenstein was a traitor.

Such was Oñate's feelings toward the end of January. Then came information that the case was worse than even he had deemed possible. Wallenstein, he learned, had been intriguing with the Bohemian exiles, who had offered, with Richelieu's consent, to place upon his head(Pg 176) the crown of Bohemia, which had fourteen years before been snatched from the unhappy Frederick. In all this there was much exaggeration. Though Wallenstein had listened to these overtures, it is almost certain that he had not accepted them. But neither had he revealed them to the government. It was his way to keep in his hands the threads of many intrigues to be used or not to be used as occasion might serve.

§ 3. Oñate informs Ferdinand.

Oñate, naturally enough, believed the worst. And for him the worst was the best. He went triumphantly to Eggenberg with his news, and then to Ferdinand. Coming alone, this statement might perhaps have been received with suspicion. Coming, as it did, after so many evidences that the general had been acting in complete independence of the government, it carried conviction with it.

§ 4. Decision of the Emperor against Wallenstein.

Ferdinand had long been tossed backwards and forwards by opposing influences. He had given no answer to Wallenstein's communication of the terms of peace arranged with Saxony. The necessity of deciding, he said, would not allow him to sleep. It was in his thoughts when he lay down and when he arose. Prayers to God to enlighten the mind of the Emperor had been offered in the churches of Vienna.

§ 5. Determination to displace Wallenstein.

All this hesitation was now at an end. Ferdinand resolved to continue the war in alliance with Spain, and, as a necessary preliminary, to remove Wallenstein from his generalship. But it was more easily said than done. A declaration was drawn up releasing the army from its obedience to Wallenstein, and provisionally appointing Gallas, who had by this time given assurances of loyalty, to the chief command. It was intended, if circumstances proved(Pg 177) favourable, to intrust the command ultimately to the young King of Hungary.

§ 6. The Generals gained over.

The declaration was kept secret for many days. To publish it would only be to provoke the rebellion which was feared. The first thing to be done was to gain over the principal generals. In the beginning of February Piccolomini and Aldringer expressed their readiness to obey the Emperor rather than Wallenstein. Commanders of a secondary rank would doubtless find their position more independent under an inexperienced young man like the King of Hungary than under the first living strategist. These two generals agreed to make themselves masters of Wallenstein's person and to bring him to Vienna to answer the accusations of treason against him.

§ 7. Attempt to seize Wallenstein.

For Oñate this was not enough. It would be easier, he said, to kill the general than to carry him off. The event proved that he was right. On February 7, Aldringer and Piccolomini set off for Pilsen with the intention of capturing Wallenstein. But they found the garrison faithful to its general, and they did not even venture to make the attempt.

§ 8. Wallenstein at Pilsen.

Wallenstein's success depended on his chance of carrying with him the lower ranks of the army. On the 19th he summoned the colonels round him and assured them that he would stand security for money which they had advanced in raising their regiments, the repayment of which had been called in question. Having thus won them to a favourable mood, he told them that it had been falsely stated that he wished to change his religion and attack the Emperor. On the contrary, he was anxious to conclude a peace which would benefit the Emperor and all(Pg 178) who were concerned. As, however, certain persons at Court had objected to it, he wished to ask the opinion of the army on its terms. But he must first of all know whether they were ready to support him, as he knew that there was an intention to put a disgrace upon him.

§ 9. The colonels engage to support him.

It was not the first time that Wallenstein had appealed to the colonels. A month before, when the news had come of the alienation of the Court, he had induced them to sign an acknowledgment that they would stand by him, from which all reference to the possibility of his dismissal was expressly excluded. They now, on February 20, signed a fresh agreement, in which they engaged to defend him against the machinations of his enemies, upon his promising to undertake nothing against the Emperor or the Catholic religion.

SECTION IV.—Assassination of Wallenstein.

§ 1. The garrison of Prague abandons him.

Wallenstein thus hoped, with the help of the army, to force the Emperor's hand, and to obtain his signature to the peace. Of the co-operation of the Elector of Saxony he was already secure; and since the beginning of February he had been pressing Oxenstjerna and Bernhard to come to his aid. If all the armies in the field declared for peace, Ferdinand would be compelled to abandon the Spaniards and to accept the offered terms. Without some such hazardous venture, Wallenstein would be checkmated by Oñate. The Spaniard had been unceasingly busy during these weeks of intrigue. Spanish gold was provided to content the colonels for their advances, and hopes of promotion were scattered broadcast amongst them. Two other of the principal generals had gone over to the Court, and on February 18, the day before the meeting(Pg 179) at Pilsen, a second declaration had been issued accusing Wallenstein of treason, and formally depriving him of the command. Wallenstein, before this declaration reached him, had already appointed a meeting of large masses of troops to take place on the White Hill before Prague on the 21st, where he hoped to make his intentions more generally known. But he had miscalculated the devotion of the army to his person. The garrison of Prague refused to obey his orders. Soldiers and citizens alike declared for the Emperor. He was obliged to retrace his steps. "I had peace in my hands," he said. Then he added, "God is righteous," as if still counting on the aid of Heaven in so good a work.

§ 2. Understanding with the Swedes.

He did not yet despair. He ordered the colonels to meet him at Eger, assuring them that all that he was doing was for the Emperor's good. He had now at last hopes of other assistance. Oxenstjerna, indeed, ever cautious, still refused to do anything for him till he had positively declared against the Emperor. Bernhard, equally prudent for some time, had been carried away by the news, which reached him on the 21st, of the meeting at Pilsen, and the Emperor's denouncement of the general. Though he was still suspicious, he moved in the direction of Eger.

§ 3. His arrival at Eger.

On the 24th Wallenstein entered Eger. In what precise way he meant to escape from the labyrinth in which he was, or whether he had still any clear conception of the course before him, it is impossible to say. But Arnim was expected at Eger, as well as Bernhard, and it may be that Wallenstein fancied still that he could gather all the armies of Germany into his hands, to defend the peace which he was ready to make. The great scheme, how(Pg 180)ever, whatever it was, was doomed to failure. Amongst the officers who accompanied him was a Colonel Butler, an Irish Catholic, who had no fancy for such dealings with Swedish and Saxon heretics. Already he had received orders from Piccolomini to bring in Wallenstein dead or alive. No official instructions had been given to Piccolomini. But the thought was certain to arise in the minds of all who retained their loyalty to the Emperor. A general who attempts to force his sovereign to a certain political course with the help of the enemy is placed, by that very fact, beyond the pale of law.

§ 4. Wallenstein's assassination.

The actual decision did not lie with Butler. The fortress was in the hands of two Scotch officers, Leslie and Gordon. As Protestants, they might have been expected to feel some sympathy with Wallenstein. But the sentiment of military honour prevailed. On the morning of the 25th they were called upon by one of the general's confederates to take orders from Wallenstein alone. "I have sworn to obey the Emperor," answered Gordon, at last, "and who shall release me from my oath?" "You, gentlemen," was the reply, "are strangers in the Empire. What have you to do with the Empire?" Such arguments were addressed to deaf ears. That afternoon Butler, Leslie, and Gordon consulted together. Leslie, usually a silent, reserved man, was the first to speak. "Let us kill the traitors," he said. That evening Wallenstein's chief supporters were butchered at a banquet. Then there was a short and sharp discussion whether Wallenstein's life should be spared. Bernhard's troops were known to be approaching, and the conspirators dared not leave a chance of escape open. An Irish captain, Devereux by name, was selected to do the deed. Followed by a few soldiers, he burst into the room where(Pg 181) Wallenstein was preparing for rest. "Scoundrel and traitor," were the words which he flung at Devereux as he entered. Then, stretching out his arms, he received the fatal blow in his breast. The busy brain of the great calculator was still forever.

§ 5. Reason of his failure.

The attempt to snatch at a wise and beneficent peace by mingled force and intrigue had failed. Other generals—Cæsar, Cromwell, Napoleon—have succeeded to supreme power with the support of an armed force. But they did so by placing themselves at the head of the civil institutions of their respective countries, and by making themselves the organs of a strong national policy. Wallenstein stood alone in attempting to guide the political destinies of a people, while remaining a soldier and nothing more. The plan was doomed to failure, and is only excusable on the ground that there were no national institutions at the head of which Wallenstein could place himself; not even a chance of creating such institutions afresh.

§ 6. Comparison between Gustavus and Wallenstein.

In spite of all his faults, Germany turns ever to Wallenstein as she turns to no other amongst the leaders of the Thirty Years' War. From amidst the divisions and weaknesses of his native country, a great poet enshrined his memory in a succession of noble dramas. Such faithfulness is not without a reason. Gustavus's was a higher nature than Wallenstein's. Some of his work, at least the rescue of German Protestantism from oppression, remained imperishable, whilst Wallenstein's military and political success vanished into nothingness. But Gustavus was a hero not of Germany as a nation, but of European Protestantism. His *Corpus Evangelicorum* was at the best a choice of evils to a(Pg 182) German. Wallenstein's wildest schemes, impossible of execution as they were by military violence, were always built upon the foundation of German unity. In the way in which he walked that unity was doubtless unattainable. To combine devotion to Ferdinand with religious liberty was as hopeless a conception as it was to burst all bonds of political authority on the chance that a new and better world would spring into being out of the discipline of the camp. But during the long dreary years of confusion which were to follow, it was something to think of the last supremely able man whose life had been spent in battling against the great evils of the land, against the spirit of religious intolerance, and the spirit of division.

SECTION V.—Imperialist Victories and the Treaty of Prague.

§ 1. Campaign of 1634.

For the moment, the House of Austria seemed to have gained everything by the execution or the murder of Wallenstein, whichever we may choose to call it. The army was reorganized and placed under the command of the Emperor's son, the King of Hungary. The Cardinal-Infant, now eagerly welcomed, was preparing to join him through Tyrol. And while on the one side there was union and resolution, there was division and hesitation on the other. The Elector of Saxony stood aloof from the League of Heilbronn, weakly hoping that the terms of peace which had been offered him by Wallenstein would be confirmed by the Emperor now that Wallenstein was gone. Even amongst those who remained under arms there was no unity of purpose. Bernhard, the daring and impetuous, was not of one mind with the cautious Horn, who commanded the Swedish forces, and both(Pg 183) agreed in thinking Oxenstjerna remiss because he did not supply them with more money than he was able to provide.

§ 2. The Battle of Nördlingen.

As might have been expected under these circumstances, the imperials made rapid progress. Ratisbon, the prize of Bernhard the year before, surrendered to the king of Hungary in July. Then Donauwörth was stormed, and siege was laid to Nördlingen. On September 2 the Cardinal-Infant came up with 15,000 men. The enemy watched the siege with a force far inferior in numbers. Bernhard was eager to put all to the test of battle. Horn recommended caution in vain. Against his better judgment he consented to fight. On September 6 the attack was made. By the end of the day Horn was a prisoner, and Bernhard was in full retreat, leaving 10,000 of his men dead upon the field, and 6,000 prisoners in the hands of the enemy, whilst the imperialists lost only 1,200 men.

§ 3. Important results from it.

Since the day of Breitenfeld, three years before, there had been no such battle fought as this of Nördlingen. As Breitenfeld had recovered the Protestant bishoprics of the north, Nördlingen recovered the Catholic bishoprics of the south. Bernhard's Duchy of Franconia disappeared in a moment under the blow. Before the spring of 1635 came, the whole of South Germany, with the exception of one or two fortified posts, was in the hands of the imperial commanders. The Cardinal-Infant was able to pursue his way to Brussels, with the assurance that he had done a good stroke of work on the way.

§ 4. French intervention.

The victories of mere force are never fruitful of good. As it had been after the successes of Tilly in 1622, and the successes of Wallenstein in 1626 and 1627, so it(Pg 184) was now with the successes of the King of Hungary in 1634 and 1635. The imperialist armies had gained victories, and had taken cities. But the Emperor was none the nearer to the confidence of Germans. An alienated people, crushed by military force, served merely as a bait to tempt foreign aggression, and to make the way easy before it. After 1622, the King of Denmark had been called in. After 1627, an appeal was made to the King of Sweden. After 1634, Richelieu found his opportunity. The bonds between France and the mutilated League of Heilbronn were drawn more closely. German troops were to be taken into French pay, and the empty coffers of the League were filled with French livres. He who holds the purse holds the sceptre, and the princes of Southern and Western Germany, whether they wished it or not, were reduced to the position of satellites revolving round the central orb at Paris.

§ 5. The Peace of Prague.

Nowhere was the disgrace of submitting to French intervention felt so deeply as at Dresden. The battle of Nördlingen had cut short any hopes which John George might have entertained of obtaining that which Wallenstein would willingly have granted him. But, on the other hand, Ferdinand had learned something from experience. He would allow the Edict of Restitution to fall, though he was resolved not to make the sacrifice in so many words. But he refused to replace the Empire in the condition in which it had been before the war. The year 1627 was to be chosen as the starting point for the new arrangement. The greater part of the northern bishoprics would thus be saved to Protestantism. But Halberstadt would remain in the hands of a Catholic bishop, and the Palatinate would be lost to Protestantism for ever. Lusatia,(Pg 185) which had been held in the hands of the Elector of Saxony for his expenses in the war of 1620, was to be ceded to him permanently, and Protestantism in Silesia was to be placed under the guarantee of the Emperor. Finally, Lutheranism alone was still reckoned as the privileged religion, so that Hesse Cassel and the other Calvinist states gained no security at all. On May 30, 1635, a treaty embodying these arrangements was signed at Prague by the representatives of the Emperor and the Elector of Saxony. It was intended not to be a separate treaty, but to be the starting point of a general pacification. Most of the princes and towns so accepted it, after more or less delay, and acknowledged the supremacy of the Emperor on its conditions. Yet it was not in the nature of things that it should put an end to the war. It was not an agreement which any one was likely to be enthusiastic about. The ties which bound Ferdinand to his Protestant subjects had been rudely broken, and the solemn promise to forget and forgive could not weld the nation into that unity of heart and spirit which was needed to resist the foreigner. A Protestant of the north might reasonably come to the conclusion that the price to be paid to the Swede and the Frenchman for the vindication of the rights of the southern Protestants was too high to make it prudent for him to continue the struggle against the Emperor. But it was hardly likely that he would be inclined to fight very vigorously for the Emperor on such terms.

§ 6. It fails in securing general acceptance.

If the treaty gave no great encouragement to anyone who was comprehended by it, it threw still further into the arms of the enemy those who were excepted from its benefits. The leading members of the League of Heilbronn were excepted from the general amnesty, though hopes of better(Pg 186) treatment were held out to them if they made their submission. The Landgrave of Hesse Cassel was shut out as a Calvinist. Besides such as nourished legitimate grievances, there were others who, like Bernhard, were bent upon carving out a fortune for themselves, or who had so blended in their own minds consideration for the public good as to lose all sense of any distinction between the two.

§ 7. Degeneration of the war.

There was no lack here of materials for a long and terrible struggle. But there was no longer any noble aim in view on either side. The ideal of Ferdinand and Maximilian was gone. The Church was not to recover its lost property. The Empire was not to recover its lost dignity. The ideal of Gustavus of a Protestant political body was equally gone. Even the ideal of Wallenstein, that unity might be founded on an army, had vanished. From henceforth French and Swedes on the one side, Austrians and Spaniards on the other, were busily engaged in riving at the corpse of the dead Empire. The great quarrel of principle had merged into a mere quarrel between the Houses of Austria and Bourbon, in which the shred of principle which still remained in the question of the rights of the southern Protestants was almost entirely disregarded.

§ 8. Condition of Germany.

Horrible as the war had been from its commencement, it was every day assuming a more horrible character. On both sides all traces of discipline had vanished in the dealings of the armies with the inhabitants of the countries in which they were quartered. Soldiers treated men and women as none but the vilest of mankind would now treat brute beasts. 'He who had money,' says a contemporary, 'was their enemy. He who had none was tortured because he had it not.' Outrages of unspeaka(Pg 187)ble atrocity were committed everywhere. Human beings were driven naked into the streets, their flesh pierced with needles, or cut to the bone with saws. Others were scalded with boiling water, or hunted with fierce dogs. The horrors of a town taken by storm were repeated every day in the open country. Even apart from its excesses, the war itself was terrible enough. When Augsburg was besieged by the imperialists, after their victory at Nördlingen, it contained an industrious population of 70,000 souls. After a siege of seven months, 10,000 living beings, wan and haggard with famine, remained to open the gates to the conquerors, and the great commercial city of the Fuggers dwindled down into a country town.

1636
§ 9. Notes of an English traveller.

How is it possible to bring such scenes before our eyes in their ghastly reality? Let us turn for the moment to some notes taken by the companion of an English ambassador who passed through the country in 1636. As the party were towed up the Rhine from Cologne, on the track so well known to the modern tourist, they passed "by many villages pillaged and shot down." Further on, a French garrison was in Ehrenbreitstein, firing down upon Coblentz, which had just been taken by the imperialists. "They in the town, if they do but look out of their windows, have a bullet presently presented at their head." More to the south, things grew worse. At Bacharach, "the poor people are found dead with grass in their mouths." At Rüdesheim, many persons were "praying where dead bones were in a little old house; and here his Excellency gave some relief to the poor, which were almost starved, as it appeared by the violence they used to get it from one another." At Mentz, the ambassador was obliged to remain "on shipboard,(Pg 188) for there was nothing to relieve us, since it was taken by the King of Sweden, and miserably battered.... Here, likewise, the poor people were almost starved, and those that could relieve others before now humbly begged to be relieved; and after supper all had relief sent from the ship ashore, at the sight of which they strove so violently that some of them fell into the Rhine, and were like to have been drowned." Up the Main, again, "all the towns, villages, and castles be battered, pillaged, or burnt." After leaving Würzburg, the ambassador's train came to plundered villages, and then to Neustadt, "which hath been a fair city, though now pillaged and burnt miserably." Poor children were "sitting at their doors almost starved to death," his Excellency giving them food and leaving money with their parents to help them, if but for a time. In the Upper Palatinate, they passed "by churches demolished to the ground, and through woods in danger, understanding that Croats were lying hereabout." Further on they stayed for dinner at a poor little village "which hath been pillaged eight-and-twenty times in two years, and twice in one day." And so on, and so on. The corner of the veil is lifted up in the pages of the old book, and the rest is left to the imagination to picture forth, as best it may, the misery behind. After reading the sober narrative, we shall perhaps not be inclined to be so very hard upon the Elector of Saxony for making peace at Prague.

CHAPTER X. THE PREPONDERANCE OF FRANCE.

SECTION I.—Open Intervention of France.

§ 1. Protestantism not yet out of danger.

The peacemakers of Prague hoped to restore the Empire to its old form. But this could not be. Things done cannot pass away as though they had never been. Ferdinand's attempt to gain a partizan's advantage for his religion by availing himself of legal forms had given rise to a general distrust. Nations and governments, like individual men, are "tied and bound by the chain of their sins," from which they can be freed only when a new spirit is breathed into them. Unsatisfactory as the territorial arrangements of the peace were, the entire absence of any constitutional reform in connexion with the peace was more unsatisfactory still. The majority in the two Upper Houses of the Diet was still Catholic; the Imperial Council was still altogether Catholic. It was possible that the Diet and Council, under the teaching of experience, might refrain from pushing their pretensions as far as they had pushed them before; but a government which refrains from carrying out its principles from motives of prudence cannot inspire confidence. A strong central power would never arise in such a way, and a strong central power to defend Germany against foreign invasion was the especial need of the hour.

§ 2. The allies of France.

In the failure of the Elector of Saxony to obtain some of the most reasonable of the Protestant demands lay the best excuse of men like Bernhard of Saxe-Weimar and William of Hesse Cassel for refusing the terms of accommodation offered. Largely as personal ambition and greed of territory found a place in the motives of these men, it is not absolutely necessary to assert that their religious enthusiasm was nothing more than mere hypocrisy. They raised the war-cry of "God with us" before rushing to the storm of a city doomed to massacre and pillage; they set apart days for prayer and devotion when battle was at hand—veiling, perhaps, from their own eyes the hideous misery which they were spreading around, in contemplation of the loftiness of their aim: for, in all but the most vile, there is a natural tendency to shrink from contemplating the lower motives of action, and to fix the eyes solely on the higher. But the ardour inspired by a military career, and the mere love of fighting for its own sake, must have counted for much; and the refusal to submit to a domination which had been so harshly used soon grew into a restless disdain of all authority whatever. The nobler motives which had imparted a glow to the work of Tilly and Gustavus, and which even lit up the profound selfishness of Wallenstein, flickered and died away, till the fatal disruption of the Empire was accomplished amidst the strivings and passions of heartless and unprincipled men.

§ 3. Foreign intervention.

The work of riving Germany in pieces was not accomplished by Germans alone. As in nature a living organism which has become unhealthy and corrupt is seized upon by the lower forms of animal life, a nation divided amongst itself, and devoid of a sense of life within it higher than the aims of parties and individuals, becomes the prey of(Pg 191)neighbouring nations, which would not have ventured to meddle with it in the days of its strength. The carcase was there, and the eagles were gathered together. The gathering of Wallenstein's army in 1632, the overthrow of Wallenstein in 1634, had alike been made possible by the free use of Spanish gold. The victory of Nördlingen had been owing to the aid of Spanish troops; and the aim of Spain was not the greatness or peace of Germany, but at the best the greatness of the House of Austria in Germany; at the worst, the maintenance of the old system of intolerance and unthinking obedience, which had been the ruin of Germany. With Spain for an ally, France was a necessary enemy. The strife for supreme power between the two representative states of the old system and the new could not long be delayed, and the German parties would be dragged, consciously or unconsciously, in their wake. If Bernhard became a tool of Richelieu, Ferdinand became a tool of Spain.

§ 4. Alsace and Lorraine.

In this phase of the war Protestantism and Catholicism, tolerance and intolerance, ceased to be the immediate objects of the strife. The possession of Alsace and Lorraine rose into primary importance, not because, as in our own days, Germany needed a bulwark against France, or France needed a bulwark against Germany, but because Germany was not strong enough to prevent these territories from becoming the highway of intercourse between Spain and the Spanish Netherlands. The command of the sea was in the hands of the Dutch, and the valley of the Upper Rhine was the artery through which the life blood of the Spanish monarchy flowed. If Spain or the Emperor, the friend of Spain, could hold that valley, men and munitions of warfare would flow freely to the Netherlands to support the Cardinal-Infant in his(Pg 192) struggle with the Dutch. If Richelieu could lay his hand heavily upon it, he had seized his enemy by the throat, and could choke him as he lay.

§ 5. Richelieu asks for fortresses in Alsace.

After the battle of Nördlingen, Richelieu's first demand from Oxenstjerna as the price of his assistance had been the strong places held by Swedish garrisons in Alsace. As soon as he had them safely under his control, he felt himself strong enough to declare war openly against Spain.

§ 6. War between France and Spain.

On May 19, eleven days before peace was agreed upon at Prague, the declaration of war was delivered at Brussels by a French herald. To the astonishment of all, France was able to place in the field what was then considered the enormous number of 132,000 men. One army was to drive the Spaniards out of the Milanese, and to set free the Italian princes. Another was to defend Lorraine whilst Bernhard crossed the Rhine and carried on war in Germany. The main force was to be thrown upon the Spanish Netherlands, and, after effecting a junction with the Prince of Orange, was to strike directly at Brussels.

SECTION II.—Spanish Successes.

§ 1. Failure of the French attack on the Netherlands.

Precisely in the most ambitious part of his programme Richelieu failed most signally. The junction with the Dutch was effected without difficulty; but the hoped-for instrument of success proved the parent of disaster. Whatever Flemings and Brabanters might think of Spain, they soon made it plain that they would have nothing to do with the Dutch. A national enthusiasm against Protestant aggression from the north made defence easy, and the French army had to return completely unsuc(Pg 193)cessful. Failure, too, was reported from other quarters. The French armies had no experience of war on a large scale, and no military leader of eminent ability had yet appeared to command them. The Italian campaign came to nothing, and it was only by a supreme effort of military skill that Bernhard, driven to retreat, preserved his army from complete destruction.

§ 2. Spanish invasion of France.

In 1636 France was invaded. The Cardinal-Infant crossed the Somme, took Corbie, and advanced to the banks of the Oise. All Paris was in commotion. An immediate siege was expected, and inquiry was anxiously made into the state of the defences. Then Richelieu, coming out of his seclusion, threw himself upon the nation. He appealed to the great legal, ecclesiastical, and commercial corporations of Paris, and he did not appeal in vain. Money, voluntarily offered, came pouring into the treasury for the payment of the troops. Those who had no money gave themselves eagerly for military service. It was remarked that Paris, so fanatically Catholic in the days of St. Bartholomew and the League, entrusted its defence to the Protestant marshal La Force, whose reputation for integrity inspired universal confidence.

§ 3. The invaders driven back.

The resistance undertaken in such a spirit in Paris was imitated by the other towns of the kingdom. Even the nobility, jealous as they were of the Cardinal, forgot their grievances as an aristocracy in their duties as Frenchmen. Their devotion was not put to the test of action. The invaders, frightened at the unanimity opposed to them, hesitated and turned back. In September, Lewis took the field in person. In November he appeared before Corbie; and the last days of the year saw the fortress again in the keeping of a French garrison. The war,(Pg 194) which was devastating Germany, was averted from France by the union produced by the mild tolerance of Richelieu.

§ 4. Battle of Wittstock.

In Germany, too, affairs had taken a turn. The Elector of Saxony had hoped to drive the Swedes across the sea; but a victory gained on October 4, at Wittstock, by the Swedish general, Baner, the ablest of the successors of Gustavus, frustrated his intentions. Henceforward North Germany was delivered over to a desolation with which even the misery inflicted by Wallenstein affords no parallel.

§ 5. Death of Ferdinand II.

Amidst these scenes of failure and misfortune the man whose policy had been mainly responsible for the miseries of his country closed his eyes for ever. On February 15, 1637, Ferdinand II. died at Vienna. Shortly before his death the King of Hungary had been elected King of the Romans, and he now, by his father's death, became the Emperor Ferdinand III.

§ 6. Ferdinand III.

The new Emperor had no vices. He did not even care, as his father did, for hunting and music. When the battle of Nördlingen was won under his command he was praying in his tent whilst his soldiers were fighting. He sometimes took upon himself to give military orders, but the handwriting in which they were conveyed was such an abominable scrawl that they only served to enable his generals to excuse their defeats by the impossibility of reading their instructions. His great passion was for keeping strict accounts. Even the Jesuits, it is said, found out that, devoted as he was to his religion, he had a sharp eye for his expenditure. One day they complained that some tolls bequeathed to them by his father had not been made over to them, and represented the value of the legacy as(Pg 195) a mere trifle of 500 florins a year. The Emperor at once gave them an order upon the treasury for the yearly payment of the sum named, and took possession of the tolls for the maintenance of the fortifications of Vienna. The income thus obtained is said to have been no less than 12,000 florins a year.

§ 7. Campaign of 1637.

Such a man was not likely to rescue the Empire from its miseries. The first year of his reign, however, was marked by a gleam of good fortune. Baner lost all that he had gained at Wittstock, and was driven back to the shores of the Baltic. On the western frontier the imperialists were equally successful. Würtemberg accepted the Peace of Prague, and submitted to the Emperor. A more general peace was talked of. But till Alsace was secured to one side or the other no peace was possible.

SECTION III.—The Struggle for Alsace.

§ 1. The capture of Breisach.

The year 1638 was to decide the question. Bernhard was looking to the Austrian lands in Alsace and the Breisgau as a compensation for his lost duchy of Franconia. In February he was besieging Rheinfelden. Driven off by the imperialists on the 26th, he re-appeared unexpectedly on March 3, taking the enemy by surprise. They had not even sufficient powder with them to load their guns, and the victory of Rheinfelden was the result. On the 24th Rheinfelden itself surrendered. Freiburg followed its example on April 22, and Bernhard proceeded to undertake the siege of Breisach, the great fortress which domineered over the whole valley of the Upper Rhine. Small as his force was, he succeeded, by a series of rapid movements, in beating off every attempt to introduce supplies, and on December 19 he entered the place in triumph.

(Pg 196)

§ 2. The capture a turning point in the war.

The campaign of 1638 was the turning point in the struggle between France and the united House of Austria. A vantage ground was then won which was never lost.

§ 3. Bernhard wishes to keep Breisach.

Bernhard himself, however, was loth to realize the world-wide importance of the events in which he had played his part. He fancied that he had been fighting for his own, and he claimed the lands which he had conquered for himself. He received the homage of the citizens of Breisach in his own name. He celebrated a Lutheran thanksgiving festival in the cathedral. But the French Government looked upon the rise of an independent German principality in Alsace with as little pleasure as the Spanish government had contemplated the prospect of the establishment of Wallenstein in the Palatinate. They ordered Bernhard to place his conquests under the orders of the King of France.

§ 4. Refuses to dismember the Empire.

Strange as it may seem, the man who had done so much to tear in pieces the Empire believed, in a sort of way, in the Empire still. "I will never suffer," he said, in reply to the French demands, "that men can truly reproach me with being the first to dismember the Empire."

§ 5. Death of Bernhard.

The next year he crossed the Rhine with the most brilliant expectations. Baner had recovered strength, and was pushing on through North Germany into Bohemia. Bernhard hoped that he too might strike a blow which would force on a peace on his own conditions. But his greatest achievement, the capture of Breisach, was also his last. A fatal disease seized upon him when he had hardly entered upon the campaign. On July 8, 1639, he died.

§ 6. Alsace in French possession.

There was no longer any question of the ownership of(Pg 197) the fortresses in Alsace and the Breisgau. French governors entered into possession. A French general took the command of Bernhard's army. For the next two or three years Bernhard's old troops fought up and down Germany in conjunction with Baner, not without success, but without any decisive victory. The French soldiers were becoming, like the Germans, inured to war. The lands on the Rhine were not easily to be wrenched out of the strong hands which had grasped them.

SECTION IV.—French Successes.

§ 1. State of Italy.

Richelieu had other successes to count besides these victories on the Rhine. In 1637 the Spaniards drove out of Turin the Duchess-Regent Christina, the mother of the young Duke of Savoy. She was a sister of the King of France; and, even if that had not been the case, the enemy of Spain was, in the nature of the case, the friend of France. In 1640 she re-entered her capital with French assistance.

§ 2. Maritime warfare.

At sea, too, where Spain, though unable to hold its own against the Dutch, had long continued to be superior to France, the supremacy of Spain was coming to an end. During the whole course of his ministry, Richelieu had paid special attention to the encouragement of commerce and the formation of a navy. Troops could no longer be despatched with safety to Italy from the coasts of Spain. In 1638 a French squadron burnt Spanish galleys in the Bay of Biscay.

§ 3. The Spanish fleet in the Downs.

In 1639 a great Spanish fleet on its way to the Netherlands was strong enough to escape the French, who were watching to intercept it. It sailed up the English Chan(Pg 198)nel with the not distant goal of the Flemish ports almost in view. But the huge galleons were ill-manned and ill-found. They were still less able to resist the lighter, well-equipped vessels of the Dutch fleet, which was waiting to intercept them, than the Armada had been able to resist Drake and Raleigh fifty-one years before. The Spanish commander sought refuge in the Downs, under the protection of the neutral flag of England.

§ 4. Destruction of the fleet.

The French ambassador pleaded hard with the king of England to allow the Dutch to follow up their success. The Spanish ambassador pleaded hard with him for protection to those who had taken refuge on his shores. Charles saw in the occurrence an opportunity to make a bargain with one side or the other. He offered to abandon the Spaniards if the French would agree to restore his nephew, Charles Lewis, the son of his sister Elizabeth, to his inheritance in the Palatinate. He offered to protect the Spaniards if Spain would pay him the large sum which he would want for the armaments needed to bid defiance to France. Richelieu had no intention of completing the bargain offered to him. He deluded Charles with negotiations, whilst the Dutch admiral treated the English neutrality with scorn. He dashed amongst the tall Spanish ships as they lay anchored in the Downs: some he sank, some he set on fire. Eleven of the galleons were soon destroyed. The remainder took advantage of a thick fog, slipped across the Straits, and placed themselves in safety under the guns of Dunkirk. Never again did such a fleet as this venture to leave the Spanish coast for the harbours of Flanders. The injury to Spain went far beyond the actual loss. Coming, as the blow did, within a few months after the surrender of Breisach,(Pg 199) it all but severed the connexion for military purposes between Brussels and Madrid.

§ 5. France and England.

Charles at first took no umbrage at the insult. He still hoped that Richelieu would forward his nephew's interests, and he even expected that Charles Lewis would be placed by the King of France in command of the army which had been under Bernhard's orders. But Richelieu was in no mood to place a German at the head of these well-trained veterans, and the proposal was definitively rejected. The King of England, dissatisfied at this repulse, inclined once more to the side of Spain. But Richelieu found a way to prevent Spain from securing even what assistance it was in the power of a king so unpopular as Charles to render. It was easy to enter into communication with Charles's domestic enemies. His troubles, indeed, were mostly of his own making, and he would doubtless have lost his throne whether Richelieu had stirred the fire or not. But the French minister contributed all that was in his power to make the confusion greater, and encouraged, as far as possible, the resistance which had already broken out in Scotland, and which was threatening to break out in England.

§ 6. Insurrection in Catalonia.

The failure of 1636 had been fully redeemed. No longer attacking any one of the masses of which the Spanish monarchy was composed, Richelieu placed his hands upon the lines of communication between them. He made his presence felt not at Madrid, at Brussels, at Milan, or at Naples, but in Alsace, in the Mediterranean, in the English Channel. The effect was as complete as is the effect of snapping the wire of a telegraph. At once the Peninsula startled Europe by showing signs of dissolution. In 1639 the Catalonians had manfully defended(Pg 200) Roussillon against a French invasion. In 1640 they were prepared to fight with equal vigour. But the Spanish Government, in its desperate straits, was not content to leave them to combat in their own way, after the irregular fashion which befitted mountaineers. Orders were issued commanding all men capable of fighting to arm themselves for the war, all women to bear food and supplies for the army on their backs. A royal edict followed, threatening those who showed themselves remiss with imprisonment and the confiscation of their goods.

§ 7. Break-up of the Spanish monarchy.

The cord which bound the hearts of Spaniards to their king was a strong one; but it snapped at last. It was not by threats that Richelieu had defended France in 1636. The old traditions of provincial independence were strong in Catalonia, and the Catalans were soon in full revolt. Who were they, to be driven to the combat by menaces, as the Persian slaves had been driven on at Thermopylæ by the blows of their masters' officers?

§ 8. Independence of Portugal.

Equally alarming was the news which reached Madrid from the other side of the Peninsula. Ever since the days of Philip II. Portugal had formed an integral part of the Spanish monarchy. In December 1640 Portugal renounced its allegiance, and reappeared amongst European States under a sovereign of the House of Braganza.

§ 9. Failure of Soissons in France.

Everything prospered in Richelieu's hands. In 1641 a fresh attempt was made by the partizans of Spain to raise France against him. The Count of Soissons, a prince of the blood, placed himself at the head of an imperialist army to attack his native country. He succeeded in defeating the French forces sent to oppose him not far from Sedan.(Pg 201) But a chance shot passing through the brain of Soissons made the victory a barren one. His troops, without the support of his name, could not hope to rouse the country against Richelieu. They had become mere invaders, and they were far too few to think of conquering France.

§ 10. Richelieu's last days.

Equal success attended the French arms in Germany. In 1641 Guebriant, with his German and Swedish army, defeated the imperialists at Wolfenbüttel, in the north. In 1642 he defeated them again at Kempten, in the south. In the same year Roussillon submitted to France. Nor was Richelieu less fortunate at home. The conspiracy of a young courtier, the last of the efforts of the aristocracy to shake off the heavy rule of the Cardinal, was detected, and expiated on the scaffold. Richelieu did not long survive his latest triumph. He died on December 4, 1642.

SECTION V.—Aims and Character of Richelieu.

§ 1. Richelieu's domestic policy.

Unlike Lewis XIV. and Napoleon, Richelieu counts amongst those few French statesmen whose fortune mounted with their lives. It is not difficult to discover the cause. As in Gustavus, love of action was tempered by extreme prudence and caution. But in Richelieu these ingredients of character were mingled in different proportions. The love of action was far less impetuous. The caution was far stronger. No man had a keener eye to distinguish the conditions of success, or was more ready to throw aside the dearest schemes when he believed them to be accompanied by insuperable difficulties. Braver heart never was. There was the highest courage in the constancy with which he, an invalid tottering for years on the brink of the grave, and supported by a king whose health was as feeble as his own, faced the whole might(Pg 202) of the aristocracy of France. If he was harsh and unpitying it was to the enemies of the nation, to the nobles who trod under their feet the peasant and the serf, and who counted the possession of power merely as the high-road to the advancement of their private fortunes. The establishment of a strong monarchical power was, as France was then constituted, the only chance for industry and commerce to lift up their heads, for the peaceable arts of life to develop themselves in security, for the intellect of man to have free course, and for the poor to be protected from oppression.

§ 2. His designs only partially accomplished.

All this was in Richelieu's heart; and some little of this he accomplished. The work of many generations was in this man's brain. Yet he never attempted to do more than the work of his own. As Bacon sketched out the lines within which science was to move in the days of Newton and of Faraday, so Richelieu sketched out the lines within which French statesmanship was to move in the days of Colbert and of Turgot, or in those of the great Revolution itself.

§ 3. The people nothing in France.

"All things for the people, nothing by the people." This maxim attributed to Napoleon embodied as well the policy of Richelieu. In it are embalmed the strength and weakness of French statesmanship. The late growth of the royal power and the long continuance of aristocratic oppression threw the people helpless and speechless into the arms of the monarchy. They were happy if some one should prove strong enough to take up their cause without putting them to the trouble or the risk of thinking and speaking for themselves. It is no blame to Richelieu if, being a Frenchman of the seventeenth century, he worked under the only conditions which(Pg 203) Frenchmen of the seventeenth century would admit. We can well fancy that he would think with scorn and contempt of the English Revolution, which was accomplishing itself under his eyes. Yet in the England of the Civil War, men were learning not merely to be governed well, but to know what good government was. It was a greater thing for a nation to learn to choose good and to refuse evil, even if the progress was slow, than to be led blindfold with far more rapid steps.

§ 4. His foreign policy.

Richelieu's foreign policy was guided by the same deep calculation as his home policy. If at home he saw that France was greater than any faction, he had not arrived at the far higher notion that Europe was greater than France, excepting so far as he saw in the system of intolerance supported by Spain an evil to be combated for the sake of others who were not Frenchmen. But there is no sign that he really cared for the prosperity of other nations when it was not coincident with the prosperity of France. As it is for the present generation a matter of complete indifference whether Breisach was to be garrisoned by Frenchmen or imperialists, it would be needless for us, if we regarded Richelieu's motives alone, to trouble ourselves much with the later years of the Thirty Years' War.

§ 5. His support of rising causes.

But it is not always by purity of motive only that the world's progress advances. Richelieu, in order to make France strong, needed help, and he had to look about for help where the greatest amount of strength was to be found. An ordinary man would have looked to the physical strength of armies, as Wallenstein did, or to the ideal strength of established institutions, as Ferdinand did. Richelieu knew better. He saw that for him who knows(Pg 204) how to use it there is no lever in the world like that of a rising cause, for a rising cause embodies the growing dissatisfaction of men with a long-established evil, which they have learned to detest, but which they have not yet learned to overthrow.

§ 6. And of those causes which were in themselves good.

In England Richelieu was on the side of Parliamentary opposition to the crown. In Germany he was on the side of the opposition of the princes against the Emperor. In Italy he was on the side of the independence of the states against Spain. In the Peninsula he was on the side of the provinces against the monarchy. There is not the slightest reason to suppose that he cared one atom for any of those causes except so far as they might promote his own ends. Yet in every case he selected those causes by which the real wants of the several countries were best expressed.

§ 7. Contrast between Richelieu and later French politicians.

It is this which distinguishes Richelieu from those who in later times have measured the foreign policy of France by French interests alone. They have taken up any cause which promised to weaken a powerful neighbour, without considering what the cause was worth. They favoured Italian division in 1860, and German division in 1870. Richelieu had a clearer insight into the nature of things than that. There can be no doubt that he would far rather have attacked Spain and Austria through the instrumentality of the League than through the instrumentality of Gustavus and the Protestants; but he saw that the future was with Gustavus and not with the League. He sacrificed his wishes to his policy. He coquetted with the League, but he supported Gustavus.

§ 8. He has no exorbitant aims.

When once Richelieu had gained his point, he was contented with his success. He never aspired to more(Pg 205) than he could accomplish: never struck, excepting for a purpose: never domineered through the mere insolence of power. He took good care to get Alsace into his hands, and to make himself master of the passes of the Alps by the possession of Pignerol; but he never dreamed of founding, like Napoleon, a French Confederation of the Rhine, or a French kingdom of Italy. His interference with his neighbours was as little obtrusive as possible.

1643
§ 9. Death of Lewis XIII.

Richelieu was quickly followed to the grave by the sovereign in whose name he had accomplished so much. Lewis XIII. died on the 14th of May, 1643.

SECTION VI.—More French Victories.

1643

§ 1. Rule of Mazarin.

His son and successor, Lewis XIV., was a mere child. His widow, Anne of Austria, claimed the regency, and forgot that she was the sister of the King of Spain and the sister-in-law of the Emperor, in the thought that she was the widow of one king of France and the mother of another. Her minister was Cardinal Mazarin, an Italian, who had commended himself to Richelieu by his capacity for business and his complete independence of French party feeling. If he was noted rather for cleverness than for strength of character, he was at least anxious to carry out the policy of his predecessor, and to maintain the predominance of the crown over aristocratic factions; and for some time Richelieu's policy seemed to carry success with it through the impetus which he had given it. On May 19 a victory came to establish the new authority of the queen-regent, the first of a long series of French victories, which was unbroken till the days of Marlborough and Blenheim.

(Pg 206)

§ 2. The Spaniards attack Rocroy.

The Spaniards had crossed the frontier of the Netherlands, and were besieging Rocroy. The command of the French forces was held by the duke of Enghien, better known to the world by the title which he afterwards inherited from his father, as the Prince of Condé. Next to Gaston, Duke of Orleans, the late king's brother, he and his father stood first in succession to the throne, and had, for this reason, attached themselves to Richelieu when he was opposed by the great bulk of the aristocracy. Those who placed him at the head of the army probably expected that a prince so young and so inexperienced would content himself with giving his name to the campaign, and would leave the direction of the troops to older heads.

§ 3. Gassion and Enghien.

The older heads, after reconnoitring the Spanish position at Rocroy, advised Enghien not to fight. But there was a certain Gassion among the officers, who had served under Gustavus, and who had seen the solid legions of Tilly break down before the swift blows of the Swedish king at Breitenfeld. Gassion had learned to look upon that close Spanish formation with contempt, and he strove hard to persuade Enghien to give orders for the attack, and, truth to say, he had no very hard task. Enghien was young and sanguine, and whether he had a genius for war or not, he had at least a genius for battles. Already conscious of the skill with which he was to direct the fortunes of many a well-fought field, he heartily adopted the views laid before him by Gassion.

§ 4. Battle of Rocroy.

Rocroy was, so to speak, a second edition of Breitenfeld, a victory gained by vigour and flexibility over solid endurance. Unreasoning obedience once more gave way before disciplined intelli(Pg 207)gence. The Spanish masses stood with all the strength of a mediæval fortress. There was no manœuvering power in them. The French artillery ploughed its way through the ranks, and the dashing charges of the infantry drove the disaster home. The glories of the Spanish armies, the glories which dated from the days of the Great Captain, were clouded for ever. Yet if victory was lost to Spain, the cherished honour of the Spanish arms was safe. Man by man the warriors fell in the ranks in which they stood, like the English defenders of the banner of Harold at Senlac. Their leader, the Count of Fuentes, an old man worn with years and gout, and unable to stand, was seated in an arm-chair to direct the battle within a square composed of his veteran troops. Death found him at his post. He had fought in the old wars of Philip II. The last of a long heroic race of statesmen and soldiers had bowed his head before the rising genius of France.

§ 5. Extension of the French frontier.

Thionville was then besieged. It surrendered in August. The cautious Richelieu had been contented to announce that he reserved all question of the ownership of his conquests till it should be finally determined by a treaty of peace. After Rocroy, Mazarin had no such scruples. Thionville was formally annexed to France. A medal was struck on which Hope was borne in the hand of Victory, and on which was inscribed the legend, *Prima finium propagatic.*

§ 6. Enghien and Turenne.
In Germany the campaign of 1643 was less successful. Maximilian of Bavaria had put forth all his resources, and his generals, the dashing John of Werth and the prudent Mercy, of whom it was said that he knew the plans of the enemy as well as if he had sat in their councils, were more than a(Pg 208) match for the French commanders. 1644. 1644 they were opposed by a soldier of a quality higher than their own. Turenne was sent amongst them, but his forces were too few to enable him to operate with success. Freiburg in the Breisgau was taken before his eyes. Breisach was threatened. Then Enghien came with 10,000 men to assume the command over the head of the modest soldier who had borne the weight of the campaign. Proud of his last year's victory he despised the counsel of Turenne, that it was better to out-manœuvre the enemy than to fight him in an almost inaccessible position.

§ 7. Battle of Freiburg.

The battle fought amongst the vineyards of Freiburg was the bloodiest battle of a bloody war. For three days Enghien led his men to the butchery. At last Mercy, unable to provide food any longer for his troops, effected his retreat. The French reaped the prizes of a victory which they had not gained.

1645
§ 8. Battle of Nördlingen.

On the 3d of August, 1645, a second battle of Nördlingen was fought. It was almost a repetition of the slaughter of Freiburg. As in the year before, Turenne had been left to do the hard work at the opening of the campaign with inferior forces, and had even suffered a check. Once more Enghien came up, gay and dashing, at the head of a reinforcement of picked men. Once more a fearful butchery ensued. But that Mercy was slain early in the fight, the day might have gone hard with the French. As it was, they were able to claim a victory. The old German bands which had served under Bernhard held out to the uttermost and compelled the enemy to retreat. But the success was not lasting. The imperialists received reinforcements, and the French were driven back upon the Rhine.

(Pg 209)

§ 9. Battle of Jankow.

The same year had opened with splendid expectations on the other side of the theatre of the war. The gouty Swedish general, Torstenson, who had taken up Baner's work in the north, burst suddenly into Bohemia, and on the 6th of March inflicted a crushing defeat on the imperialists at Jankow. He then harried Moravia, and pressed on to lay siege to Vienna, as if to repair the fault which it was the fashion to ascribe to Gustavus. But Vienna was unassailable, and Torstenson, like Turenne, was driven to retreat. He next tried to reduce Brünn. Failing in this he returned to Bohemia, where, worn out with his maladies, he delivered over the command to Wrangel, his appointed successor.

CHAPTER XI. THE END OF THE WAR.

SECTION I.—Turenne's Strategy.

1643

§ 1. Thoughts of peace.

At last the thought entered into men's minds that it was time to put a stop to this purposeless misery and slaughter. It was hopeless to think any longer of shaking the strong grasp of France upon the Rhine; and if Sweden had been foiled in striking to the heart of the Austrian monarchy, she could not be driven from the desolate wilderness which now, by the evil work of men's hands, stretched from the Baltic far away into the interior of Germany. Long ago the disciplined force which Gustavus had brought across the sea had melted away, and a Swedish army was now like other armies—a mere collection of mercenaries, without religion, without pity, and without remorse.

(Pg 210)

§ 2. Meeting of diplomatists.

Negotiations for peace were spoken of from time to time, and preparations were at last made for a great meeting of diplomatists. In order to prevent the usual quarrel about precedency it was decided that some of the ambassadors should hold their sittings at Osnabrück and others at Münster, an arrangement which was not likely to conduce to a speedy settlement. 1644, 1645. Emperor proved his sincerity by sending his representative early enough to arrive at Münster in July, 1643, whilst the Swedish and French ambassadors only made their appearance in the March and April of the following year, and it was only in June, 1645, that the first formal proposition was handed in.

§ 3. Reluctance of the Emperor to give up all that is asked.

All who were concerned were in fact ready to make peace, but they all wished it made on their own terms. Ferdinand III. was not bound by his father's antecedents. The Edict of Restitution had been no work of his. Long before this he had been ready to give all reasonable satisfaction to the Protestants. He had declared his readiness to include Calvinists as well as Lutherans in the religious peace. He had offered to restore the Lower Palatinate to Frederick's son, and he actually issued a general amnesty to all who were still in arms; but he shrank from the demand that these arrangements of the Empire should be treated of, not in the constitutional assemblies of the Empire, but in a congress of European powers. To do so would be to tear the last veil from the sad truth that the Empire was a mere shadow, and that the states of which it was composed had become practically independent sovereignties. And behind this degradation lay another degradation, hardly less bitter to Ferdinand. The proudest title of the great emperors of old had been(Pg 211) that of Increaser of the Empire. Was he to go down to posterity with the title of Diminisher of the Empire? And yet it was beyond his power to loosen the hold of France upon Alsace, or of Sweden upon Pomerania.

§ 4. Especially the Breisgau.

Nor was it only as Emperor that Ferdinand would feel the loss of Alsace deeply. Together with the Breisgau it formed one of territories of the House of Austria, but it was not his own. It was the inheritance of the children of his uncle Leopold, and he was loth to purchase peace for himself by agreeing to the spoliation of his orphan nephews.

§ 5. Aims of the Elector of Bavaria.

Maximilian of Bavaria viewed the question of peace from another point of view. To him Alsace was nothing, and he warmly recommended Ferdinand to surrender it for the sake of peace. If concessions were to be made at all, he preferred making them to Catholic France rather than to the Protestants in the Empire, and he was convinced that if Alsace remained under French rule, the motive which had led France to support the Protestants would lose its chief weight. But besides these general considerations, Maximilian, like Ferdinand, had a special interest of his own. He was resolved, come what might, to retain at least the Upper Palatinate, and he trusted to be seconded in his resolve by the good offices of France.

§ 6. The campaign of 1646.

The position of Maximilian was thus something like that of John George of Saxony in 1632. He and his chief ally were both ready for peace, but his ally stood out for higher terms than he was prepared to demand. And as in 1632 Wallenstein saw in the comparative moderation of the Elector of Saxony only a reason for driving him by force to separate his cause from that of Gustavus, so in(Pg 212) 1646 the French government resolved to fall upon Bavaria, and to force the elector to separate his cause from that of Ferdinand.

§ 7. Turenne out-manœuvres the Bavarians.

The year before, the Elector of Saxony, crushed and ruined by the Swedes, had consented to a separate truce, and now Turenne was commissioned to do the same with Bavaria. In August he effected a junction on the Lahn with Wrangel and the Swedes, and if Enghien had been there, history would doubtless have had to tell of another butchery as resultless as those of Freiburg and Nördlingen. But Enghien was far away in Flanders, laying siege to Dunkirk, and Turenne, for the first time at the head of a superior force, was about to teach the world a lesson in the art of war. Whilst the enemy was preparing for the expected attack by entrenching his position, the united French and Swedish armies slipped past them and marched straight for the heart of Bavaria, where an enemy had not been seen since Bernhard had been chased out in 1634. That one day, as Turenne truly said, altered the whole face of affairs. Everywhere the roads were open. Provisions were plentiful. The population was in the enjoyment of the blessings of peace. Turenne and Wrangel crossed the Danube without difficulty. Schorndorf, Würzburg, Nördlingen, Donauwörth made no resistance to them. It was not till they came to Augsburg that they met with opposition.

The enemy had time to come up. But there was no unanimity in the councils of the enemy. The Bavarian generals wanted to defend Bavaria. The imperialist generals wanted to defend the still remaining Austrian possessions in Swabia. The invaders were allowed to accomplish their purpose. They arrived at the gates of Munich before the citizens knew what had become of(Pg 213) their master's army. With grim purpose Turenne and Wrangel set themselves to make desolate the Bavarian plain, so that it might be rendered incapable of supporting a Bavarian army. Maximilian was reduced to straits such as he had not known since the time when Tilly fell at the passage of the Lech. Sorely against his will he signed, in May, 1647, a separate truce with the enemy.

§ 8. Last struggles of the war.

The truce did not last long. In September Maximilian was once more on the Emperor's side. Bavaria paid dearly for the elector's defection. All that had been spared a year before fell a sacrifice to new devastation. The last great battle of the war was fought at Zusmarshausen on May 17, 1648. The Bavarians were defeated and the work of the destroyer went on yet for a while unchecked. In Bohemia half of Prague fell into the hands of the Swedes, and the Emperor was left unaided to bear up in the unequal fight.

SECTION II.—The Treaty of Westphalia.

§ 1. The Peace of Westphalia.

Ferdinand could resist no longer. On the 24th of October, 1648, a few months before Charles I. ascended the scaffold at Whitehall, the Peace of Westphalia was signed.

§ 2. Religious settlement.

The religious difficulty in Germany was settled as it ought to have been settled long before. Calvinism was to be placed on the same footing as Lutheranism. New-Year's day 1624 was fixed upon as the date by which all disputes were to be tested. Whatever ecclesiastical benefice was in Catholic hands at that date was to remain in Catholic hands forever. Ecclesiastical benefices in Protestant hands at that date were to remain in Protestant keeping. Catholics would never again be able to lay(Pg 214) claim to the bishoprics of the north. Even Halberstadt, which had been retained at the Peace of Prague, was now lost to them. To make this settlement permanent, the Imperial Court was reconstituted. Protestants and Catholics were to be members of the court in equal numbers. And if the judicial body was such as to make it certain that its sanction would never be given to an infringement of the peace, the Catholic majority in the Diet became powerless for evil.

§ 3. Political settlement.

In political matters, Maximilian permanently united the Upper Palatinate to his duchy of Bavaria, and the Electorate was confirmed to him and his descendants. An eighth electorate was created in favour of Charles Lewis, the worthless son of the Elector, Frederick, and the Lower Palatinate was given up to him. Sweden established herself firmly on the mouths of the great northern rivers. The Eastern part of Pomerania she surrendered to Brandenburg. But Western Pomerania, including within its frontier both banks of the lower Vistula, was surrendered to her; whilst the possession of the bishoprics of Bremen and Verdun, on which Christian of Denmark had set his eyes at the beginning of the war, gave her a commanding position at the mouths of the Elbe and the Weser. The bishoprics of Halberstadt, Camin, Minden, and the greater part of the diocese of Magdeburg, were made over to Brandenburg as a compensation for the loss of its claims to the whole of Pomerania, whilst a smaller portion of the diocese of Magdeburg was assigned to Saxony, that power, as a matter of course, retaining Lusatia.

§ 4. Gains of France.

France, as a matter of course, retained its conquests. It kept its hold upon Austrian Alsace, Strasburg, as a free city, and the immediate(Pg 215) vassals of the Empire being, however, excluded from the cession. The strong fortress of Philippsburg, erected by the warlike Elector of Treves, received a French garrison, and the three bishoprics, Metz, Toul, and Verdun, which had been practically under French rule since the days of Henry II. of France, were now formally separated from the Empire. Equally formal was the separation of Switzerland and the Netherlands, both of which countries had long been practically independent.

§ 5. The question of toleration left to the German princes.

The importance of the peace of Westphalia in European history goes far beyond these territorial changes. That France should have a few miles more and Germany a few miles less, or even that France should have acquired military and political strength whilst Germany lost it, are facts which in themselves need not have any very great interest for others than Frenchmen or Germans. That which gives to the Peace of Westphalia its prominent place amongst treaties is that it drew a final demarcation between the two religions which divided Europe. The struggle in England and France for the right of settling their own religious affairs without the interference of foreign nations had been brought to a close in the sixteenth century. In Germany it had not been brought to a close for the simple reason that it was not decided how far Germany was a nation at all. The government of England or France could tolerate or persecute at home as far as its power or inclination permitted. But the central government of Germany was not strong enough to enforce its will upon the territorial governments; nor on the other hand were the territorial governments strong enough to enforce their will without regard for the central government. Thirty years of war ended by a compromise under which the religious(Pg 216) position of each territory was fixed by the intervention of foreign powers, whilst the rights of the central government were entirely ignored.

§ 6. How toleration was the result of this.

Such a settlement was by no means necessarily in favour of religious toleration. The right of an Elector of Bavaria or an Elector of Saxony to impose his belief by force upon his dissident subjects was even more fully acknowledged than before. He could still give them their choice between conversion or banishment. As late as in 1729 an Archbishop of Salzburg could drive thousands of industrious Protestants into exile from his Alpine valleys, leaving a void behind them which has not been filled up to this day. But if such cases were rare, their rarity was indirectly owing to the Peace of Westphalia. In 1617 a bishop who had to consider the question of religious persecution, had to consider it with the fear of Christian of Anhalt before his eyes. Every Protestant in his dominions was a possible traitor who would favour, if he did not actively support, the revolutionary attacks of the neighbouring Protestants. In 1649 all such fear was at an end for ever. The bishop was undisputed master of his territory, and he could look on with contemptuous indifference if a few of his subjects had sufficient love of singularity to profess a religion other than his own.

§ 7. The Peace of Westphalia compared with the Peace of Augsburg.

It may perhaps be said that the assurance given by the Peace of Westphalia was after all no better than the assurance given by the Peace of Augsburg, but even so far as the letter of the two documents was concerned, this was very far from being the case. The Peace of Augsburg was full of uncertainties, because the contracting parties were unable to abandon their respective desires.(Pg 217) In the Peace of Westphalia all was definite. Evasion or misinterpretation was no longer possible.

§ 8. General desire for the continuance of peace.

If the letter of the two treaties was entirely different, it was because the spirit in which they were conceived was also entirely different. In 1555 Protestantism was on the rise. The peace of 1555 was a vain attempt to shut out the tide by artificial dykes and barriers. In 1648 the tide had receded. The line which divided the Protestant from the Catholic princes formed almost an exact division between the Protestant and Catholic populations. The desire for making proselytes, once so strong on both sides, had been altogether extinguished by the numbing agony of the war. All Germany longed for peace with an inexpressible longing. The mutual distrust of Catholic and Protestant had grown exceedingly dull. The only feeling yet alive was hatred of the tyranny and exactions of the soldiers.

SECTION III.—Condition of Germany.

§ 1. Effects of the war.

What a peace it was when it really came at last! Whatever life there was under that deadly blast of war had been attracted to the camps. The strong man who had lost his all turned soldier that he might be able to rob others in turn. The young girl, who in better times would have passed on to a life of honourable wedlock with some youth who had been the companion of her childhood in the sports around the village fountain, had turned aside, for very starvation, to a life of shame in the train of one or other of the armies by which her home had been made desolate. In the later years of the war it was known that a body of 40,000 fighting men drew along with it a loathsome following of no less than 140,000 men, women,(Pg 218) and children, contributing nothing to the efficiency of the army, and all of them living at the expense of the miserable peasants who still contrived to hold on to their ruined fields. If these were to live, they must steal what yet remained to be stolen; they must devour, with the insatiable hunger of locusts, what yet remained to be devoured. And then, if sickness came, or wounds—and sickness was no infrequent visitor in those camps—what remained but misery or death? Nor was it much better with the soldiers themselves. No careful surgeons passed over the battle-field to save life or limb. No hospitals received the wounded to the tender nursing of loving, gentle hands. Recruits were to be bought cheaply, and it cost less to enrol a new soldier than to cure an old one.

§ 2. Decrease of the population.

The losses of the civil population were almost incredible. In a certain district of Thuringia which was probably better off than the greater part of Germany, there were, before the war cloud burst,

1,717 houses standing in nineteen villages. In 1649, only 627 houses were left. And even of the houses which remained many were untenanted. The 1,717 houses had been inhabited by 1,773 families. Only 316 families could be found to occupy the 627 houses. Property fared still worse. In the same district 244 oxen alone remained of 1,402. Of 4,616 sheep, not one was left. Two centuries later the losses thus suffered were scarcely recovered.

§ 3. Moral decadence.

And, as is always the case, the physical decline of the population was accompanied by moral decadence. Men who had been accustomed to live by the strong arm, and men who had been accustomed to suffer all things from those who were strong, met one another, even in the days of peace,(Pg 219) without that mutual respect which forms the basis of well-ordered life. Courts were crowded with feather-brained soldiers whose highest ambition was to bedeck themselves in a splendid uniform and to copy the latest fashion or folly which was in vogue at Paris or Versailles. In the country district a narrow-minded gentry, without knowledge or culture, domineered over all around, and strove to exact the uttermost farthing from the peasant in order to keep up the outward appearance of rank. The peasant whose father had been bullied by marauding soldiers dared not lift up his head against the exactions of the squire. The burden of the general impoverishment fell heavily upon his shoulders. The very pattern of the chairs on which he sat, of the vessels out of which he ate and drank, assumed a ruder appearance than they had borne before the war. In all ranks life was meaner, poorer, harder than it had been at the beginning of the century.

§ 4. Intellectual decline even before the war.

If much of all this was the result of the war, something was owing to causes antecedently at work. The German people in the beginning of the seventeenth century was plainly inferior to the German people in the beginning of the sixteenth century. During the whole course of the war Maximilian of Bavaria was the only man of German birth who rose to eminence, and even he did not attain the first rank. The destinies of the land of Luther and Göthe, of Frederick II. and Stein were decided by a few men of foreign birth. Wallenstein was a Slavonian, Tilly a Walloon, Gustavus a Swede, Richelieu a Frenchman. The penalty borne by a race which was unable to control individual vigour within the limits of a large and fruitful national life was that individual vigour itself died out.

(Pg 220)

§ 5. Difficulties inherited from early times.

We may well leave to those who like such tasks the work of piling up articles of accusation against this man or that, of discovering that the war was all the fault of Ferdinand, or all the fault of Frederick, as party feeling may lead them. Probably the most lenient judgment is also the truest one. With national and territorial institutions the mere chaos which they were, an amount of political intelligence was needed to set them right which would be rare in any country or in any age.

§ 6. Total disintegration of Germany.

As far as national institutions were concerned the Thirty Years' War made a clean sweep in Germany. Nominally, it is true, Emperor and Empire still remained. Ferdinand III. was still according to his titles head of all Christendom, if not of the whole human race. The Diet still gathered to discuss the affairs of the Empire. The imperial court, re-established on the principle of equality between the two religions, still met to dispense justice between the estates of the Empire. But from these high-sounding names all reality had fled. The rule over German men had passed for many a long day into the hands of the princes. It was for the princes to strive with one another in peace or war under the protection of foreign alliances; and by and by, half consciously, half unconsciously, to compete for the leadership of Germany by the intelligence and discipline which they were able to foster under their sway.

§ 7. Protestantism saved.

When the days of this competition arrived it was of inestimable advantage to Germany that, whatever else had been lost, Protestantism had been saved. Wherever Protestantism had firmly rooted itself there sprang up in course of time a mighty race of intellectual giants. Göthe and(Pg 221) Schiller, Lessing and Kant, Stein and Humboldt, with thousands more of names which have made German intellect a household word in the whole civilized world, sprung from Protestant Germany. When Bavaria, scarcely more than two generations ago, awoke to the consciousness that she had not more than the merest rudiments of education to give to her children, she had to apply to the Protestant north for teachers.

§ 8. The worst over for Germany.

For Germany in 1648 the worst was over. Physically, at least she had no more to suffer. One page of her history was closed and another had not yet been opened. She lay for a time in the insensibility of exhaustion.

SECTION IV.—Continuance of the War between France and Spain.

§ 1. Peace between Spain and the Dutch.

For France 1648 is hardly a date at all. She was rid of the war in Germany. But her war with Spain was not brought to an end. And if Spain would no longer have the support of the imperialists of Germany, France was at the same time deprived of the support of a far more vigorous ally. Spain at last lowered its haughty neck to accept conditions of peace on terms of equality from the Dutch republic. The eighty years' war of the Netherlands was brought to a conclusion simultaneously with the thirty years' war of Germany. Spain could now send reinforcements to Flanders by sea without fearing the overwhelming superiority of the Dutch marine, and could defend the southern frontier of the obedient provinces without having to provide against an attack in the rear.

§ 2. France and Spain.

In the long run, a duel between France and Spain could be of no doubtful issue. It was a contest between the old system of immobility and intolerance and the(Pg 222) new system of intelligence and tolerance; between a government which despised industry and commerce, and a government which fostered them. But however excellent might be the aims which the French government kept in view, it was still in its nature an absolute government. No free discussion enlightened its judgment. No popular intervention kept in check its caprices. It was apt to strike roughly and ignorantly, to wound many feelings and to impose grievous burdens upon the poor and the weak whose lamentations never reached the height of the throne.

§ 3. The Fronde.

Suddenly, when Mazarin's government appeared most firmly rooted, there was an explosion which threatened to change the whole face of France. An outcry arose for placing restrictions upon rights of the crown, for establishing constitutional and individual liberties. The Fronde, as the party which uttered the cry was called, did its best to imitate the English Long Parliament whose deeds were then ringing through the world. But there were no elements in France upon which to establish constitutional government. The Parliament of Paris, which wished itself to be considered the chief organ of that government, was a close corporation of lawyers, who had bought or inherited judicial places; and of all governments, a government in the hands of a close corporation of lawyers is likely, in the long run, to be the most narrow-minded and unprogressive of all possible combinations; for it is the business of a lawyer to administer the law as it exists, not to modify it in accordance with the new facts which rise constantly to the surface of social and political life. Nor were the lawyers of the parliament fortunate in their supporters. The Paris mob, combined with a knot of intriguing courtiers, could form no firm basis for a healthy revolu(Pg 223)tion. It was still worse when Condé, quarrelling on a personal question with Mazarin, raised the standard of aristocratic revolt, and threw himself into the arms of the Spanish invader. Mazarin and the young king represented the nation against aristocratic selfishness and intrigue; and when they obtained the services of Turenne, the issue was hardly doubtful. In 1652 Lewis XIV. entered Paris in triumph. In 1653 Condé, in conjunction with a Spanish army, invaded France, and pushed on hopefully for Paris. But Turenne was there with a handful of troops; and if Condé was the successor of Gustavus in the art of fighting battles, Turenne was Wallenstein's successor in the art of strategy. Condé could neither fight nor advance with effect. The siege and reduction of Rocroy was the only result of a campaign which had been commenced in the expectation of reducing France to submission.

§ 4. The war with Spain.

In 1654 Condé and the Spaniards laid siege to Arras, whilst the French were besieging Stenay. Stenay was taken; Arras was relieved. In 1655 further progress was made by the French on the frontier of the Netherlands; but in 1656 they failed in the siege of Valenciennes.

§ 5. France, Cromwell, and Spain.

With the check thus inflicted, a new danger appeared above the horizon. In England there had arisen, under Cromwell, a new and powerful military state upon the ruins of the monarchy of the Stuarts. To Cromwell Spain addressed itself with the most tempting offers. The old English jealousy of France, and the political advantage of resisting its growing strength, were urged in favour of a Spanish alliance. Cromwell might renew the old glories of the Plantagenets, and might gather round him the forces of the Huguenots of the south. If Charles I. had failed at Rochelle, Cromwell might establish himself firmly at Bordeaux.

(Pg 224)

§ 6. Spain refuses Cromwell's terms.

For a moment Cromwell was shaken. Then he made two demands of the Spanish ambassador. He must have, he said freedom for Englishmen to trade in the Indies, and permission for Englishmen carrying on commercial intercourse with Spain to profess their religion openly without interference. "To give you this," was the Spaniard's cool reply, "would be to give you my master's two eyes."

§ 7. Alliance between France and England.

To beat down religious exclusiveness and commercial exclusiveness was the work to which Cromwell girded himself. An alliance with France was quickly made. The arrogant intolerance of Spain was to perish through its refusal to admit the new principle of toleration. The politic tolerance of France was to rise to still higher fortunes by the admission of the principle on which all its successes had been based since Richelieu's accession to power. In 1657, six thousand of Cromwell's Ironsides landed to take part in continental warfare. The union of Turenne's strategy with the valour and discipline which had broken down opposition at Naseby and Worcester was irresistible. That autumn the small Flemish port of Mardyke surrendered. In 1658 Dunkirk was taken, and given over, according to compact, to the English auxiliaries. But France, too, reaped an ample harvest. Gravelines, Oudenarde, Ypres saw the white flag of France flying from their ramparts.

§ 8. The Treaty of the Pyrenees.

Spain was reduced to seek for peace. In 1660 the Treaty of the Pyrenees, a supplement as it were to the Treaty of Westphalia, put an end to the long war. The advantages of the peace were all on the side of France. Roussillon and Artois, with Thionville, Landrecies, and Avesnes,(Pg 225) were incorporated with France. Another condition was pregnant with future evil. Lewis XIV. gave his hand to the sister of Philip IV. of Spain, the next heiress to the Spanish monarchy after the sickly infant who became afterwards the imbecile and childish Charles II. At her marriage she abandoned all right to the great inheritance; but even at the time there were not wanting Frenchmen of authority to point to circumstances which rendered the renunciation null and void.

§ 9. The greatness of France based on its tolerance.

Richelieu's power had been based upon tolerance at home and moderation abroad. Was it likely that his successors would always imitate his example? What guarantee could be given that the French monarchy would not turn its back upon the principles from which its strength had been derived? In a land of free discussion, every gain is a permanent one. When Protestantism, or toleration, or freedom of the press, or freedom of trade had been once accepted in England, they were never abandoned; they became articles of popular belief, on which no hesitation, except by scattered individuals, was possible. Multitudes who would find it difficult to give a good reason why they thought one thing to be true and another untrue, had yet a hazy confidence in the result of the battle of reason which had taken place, much in the same way as there are millions of people in the world who believe implicitly that the earth goes round the sun, without being able to give a reason for their belief.

§ 10. But this depended on the will of the king.

In France it was hard for anything of the kind to take place. Tolerance was admitted there by the mere will of the government in the seventeenth century, just as free trade was admitted by the mere will of the government in the nineteenth century. The hand that gave could also(Pg 226) take away; and it depended on the young king to decide whether he would walk in the steps of the great minister who had cleared the way before him, or whether he would wander into devious paths of his own seeking.

§ 11. Intolerance of Lewis XIV.

At first everything promised well. A great statesman, Colbert, filled the early part of the manhood of Lewis XIV. with a series of domestic reforms, the least of which would have gladdened the heart of Richelieu. Taxation was reduced, the tolls taken upon the passage of goods from one province to another were diminished in number, trade and industry were encouraged, the administration of justice was improved; all, in short, that it was possible to do within the circle of one man's activity was done to make France a prosperous and contented land. But the happy time was not of long duration. The war fever took possession of Lewis; the lust of absolute domination entered into his heart. He became the tyrant and bully of Europe; and as abroad he preferred to be feared rather than to be loved, at home he would be content with nothing else than the absolute mastery over the consciences as well as over the hearts of his subjects. The Edict of Nantes, issued by Henry IV. and confirmed by the policy of Richelieu, was revoked, and intolerance and persecution became the law of the French monarchy, as it had been the law of the Spanish monarchy.

§ 12. Fate of the French monarchy.

It was not for this that Henry IV. and Richelieu had laboured. The tree that bears no fruit must be cut down to the ground, or it will perish by its own inherent rottenness. As the Empire had fallen, as the Spanish monarchy had fallen, the French monarchy, shaken by the thunders of La Hogue and Blenheim, fell at last, when, amidst the corruption of Versailles, it ceased to do any useful work for man.

(Pg 227)

INDEX.

- Aachen (*Aix-la-Chapelle*) place of coronation, 2.
- Administrators. *See* Bishoprics.
- Aix-la-Chapelle. *See* Aachen.
- Aldringer, offers to assist Wallenstein, 175;
    - declares against him, 177;
    - tries to seize him, 177.
- Alsace, Mansfeld in, 50;
    - his designs there, 56;
    - Mansfeld returns to, 60;
    - proposed march of Mansfeld to, 75;
    - its possession of importance to France, 191;
    - comes into French possession, 197.
- Anhalt, Prince of. *See* Christian of Anhalt.
- Anne of Austria, Regent of France, 205.

- Anspach, the Margrave of, hopes for a revolution, 135.
- Anstruther, Sir Robert, his mission to the King of Denmark, 84.
- Arnim, ordered by Wallenstein to besiege Stralsund, 108;
    - commands the Saxons at Breitenfeld, 139;
    - his conference with Wallenstein, 153;
    - is expected to meet Wallenstein at Eger, 179.
- Arras, besieged by Condé, 223.
- Augsburg, city of, swears obedience to Gustavus, 150;
    - besieged by the imperialists, 187;
    - resists Turenne, 212.
- Augsburg, Peace of, 9;
    - questions arising out of it, 10;
    - evaded by the Protestants, 11.
- Austria, Lower, estates of, attempt to wring concessions from Ferdinand, 36.
- Austria, Upper, surrenders to Maximilian, 42;
    - pledged to Maximilian, 46;
    - restored to Ferdinand, 119.
- Austria, the House of, territories governed by it, 9;
    - its branches, 24.
- Avesnes incorporated with France, 225.
- Bautzen, besieged by John George, 42.
- Bergen-op-zoom, siege of, 63.
- Bernhard of Weimar, joins the King of Denmark, 101;
    - joins Gustavus, 138;
    - takes the command of the Swedes at Lützen, 163;
    - his expectations after the death of Gustavus, 166;
    - his duchy of Franconia, 167;
    - takes Ratisbon, 173;
    - is invited to assist Wallenstein, 179;
    - prepares to march to Eger, 179;
    - is defeated at Nördlingen, 183;
    - loses his duchy of Franconia, 183;
    - his alliance with France, 190;
    - defeats the imperialists at Rheinfelden and takes Rheinfelden, Freiburg, and Breisach, 195;
    - his death, 196.
- Bachararch, misery at, 187.
- Baden-Durlach, Margrave of, joins Frederick, 54;
    - defeated at Wimpfen, 57;
    - abandons his allies, 60;
    - aids the King of Denmark, 101.
- Bamberg and Würzburg, Bishop of;
    - attacked by Mansfeld, 49.
- Baner, defeats the Imperialists at Wittstock, 194;
    - is driven back to the coast of the Baltic, 195;
    - fights in different parts of Germany, 196.

- Bärwalde, treaty of, 132.
- Bethlen Gabor, Prince of Transylvania, attacks Austria, 40;
    - prepares to aid Frederick, 44;
    - defeats Bucquoi, 49;
    - threatens Austria, 88, 94;
    - is joined by Mansfeld, 97;
    - withdraws from the contest, 101.
- (Pg 228)Bishoprics, question connected with them left unsettled at the Peace of Augsburg, 10;
    - in the north they mainly fall under Protestant administrators, 12;
    - forcible reconversion of the population where this is not the case, 14;
    - Protestant administrators not acknowledged by the Diet, 14;
    - attempt to bring over Cologne and Strasburg to Protestantism, 14;
    - questions relating to them settled for a time at Mühlhausen, 41;
    - reopened after the battle of Stadtlohn, 67;
    - names of those reclaimed in the Edict of Restitution, 121;
    - arrangement for them at the treaty of Prague, 184.
- Boguslav, Duke of Pomerania, compelled to accept a garrison by Wallenstein, 108;
    - supports Wallenstein in the siege of Stralsund, 110;
    - complains of Wallenstein's soldiers, 127;
    - submits to Gustavus, 130.
- Bohemia, the Royal Charter granted in, 25;
    - its infringement, 27;
    - acknowledgment of Ferdinand as its king, 28;
    - revolution in, 29;
    - directors appointed, 32;
    - war begins in, 32;
    - political incapacity of the revolutionary government, 32;
    - it makes application to foreign powers, 35;
    - election of Frederick as king, 38;
    - suppression of the Revolution, 45;
    - occupied by John George, 151;
    - the Saxons driven out of, 155;
    - Torstenson's occupation of, 209.
- Bohemia, King of, his functions as an Elector, 1.
    - *See* also Rudolph II., Matthias, Frederick V., and Ferdinand II.
- Bohemian Brethren expelled from Bohemia, 46.
- Brandenburg, bishopric of, named in the Edict of Restitution, 131.
- Brandenburg, Elector of, 1.
    - *See* also John Sigismund, and George William.
- Braunau, Protestant church at, 27.
- Breda, siege of, 76.
- Breisach, taken by Bernhard, 195.
- Breisgau, taken possession of by the French, 195.
- Breitenfeld, battle of, 141.
- Bremen, archbishopric of, connexion of, with Christian IV., 78;

- named in the Edict of Restitution, 120;
- given up to Sweden, 214.
- Bridge of Dessau, battle of, 96.
- Brünn, besieged by Torstenson, 209.
- Brunswick, peace negotiations at, 93.
- Brussels, conferences for peace at, 52, 57, 60.
- Bucquoi, commands the army invading Bohemia, 32;
  - defeats Mansfeld, 37;
  - joined by Maximilian, 43;
  - advises to delay a battle, 44;
  - is killed, 49.
- Buckingham, Duke of, his expedition to Rhé, 114;
  - intends to raise the siege of Rochelle, 115;
  - is murdered, 115.
- Budweis, attacked by the Bohemians, 32.
- Burgundy, Eastern. *See* Franche Comté.
- Butler, receives orders to capture Wallenstein, 180;
  - consults on the murder with Leslie and Gordon, 180.
- Calvinism in Germany, 18.
- Camin, bishopric of, named in the Edict of Restitution, 121.
- Casale, sieges of, 122, 123.
- Catalonia, insurrection of, 199.
- Charles I., King of England, forms an alliance with Christian IV., 86;
  - is unable to fulfil his engagement, 95;
  - sends Sir C. Morgan to aid Christian IV., 101;
  - quarrels with France, 111;
  - attempts to succour Rochelle, 113;
  - his arrangements about the Spanish fleet in the Downs, 198.
- Charles V., his strength external to the empire, 8;
  - his meeting with Luther, 9;
  - forced to yield to the Protestants, 9.
- Charles Emanuel, Duke of Savoy, helps the Bohemians, 33;
  - plans for his advancement in Germany, 35;
  - attacks Genoa, 76;
  - reduced to submission by Richelieu, 122.
- Charles Lewis, Elector Palatine, claims his father's dominion, 198;
  - receives the Lower Palatinate, 214.
- Charles, Prince of Wales, proposed marriage with an Infanta, 51;
  - treaty with Spain broken off, 70;
  - proposed marriage with Henrietta Maria, 74.
  - *See* Charles I., King of England.
- Charles the Great (*Charlemagne*), nature of his authority, 2.
- Cherasco, treaty of, 135.
- (Pg 229)Chichester, Lord, his embassy to the Palatinate, 59.
- Christian IV., King of Denmark, his connection with Germany, 78;
  - his views on the course of the war, 79;

- his offers to England to make war, 84;
- his offer accepted, 85;
- attacked by Tilly, 94;
- defeated at Lutter, 96;
- refuses Wallenstein's terms of peace, 101;
- sends agents to Stralsund, 109;
- makes peace at Lübeck, 117.
- Christian of Anhalt, leader of the German Calvinists, 18;
  - his character and policy, 18;
  - his part in the foundation of the Union, 21;
  - his intrigues in Austria, 26;
  - his plan for supporting the Bohemians, 34;
  - commands the Bohemian army, 44.
- Christian of Brunswick, administrator of Halberstadt, his instalment in the cathedral, 54;
  - resolves to take part in the war, 55;
  - invades the diocese of Paderborn, 55;
  - defeated at Höchst, 59;
  - retreats to Alsace, 60;
  - marches through Lorraine, 63;
  - loses his arm at Fleurus, 64;
  - threatens the Lower Saxon Circle, 65;
  - negotiates with the Emperor, 66;
  - is defeated at Stadtlohn, and resigns the See of Halberstadt, 67;
  - joins Christian IV., 95;
  - dies, 96.
- Christina, Queen of Sweden, 166.
- Christina, Regent of Savoy, assisted by the French, 197.
- Church lands secularized, 10, 11;
  - legal decision about them against the Protestants, 14.
- Cities, free imperial, their part in the Diet, 6.
- Cleves, war of succession in, 21.
- Coblentz, fired at by the French in Ehrenbreitstein, 187.
- Colbert, his reforms, 226.
- Cologne, Elector of, 1;
  - failure of an attempt by him to bring over the electorate to Protestantism, 14.
- Condé, Prince of, takes part with Spain, 223.
- Convention of Passau. *See* Passau.
- Corbie, taken by the Spaniards, and retaken by the French, 193.
- Cordova, Gonzales de, commands the Spaniards in the Lower Palatinate, 50;
  - takes part in the battle of Wimpfen, 57;
  - joins in defeating Christian of Brunswick at Höchst, 59;
  - commands at Fleurus, 63.
- Corneille, writes "The Cid," 169.
- Cromwell, courted by France and Spain, 223;
  - decides to help France, 224.
- Dänholm, seized by Wallenstein's soldiers, 109.

- Darmstadt, entered by Mansfeld, 58.
- Descartes, his first work published, 169.
- Dessau, the Bridge of, battle of, 96.
- Devereux, murders Wallenstein, 180.
- Diet of the Empire, 1;
  - its reform in the 15th century, 5;
  - its constitution, 5;
  - how far opposed to Protestantism, 8;
  - its meeting in 1608, 21.
- Directors of Bohemia appointed, 31.
- Donauwörth, occupation of, 20;
  - entered by Gustavus, 149;
  - surrenders to Turenne, 212.
- Downs, the Spanish fleet takes refuge in the, 198.
- Dunkirk, surrender of, 224.
- East Friesland, invaded by Mansfeld, 64.
- Ecclesiastical reservation, the, *See* Bishoprics.
- Edict of Restitution, issued, 120.
- Eger, Wallenstein summons his colonels to, 179.
- Eggenberg confers with Wallenstein, 99;
  - favours Wallenstein's restoration, 151;
  - joins Oñate against Wallenstein, 176.
- Ehrenbreitstein, receives a French garrison, 170;
  - fires on Coblentz, 187.
- Elector Palatine, 1.
  - *See* also Frederick IV., and Frederick V.
- Electors, functions of, 1;
  - their part in the Diet, 6;
  - their quarrel with Wallenstein, 103, 124;
  - demand Wallenstein's dismissal, 127.
- Eliot, Sir John, his satisfaction at the victories of Gustavus, 142.
- Elizabeth, Electress Palatine, encourages her husband to accept the crown of Bohemia, 39.
- Emperor, functions of, 1;
  - he is practically scarcely more than a German king, 2.
- (Pg 230)Enghien, Duke of (afterwards Prince of Condé), defeats the Spaniards at Rocroy, 206;
  - commands at the battle of Freiburg and Nördlingen, 208.
  - *See* Condé, Prince of.
- England. *See* James I., Charles I., Charles, Prince of Wales.
- English ambassador (the Earl of Arundel), notes of his journey through Germany, 187.
- Erfurt, Gustavus at, 147.
- Fabricius, thrown out of window, 30.
- Felton, murders Buckingham, 115.
- Ferdinand, the Archduke, afterwards the Emperor Ferdinand I., represents Charles V., at Augsburg, 10.

- Ferdinand, Archduke (afterwards the Emperor Ferdinand II.), rules Styria, Carinthia, and Carniola, 24;
    - puts down Protestantism there, 24;
    - acknowledged as King of Bohemia, 28;
    - his character, 28;
    - swears to the Royal Charter, 29;
    - elected King of Hungary, 32;
    - receives help from Spain, 33;
    - promises to respect the Royal Charter, 36;
    - besieged by Mansfeld, 37;
    - elected Emperor, 38;
    - comes to terms with Maximilian, 40;
    - puts Frederick to the ban, 46;
    - refuses to go beyond the agreement of Mühlhausen, 68;
    - accepts Wallenstein's offer to raise an army, 89;
    - grants Mecklenburg to Wallenstein, 105, 118;
    - oppresses the Protestants, 120;
    - recovers Upper Austria, 119;
    - takes part in the Mantuan war, 121;
    - carries out the Edict of Restitution, 126;
    - despises Gustavus, 134;
    - refuses to abandon the Edict, 137;
    - looks to Spain for help, 151;
    - hesitates what to do about Wallenstein, 174;
    - decides against him, 176;
    - consents to the Peace of Prague, 184;
    - his death, 194.
- Ferdinand, King of Hungary (afterwards the Emperor Ferdinand III.), his marriage, 174;
    - commands the army after Wallenstein's death, 182;
    - becomes Emperor, 194;
    - reluctance to surrender Alsace to the French, 210.
- Ferdinand, the Cardinal-infant, proposed command of, resisted by Wallenstein, 171;
    - joins the King of Hungary before the battle of Nördlingen, 182;
    - proceeds to Brussels, 183;
    - invades France, 192.
- Fleurus, battle of, 63.
- France, takes precautions against Mansfeld, 63;
    - its internal dissensions, 77, 112;
    - at war with England, 113;
    - intervenes in Italy and makes peace with England, 122;
    - supremacy of Richelieu in, 168;
    - places itself at the head of a German alliance, 189;
    - declares war openly against Spain, 192;
    - continues the war with Spain, 197;
    - its victories over Spain, 205;
    - its victories in Germany, 207;

- its gains by the Peace of Westphalia, 214;
- continuance of its war with Spain, 221;
- successes of, in Flanders, 224;
- its gains by the treaty of the Pyrenees, 224;
- its condition under Lewis XIV., 226.
- Franche Comté, included in the Empire, 2.
- Franconia, duchy of, assigned to Bernhard, 167;
    - taken from him, 183.
- Frankenthal, garrisoned by Vere's troops, 57;
    - given up to the Spaniards, 60.
- Frankfort-on-the Main, place of coronation, 2.
- Frankfort-on-the-Oder, taken by Gustavus, 134.
- Frederick III., the Emperor, words used to him, 2.
- Frederick IV., Elector Palatine, nominal leader of the Calvinists, 18;
    - his death, 31.
- Frederick V., Elector Palatine, his marriage, 31;
    - encourages the Bohemians, 31;
    - proposal that he shall mediate in Bohemia, 34;
    - is elected King of Bohemia, 38;
    - becomes unpopular at Prague, 43;
    - his defeat at the White Hill, 45;
    - takes refuge at the Hague, 45;
    - put to the ban, 46;
    - maintains his claims to Bohemia, 48;
    - proposal that his eldest son shall be educated at Vienna, 52;
    - his prospects in 1622, 53;
    - joins Mansfeld in Alsace, 57;
    - seizes the Landgrave of Darmstadt, 58;
    - driven back to Mannheim, 59;
    - returns to the Hague, 60;
    - (Pg 231)enters Munich with Gustavus, 150;
    - his death, 171.
- Freiburg (in the Breisgau), surrenders to Bernhard, 195;
    - retaken, 208;
    - battle of, 208.
- Friedland, Prince and Duke of. *See* Wallenstein.
- Friesland. *See* East Friesland.
- Fronde, the, 217.
- Fuentes, Count of, killed at Rocroy, 207.
- Fürth, Wallenstein's entrenchments at, 158.
- Gallas, offers to assist Wallenstein, 175.
- Gassion, advises the French to give battle at Rocroy, 206.
- Gaston, Duke of Orleans, leaves France, 167;
    - takes part in a rebellion, 168.
- George of Lüneburg, a Lutheran in Wallenstein's service, 98;
    - sent into Silesia, 101.

- George William, Elector of Brandenburg, consents to his sister's marriage with Gustavus, 81;
  - refuses to join Gustavus, 131;
  - compelled to submit to him, 135.
- Germany, its political institutions, 1-7;
  - what it included, 2;
  - divided into circles, 6;
  - its miserable condition, 186;
  - its condition after the Peace of Westphalia, 217.
- Glückstadt, fortified by Christian IV., 78;
  - siege of, 117.
- Gordon, his part in Wallenstein's murder, 180.
- Gravelines surrenders to the French, 224.
- Guebriant, defeats the Imperialists at Wolfenbüttel and Kempten, 201.
- Guise, the Duke of, leaves France, 168.
- Guiton, Mayor of Rochelle, 115.
- Gustavus Adolphus, King of Sweden, his character, 79;
  - early struggles, 80;
  - visits Germany, 81;
  - hostile to the growth of the Empire, 82;
  - views on religion and politics, 83;
  - projects a general league against the House of Austria, 84;
  - refuses to take part in it on the terms offered, and attacks Poland, 86;
  - sends help to Stralsund, 104;
  - makes peace with Poland, 124;
  - negotiates with France, 124;
  - lands in Pomerania, 127;
  - gains possession of the lands on the Baltic coast, 131;
  - negotiates with France, 131;
  - signs the treaty of Bärwalde, 132;
  - compels the Elector of Brandenburg to join him, 135;
  - fails to relieve Magdeburg, 136;
  - entrenches himself at Werben, 138;
  - allies himself with Saxony, 139;
  - his skill as a commander, 140;
  - defeats Tilly at Breitenfeld, 141;
  - receives overtures from Wallenstein, 143;
  - his political plans, 144;
  - determines to march to the Rhine, 145;
  - keeps Christmas at Mentz, 147;
  - his reception at Nüremberg, 148;
  - enters Donauwörth, and defeats Tilly at the Lech, 149;
  - occupies Munich, 150;
  - lays down terms of peace, 156;
  - proposes a league of the cities, 157;
  - rebukes his officers, 159;

- fails in storming Wallenstein's entrenchments, 160;
- follows Wallenstein into Saxony, 161;
- attacks Wallenstein at Lützen, 162;
- his death, 163;
- his future plans, 165.
- Hagenau, seized by Mansfeld, 50.
- Hague, the, Frederick takes refuge there, 45;
    - returns after his campaign in Germany, 60.
- Halberstadt, diocese of, Christian of Brunswick Bishop of it, 54;
    - forfeited by his treason, 65;
    - occupied by Wallenstein, 92;
    - named in the Edict of Restitution, 120;
    - execution of the Edict at, 125;
    - not recovered by the Protestants at the treaty of Prague, 184;
    - restored at the peace of Westphalia, 214.
- Halle, Pappenheim's march to, 162.
- Hamburg, its commerce, 78;
    - refuses to submit to Wallenstein, 110.
- Hanse Towns, offers made them by the Emperor, 106.
- Havelberg, bishopric of, named in the Edict of Restitution, 121.
- Heidelberg, garrisoned by Vere, 57;
    - taken by Tilly, 61;
    - treatment of Protestants at, 119.
- Heilbronn, the league of, 167;
    - its leading members excepted from the amnesty of the treaty of Prague, 184.
- Heiligenhafen, combat of, 102.
- Henry IV., King of France, plans intervention in Germany, 22.
- (Pg 232)Henry the Fowler, not an emperor, 2.
- Hesse Cassel, Landgrave of. *See* Maurice, and William.
- Hesse Darmstadt. *See* Lewis.
- Höchst, battle of, 59.
- Horn, commands a Swedish force in Mecklenburg, 134;
    - is defeated at Nördlingen, 183.
- Huguenots, nature of toleration granted to, 173;
    - insurrection of, 77, 112;
    - tolerated by Richelieu, 116.
- Hungary, political divisions of, 40.
- Imperial Council (*Reichshofrath*) intervenes in the case of Donauwörth, 20.
- Imperial Court (*Reichskammergericht*), institution, 6;
    - out of working order, 19.
- Ingolstadt, Tilly's death at, 149.
- Italy, kingdom of, 3, 122.
- James I., King of England, offers to mediate in Bohemia and Germany, 35, 47;
    - proposes to pay Mansfeld, 51;
    - his negotiations with Spain, 51, 70;
    - desires aid from France, 71;

- supports Mansfeld, 75;
- orders him not to relieve Breda, 76;
- agreement with Christian IV., 85;
- death of, 86.
- Jankow, battle of, 209.
- Jesuits, the, appear in Germany, 13.
- John Ernest, Duke of Saxe-Weimar, ideas of religious liberty, 94;
  - supports Mansfeld, 96;
  - dies, 101.
- John George, Elector of Saxony, at the head of the Lutheran and neutral party, 15, 22;
  - wishes to pacify Bohemia, 31;
  - his share in Ferdinand's election to the Empire, 38;
  - is gained over by Maximilian, 41;
  - his vacillations in 1622, 62;
  - refuses to join in the Danish war, 87;
  - his son elected administrator of Magdeburg, 126;
  - attempts to mediate between Gustavus and the Emperor, 133, 134;
  - joins Gustavus, 139;
  - failure of his army at Breitenfeld, 141;
  - despatched into Bohemia, 151;
  - enters Prague, 151;
  - is driven out of Bohemia, 155;
  - proposes terms of peace to Gustavus, 156;
  - refuses to join the League of Heilbronn, 167;
  - negotiates with Wallenstein, 170;
  - hopes for peace, 184;
  - agrees to the Peace of Prague, 185;
  - his troops defeated at Wittstock, 194.
- John Sigismund, Elector of Brandenburg, his claim to the duchy of Cleves, 21;
  - turns Calvinist, 22.
- Joseph, Father, employed as Richelieu's agent, 128.
- Kempten, battle of, 201.
- Klostergrab, Protestant church at, 27.
- Köln. *See* Cologne.
- La Force, commands at Paris, 193.
- Lamormain, Father, Ferdinand's confessor, declares against peace, 171.
- Landrecies incorporated with France, 224.
- League, the Catholic, its formation, 21;
  - agrees to the treaty of Ulm, 42.
  - *See* Maximilian, Duke of Bavaria.
- Lebus, bishopric of, 121.
- Lech, battle at the passage of the, 149.
- Leipzig, assembly at, 133.
- Leipzig, battle of. *See* Breitenfeld.
- Leslie, his part in Wallenstein's murder, 180.
- Leuchtenberg, Landgrave of, taken prisoner by Mansfeld, 49.

- Lewis XIII., King of France, his character, 72;
    - his jealousy of Spain, 73;
    - summons Richelieu to his council, 74;
    - takes part against Spain, 75;
    - his policy towards the Huguenots, 112;
    - at war with England, 113;
    - invades Italy, 122;
    - dislikes the success of Gustavus, 148;
    - takes the field against Spain, 193;
    - dies, 205.
- Lewis XIV., King of France, accession of, 205.
- Lewis, Landgrave of Hesse Darmstadt, taken prisoner, 58.
- Lombardy, the iron crown of, 3.
- Lorraine (*Lothringen*), included in the Empire, 2;
    - Mansfeld and Christian of Brunswick, in, 63.
- Lorraine, Duke of, joins the Spaniards against Gustavus, 158;
    - is reduced to subjection by France, 170.
- (Pg 233)Lower Saxony, Circle of, threatened by Christian of Brunswick and Tilly, 64;
    - refuses to support Christian, 65;
    - disunion amongst its members, 68;
    - attacked by Tilly, 87.
- Lübeck, bishopric of, named in the Edict of Restitution, 121.
- Lübeck, Peace of, 117.
- Lusatia, invaded by the Saxons, 42.
- Luther, his meeting with Charles V., 9.
- Lutherans, 17;
    - their estrangements from Frederick in Bohemia, 43;
    - still remain in Paderborn, 55.
- Lutter, battle of, 96.
- Lützen, battle of, 161.
- Magdeburg, city of, refuses to admit Wallenstein's troops, 105, 126;
    - declares for Gustavus, 134;
    - stormed and sacked, 136.
- Magdeburg, diocese of, occupied by Wallenstein, 92;
    - included in the Edict of Restitution, 120;
    - execution of the Edict at, 126.
- Magdeburg, Protestant administrator of, not acknowledged as Archbishop by the Diet, 14.
- Maintz. *See* Mentz.
- *Majestätsbrief. See* Royal Charter.
- Manheim, garrisoned by Vere, 57;
    - retreat of Frederick and Mansfeld to, 59;
    - taken by Tilly, 60.
- Mansfeld, Count Ernest of, takes service with the Bohemians and besieges Pilsen, 33;
    - takes the field against Bucquoi, 36;
    - is defeated by him, 37;

- character of his army, 48;
- occupies the Upper Palatinate, 49;
- marches into Alsace, 50;
- aims at becoming master of part of it, 56;
- invades the Lower Palatinate, 57;
- seizes the Landgrave of Darmstadt, 58;
- state of his army, 59;
- retreats to Alsace, 60;
- occupies Lorraine, 63;
- cuts his way through the Spanish Netherlands, relieves Bergen-op-zoom, and invades East Friesland, 64;
  - returns to the Netherlands, 69;
  - assisted by France, 74;
  - proposed march into Alsace, 75;
  - fails to relieve Breda, 76;
  - sent to help the King of Denmark, 86;
  - joins Christian IV., 94;
  - defeated at the Bridge of Dessau, 96;
  - marches through Silesia into Hungary, 96;
  - dies, 97.
- Mantua and Montferrat, war of succession in, 121.
- Mardyke, surrender of, 224.
- Martinitz, one of the Regents of Bohemia, thrown out of window, 30.
- Mary of Medici, opposes Richelieu, 132;
  - obliged to leave France, 160.
- Matthias, Archduke, rises against Rudolph II., 25;
  - succeeds as Emperor, 26.
  - *See* Matthias, Emperor.
- Matthias, Emperor, his election, 26;
  - his attempts to break the Royal Charter, 27;
  - his death, 36.
- Maurice, Landgrave of Hesse Cassel, submits to Spinola, 47.
- Maximilian, Archduke, governs Tyrol, 24.
- Maximilian, Duke of Bavaria, his character and policy, 15;
  - his part in the formation of the League, 21;
  - prepares to attack Bohemia, 39;
  - proposed transference of the Palatinate Electorate to, 40;
  - gains over the North German princes, 41;
  - attaches Austria and Bohemia, 42;
  - receives Upper Austria in pledge, 46;
  - receives the Electorate, 60;
  - his policy after the peace of Lübeck, 118;
  - makes an effort against the French, 207;
  - is ready to surrender Alsace to the French, 211;
  - but refuses to surrender the Upper Palatinate, 211;
  - makes a truce, which does not last long, 213.

- Mayence. *See* Mentz.
- Mazarin, Cardinal, Minister of Anne of Austria, 205.
- Mecklenburg, Dukes of their land pledged to Wallenstein, 105;
    - formally given to Wallenstein, 118.
- Meissen. *See* Misnia.
- Melancthon, his protest against theological disputation, 13.
- Mentz, entered by Spinola, 42;
    - treaty for the dissolution of the Union signed at, 47.
- Mentz, Archbishop of, one of the Electors, 6;
    - lays claim to lands in North Germany, 98.
- Mentz, city of, Gustavus at, 147;
    - given over to Oxenstjerna, 148;
    - misery at, 187.
- Mercy, prudence of, 208;
    - is killed, 208.
- Merseburg, bishopric of, named in the Edict of Restitution, 121.
- (Pg 234)Merseburg, city of, taken by Pappenheim, 139.
- Metz, annexed by France, 215.
- Minden, bishopric of, named in the Edict of Restitution, 121.
- Misnia, bishopric of, named in the Edict of Restitution, 121.
- Montmorenci, Duke of, his rebellion, 168.
- Morgan, Sir Charles, commands an English force sent in aid of Denmark, 101.
- Mühlhausen (in Thuringia), agreement of, 41;
    - meeting of the Electors at, 103.
- Munich, occupied by Gustavus, 150.
- Münster, meeting of diplomatists at, 210.
- Münster, diocese of, threatened by Mansfeld, 64.
- Nancy, taken possession of by the French, 180.
- Nantes, Edict of, 71;
    - its revocation, 226.
- Naumburg, bishopric of, named in the Edict of Restitution, 121.
- Naumburg, city of, entered by Gustavus, 161.
- Netherlands, the, included in the Empire, 2.
- Netherlands, the Spanish, defended against a French attack, 191.
- Netherlands, United States of the, end of their truce with Spain, 51;
    - acknowledgment of their independence, 221.
- Neuberg, Wolfgang Wilhelm, Count Palatine of, lays claim to the duchy of Cleves, 22;
    - has his ears boxed, 22.
- Neustadt, misery at, 188.
- Nevers, Duke of, his claims to the succession in Mantua, 122.
- New Brandenburg, taken by Tilly, 134.
- Nienburg, holds out for Christian IV., 101.
- Nordheim, holds out for Christian IV., 101.
- Nördlingen, treatment of the Protestants at, 120;
    - battle of, 183;
    - second battle of, 208;

- surrenders to Turenne, 213.
- Nüremberg, joins the Union, 20, 21;
  - meeting of the Union at, 41;
  - deserts the Union, 47;
  - welcomes Gustavus, 148;
  - despatches Gustavus against Wallenstein, 158;
  - sufferings of, 158.
- Oñate, opposes Wallenstein, 175;
  - proposes to kill Wallenstein, 177.
- Oppenheim, stormed by Gustavus, 147.
- Osnabrück, election of a Catholic Bishop of, 67;
  - meeting of diplomatists at, 217.
- Otto the Great, becomes Emperor, 2.
- Oudenarde, surrender to the French, 224.
- Oxenstjerna, his view of Gustavus' march upon the Rhine, 145;
  - receives the government of Mentz, 148;
  - his position after the death of Gustavus, 166;
  - asked to help Wallenstein, 172;
  - keeps his doubts till the last, 179;
  - surrenders fortresses in Alsace to Richelieu, 192.
- Paderborn, attack upon by Christian of Brunswick, 55.
- Palatinate, the Lower, attacked by Spinola, 43;
  - defended by Vere, 49;
  - invaded by Tilly, 50;
  - conquered by Tilly, 60;
  - the eastern part made over to Maximilian, 119;
  - the whole restored to Charles Lewis, 214.
- Palatinate, the Upper, Mansfeld's occupation of, 50;
  - its conquest by Tilly, 50;
  - made over to Maximilian, 119;
  - secured to him by the peace of Westphalia, 214.
- Pappenheim, confidence that Gustavus will be beaten, 139;
  - storms Magdeburg, 135;
  - commands on the Rhine, 161;
  - leaves Wallenstein before the battle of Lützen, 161;
  - is killed at Lützen, 161.
- Passau, convention of, 9.
- Peace of Augsburg. *See* Augsburg.
- Peace of Phillipsburg, French garrison of, 215.
- Piccolomini, offers to join Wallenstein, 175;
  - declares against him, 177;
  - tries to seize him, 177;
  - orders Butler to capture Wallenstein, 180.
- Pignerol, seized by Richelieu, 124.
- (Pg 235)Pilsen refuses to take part with the Bohemian directors, 32;
  - besieged and taken by Mansfeld, 33;

- - Wallenstein holds a meeting of officers at, 177.
- Pomerania laid waste by Wallenstein's troops, 127;
  - Gustavus lands in, 128;
  - divided between Brandenburg and Sweden, 214.
- Pomerania, Duke of, *See* Boguslav.
- Portugal, independence of, 200.
- Prague, revolution at, 29;
  - Frederick crowned King of Bohemia at, 38;
  - Frederick's growing unpopularity there, 43;
  - battle at the White Hill near, 45;
  - entered by the Saxons, 151;
  - recovered by Wallenstein, 155;
  - part of it taken by the Swedes, 213.
- Prague, the treaty of, 184.
- Princes of the Empire, their increasing power, 3;
  - compared with the French vassals, 4;
  - care little for the Diet, 5;
  - their part in the Diet, 6;
  - the majority opposed to Protestantism, 9.
- Protestantism, its rise in Germany, 7;
  - its position in North Germany, 12;
  - its division, 12;
  - contrast between it in the north and the south, 17.
- Pyrenees, treaty of the, 224.
- Ratisbon, diets held at, 61, 127;
  - taken by Bernhard, 173.
- Ratseburg, bishopric of, named in the Edict of Restitution, 121.
- Regensburg. *See* Ratisbon.
- *Reichshofrath*. *See* Imperial Council.
- *Reichskammergericht*. *See* Imperial Court.
- Rhé, Isle of, Buckingham's expedition to, 114.
- Rheinfelden, battle of, 195.
- Richelieu, becomes a minister of Lewis XIII., 74;
  - recovers the Valtelline, 75;
  - his plans frustrated by the insurrection of the Huguenots, 77;
  - wishes to make peace with them, 112;
  - causes of his success, 116;
  - his policy of toleration, 116;
  - takes part in the Mantuan War, 122;
  - negotiates with Sweden, 124;
  - is startled by the victories of Gustavus, 148;
  - defends himself against the French aristocracy, 167;
  - nature of the government established by him, 168;
  - his aims in Europe, 169;
  - intervenes more decidedly in Germany, 184, 190;
  - aims at the conquest of Alsace, 191;

- obtains control over fortresses in Alsace, 192;
- failure of his attack upon the Spanish Netherlands, 192;
- successfully resists a Spanish invasion, 193;
- continues the struggle with Spain, 197;
- his successes, 197, 201;
- his death and policy, 201.
- Rochelle, insurrection of, 77, 112;
  - siege of, 114;
  - surrender of, 115;
  - subsequent treatment of, 116.
- Rocroy, attacked by the Spaniards, 206;
  - battle of, 207.
- Rohan, Duke of, insurrection of, 123.
- Rostock, its harbour blocked up by Wallenstein, 108.
- Roussillon, conquered by France, 200, 201;
  - annexed to France, 224.
- Royal Charter, the (*Majestätsbrief*), granted by Rudolph II., 25;
  - its forfeiture declared, 45.
- Rüdesheim, misery at, 187.
- Rudolph II., Emperor, his part in the Austrian territories, 24;
  - grants the Royal Charter of Bohemia, 25;
  - tries to withdraw it, 26;
  - dies, 26;
  - fate of his art-treasures, 43.
- Rupert, Prince, his birth at Prague, 43.
- Saluces, seized by Richelieu, 124.
- Salzburg, persecution of Protestants of, 216.
- Saxony, Elector of, 1. *See* also John George.
- Savoy, Duke of. *See* Charles Emanuel.
- Schorndorf, surrenders to Turenne, 212.
- Sigismund, King of Poland, a claimant to the crown of Sweden, 81.
- Sigismund, the Emperor, anecdote of, 2.
- Slawata, one of the Regents of Bohemia, 30;
  - thrown out of window, 30.
- Soissons, Count of, rebels in France, 200.
- Soubise, Duke of, rebels, 77.
- Spain, intervenes in the war, 42;
  - anxious for peace, 43;
  - military position of in 1624, 74;
  - loses the Valtelline, 75;
  - takes part in the Mantua war, 121;
  - (Pg 236)supports Wallenstein, 151;
  - takes part in the war on the Rhine, 158;
  - turns against Wallenstein, 171;
  - at war with France, 192;
  - invades France, 193;

- naval inferiority of, 197, 198;
- rebellion of the Catalans, 199;
- loss of Portugal, 200;
- continues the war with France after the Peace of Westphalia, 221;
- agrees to the Peace of the Pyrenees, 224.
- Spens, Sir James, his mission to Sweden, 84.
- Spinola, attacks the Palatinate, 42;
  - returns to Brussels, 50;
  - besieges Bergen-op-zoom, 63;
  - besieges Breda, 75;
  - besieges Casale, 123.
- Spires, Bishop of, attacked by Vere, 50.
- Stade, taken by Tilly, 117.
- Stadtlohn, battle of, 66.
- Stenay, besieged by Condé, 223.
- Stralsund, siege of, 108.
- Strasburg, Bishopric of, failure of an attempt to place it in Protestant hands, 14.
- Strasburg, city of, joins the Union, 20, 21;
  - deserts it, 47.
- Sweden, her gains at the Peace of Westphalia, 214.
- Switzerland included in the Empire, 21.
- Tabor, occupied by Mansfeld, 48.
- Thionville, besieged by the French, 207;
  - annexed to France, 224.
- Thirty Years' War, the disputes which led to it, 14;
  - commencement of, 30;
  - end of, 213.
- Thurn, Count Henry of, his part in the Bohemian Revolution, 30;
  - his operations against Bucquoi, 33;
  - besieges Vienna, 36;
  - aids Christian IV., 101.
- Tilly, commands the army of the League, 42;
  - his part in the conquest of Bohemia, 44;
  - his army, 48;
  - conquers the Upper Palatinate, 50;
  - invades the Lower Palatinate, 51;
  - his prospects in 1622, 55;
  - defeats the Margrave of Baden at Wimpfen, 57;
  - defeats Christian of Brunswick at Höchst, 59;
  - conquers the Lower Palatinate, 61;
  - threatens the Lower Saxon Circle, 64;
  - defeats Christian of Brunswick at Stadtlohn, 66;
  - attacks Lower Saxony, 87;
  - makes head against Christian IV., 95;
  - defeats him at Lutter, 96;
  - besieges Stade and Glückstadt, 117;

- his campaign against Gustavus, 134;
- takes Magdeburg, 136;
- attacks Saxony, 139;
- defeated at Breitenfeld, 141;
- his defeat and death at the passage of the Lech, 149.
- Torgau, holds out against Wallenstein, 161.
- Torstenson, his campaign of 1645, 209.
- Toul, annexed to France, 215.
- Treves, Elector of, 1;
    - makes an alliance with France, 170.
- Trier. *See* Treves.
- Tübingen, university of, 17.
- Turenne, his part in the campaigns of 1644 and 1645, 208;
    - his strategy in Bavaria in 1646, 212.
- Turin, changes of government in, 197.
- Ulm, joins the Union, 20, 21;
    - deserts it, 47.
- Ulm, treaty of, 42.
- Union, the Protestant, formation of, 21;
    - enters into an agreement with the Duke of Savoy, 33;
    - its coolness in the cause of the Bohemians, 34;
    - refuses to support Frederick
    - in Bohemia, 41;
    - agrees to the treaty of Ulm, 42;
    - its dissolution, 47.
- Valtelline, the Spaniards driven from the, 75.
- Verden, bishopric of, occupied by a son of Christian IV., 78;
    - named in the Edict of Restitution, 121;
    - given up to Sweden, 215.
- Verdun, annexed to France, 214.
- Vere, Sir Horace, defends the Lower Palatinate, 49, 57.
- Vienna, besieged by Thurn, 36;
    - attacked by Bethlen Gabor, 40;
    - attacked by Torstenson, 209.
- Wallenstein, his birth and education, 88;
    - (Pg 237)raises an army for the Emperor, and is created Prince of Friedland, 89;
    - his mode of carrying on war, 90;
    - enters Magdeburg and Halberstadt, 92;
    - defeats Mansfeld at the Bridge of Dessau, 96;
    - his quarrel with the League, 98;
    - confers with Eggenberg, 99;
    - is created Duke of Friedland, 100;
    - subdues Silesia, 101;
    - conquers Schleswig and Jutland, 102;
    - complaints of the Electors against him, 103;
    - his fresh levies, 104;

- Mecklenburg pledged to him, 105;
- named Admiral of the Baltic, 108;
- attempts to burn the Swedish fleet, 108;
- besieges Stralsund, 108;
- assists in the siege of Glückstadt, 117;
- his investiture with the Duchy of Mecklenburg, 118;
- his breach with the Electors, 124;
- talks of sacking Rome, 127;
- his deprivation demanded, 127;
- his dismissal, 129;
- makes overtures to Gustavus, 142;
- breaks off his intercourse with Gustavus, 152;
- is reinstated in command by the Emperor, 153;
- character of his army, 153;
- drives the Saxons out of Bohemia, 155;
- entrenches himself near Nüremberg, 158;
- repulses Gustavus and marches into Saxony, 160;
- takes up a position at Lützen, is defeated, 161;
- negotiates with the Saxons, 170;
- hopes to bring about peace, 171;
- negotiates with the Swedes, 172;
- prepares to force the Emperor to accept peace from him, 174;
- opposition to him, 175;
- the Emperor decides against him, 176;
- throws himself upon his officers, 177;
- is declared a traitor, and abandoned by the garrison of Prague, 178;
- his murder, 181;
- causes of his failure, 181.
- Werben, camp of Gustavus at, 138.
- Werth, John of, general in Maximilian's service, 207.
- Weston, Sir Richard, represents England at the Congress at Brussels, 57.
- Westphalia, the Peace of, opening of negotiations for, 209;
    - signature of, 213;
    - its results, 215.
- White Hill, battle of the, 45.
- Wiesloch, combat of, 57.
- William, Landgrave of Hesse Cassel, joins Gustavus, 138;
    - shut out from the benefits of the treaty of Prague, 186;
    - his alliance with France, 190.
- Wimpfen, battle of, 57.
- Winter-king, nickname of Frederick, 39.
- Wismar in Wallenstein's hands, 108.
- Wittingau, occupied by Mansfeld, 48.
- Wittstock, battle of, 194.
- Wolfenbüttel holds out for Christian IV., 101;
    - battle at, 201.

- Wrangel, succeeds Torstenson as commander of the Swedes, 209;
  - joins Turenne, 212.
- Würtemberg, accepts the terms of the treaty of Prague, 195.
- Würzburg taken by Gustavus, 147;
  - surrenders to Turenne, 212.
- Ypres, surrenders to the French, 224.
- Znaim, Wallenstein confers with Eggenberg at, 153.
- Zusmarshausen, battle of, 231.